The Brothers Singer

by

CLIVE SINCLAIR

Allison & Busby

London · New York

First published 1983 by
Allison and Busby Limited
6a Noel Street, London W1V 3RB, England
and distributed in the USA by
Schocken Books Inc.
200 Madison Avenue, New York, NY 10016

British Library Cataloguing in Publication Data:

Sinclair, Clive
    The Brothers Singer
    1. Singer, Isaac Bashevis
    2. Singer, Israel Joshua
    I. Title
    839'.0933   PJ5129.S5Z/

ISBN 0-85031-275-2

Set in 10/11 Plantin by
Top Type Phototypesetting Co. Ltd., London W1.
and printed and bound in Great Britain by
Billings & Sons Limited, Worcester.

THE BROTHERS SINGER

Also by Clive Sinclair:
Bibliosexuality (1973)
Hearts of Gold (1979)
Bedbugs (1982)

Contents

Acknowledgements

I should like to thank the faculty of the School of English and American Studies at the University of East Anglia — Eric Homberger and Ellman Crasnow in particular — for much good advice, some of which I have taken. I am also grateful to my colleagues at the University of California at Santa Cruz, where I was a Visiting Lecturer during 1980–81, for many stimulating discussions — those with Murray Baumgarten being the most rewarding. Thanks also to Isaac Bashevis Singer, Maurice Carr, Yosl Bergner, the Friends of Yiddish, and those others who gave me invaluable information, and to Anthony Thwaite who first published my interview with Singer (*Encounter,* February 1979).

No less important than the mental stimulation from the aforementioned was the encouragement I received from my wife, Fran, my parents, my brother, my friends and my publishers. Lastly I must mention my son, Seth Benjamin, whose imminent arrival prompted me to complete the manuscript. We were in Santa Cruz, at the time, on a Bicentennial Arts Fellowship.

I dedicate this book to my grandmother, Eva Jacobs.

Clive Sinclair
St Albans, January 1983

Author's Note

Because they have been transliterated, several Yiddish and Hebrew words — for example, hasidim, zaddik, cabbala — and also names have more than one spelling. These have been standardized in the main text but within quotations the original spellings have been retained.

I have also taken the liberty of referring to I. B. Singer as Bashevis and I. J. Singer as Joshua throughout for the sake of readability.

Introduction

THE FOLLOWING conversation was broadcast by the BBC moments after the announcement of the award of the 1978 Nobel Prize for Literature:

> INTERVIEWER [astounded]: Professor Bradbury, are you surprised by this award?
>
> PROF. BRADBURY [caught off balance, but quick to steady himself]: No, I'm not surprised. I'm a little disappointed that it didn't turn out to be Graham Greene.... But Singer clearly deserves the prize and I think it's a just honour.
>
> INTERVIEWER [suspicious]: Is there some kind of American Mafia at work, do you think, in the Nobel Committee?
>
> PROF. BRADBURY [serious]: No. I think it's a reflection of the domination of American writing in the world today....
>
> INTERVIEWER [resigned]: Now, what kind of work does he do?[1]

The Brothers Singer will provide an extended answer to that question. But first I must introduce the older brother, Israel Joshua Singer.

It is a shame that he is so little known. Only one of his books — his masterpiece, *The Brothers Ashkenazi* — has a British publisher at present. However, his name is remembered in Stepney, as this reply from the Friends of Yiddish testifies:

> The President thanks you for your very interesting letter of 21st November 1977. I am writing for the President, who does not write in English. (Re: *The Brothers Singer*). Both brothers belong to the well known Yiddish writers of Yiddish prose. If Isaac Bashevis Singer now makes more of an impression that his brother, Israel Joshua Singer, is it because he has lived longer (till 120) than his brother who died young? Also it is because of his erotic-mystic short stories, that he understands so well to write.[2]

As in Henry Roth's *Call It Sleep*, the fractured English disguises a mind capable of more elegant expression in another language. Reading between the lines reveals an attitude to the Singer brothers at variance with their present reputation in the outside world. The writer of the letter knows that longevity cannot really account for Bashevis's uncanny popularity. Those "erotic-mystic" short stories are closer to the truth. There is a hint of censure in the words, "that he understands so well to write", as if Bashevis were pandering to his English-speaking readers, unlike the President "who does not write in English". The Friends of Yiddish would not have been impressed by Professor Bradbury's appreciation of Bashevis's work, with its sophisticated references to "metaphysics". In fact, Bashevis is considered a prodigal son by many of his peers, while Joshua is mourned as a lost champion, whose premature death in 1944 at the height of a brilliant career symbolized the fate of Yiddish, not to mention the majority of its speakers.

Old feuds flicker among the survivors, just as they do within the Singer family itself. Yiddish links them, but also separates them. Nevertheless, when Bashevis accepted the Nobel Prize he interpreted the honour bestowed upon him as a "recognition of the Yiddish language". Moreover, he spoke of Joshua, calling him "my older brother and master".[3] "Older brother" is pregnant with possibilities of sibling rivalry, but "master" is unambiguous. When I began work on *The Brothers Singer* I wrote to Bashevis. This was his response:

> I am absolutely delighted that you want to write a book about my brother and that you like my own works. All I can say is God bless you and God bless your publisher. At this moment I am busy with my work but whatever information you will need from me I will be happy to send you or to give you personally if you come to the States.[4]

I interviewed him in May 1978. Seated beside me on a sofa in his New York apartment he called Joshua, "the only hero that I ever worshipped".[5]

Bashevis's Nobel-Prize tribute to his brother echoed an earlier dedication in *The Family Moskat:* "To me he was not only the older brother, but a spiritual father and master as well." He dedicated *The Séance and Other Stories* to the memory of his "beloved sister Minda Esther". It was typical of Hinda Esther's ill-starred life that the printers mis-spelt her name. Thirteen years older than Bashevis, she figures briefly in his memoirs as a near hysteric. During *A Day of Pleasure* he mentions that she was a writer, but gives no titles. It was the Friends of Yiddish who led me to her fiction. "In London a sister of theirs lived, Esther Kreitman, who died. She also wrote good prose. She wrote a romance called *Diamonds,* and a book of short stories." Neither was translated. But listed under Kreitman Esther in the British Library catalogue was an autobiographical novel: *Der Szejdym Tanc* in Yiddish, *Deborah* in English. It filled the gap between Joshua's only volume of memoirs and Bashevis's earliest recollections. By reading all the autobiographical works in sequence it is possible to reconstruct the history of the Singer Family from the 1890s to the 1930s.

It began when Pinchos Mendel Singer married Bathsheba, daughter of Reb Mordecai, the Bilgoray rabbi, thus uniting two ancient rabbinic houses. According to custom the couple lodged with the bride's parents until the husband had the means to support his new family.

1
Fathers and Sons

PINCHOS MENDEL and Bathsheba had four children: Esther, Joshua, Bashevis and Moshe. Another two died of scarlet fever. Only Moshe remained faithful to the teachings of his parents. As a result he starved to death with his mother during the Second World War, caught between the German and Russian armies. Fortunately his father did not live to see the tragic end of his illustrious rabbinic line. Pinchos Mendel preached in the ramshackle *shtetlach* of Leoncin and Radzymin, before finding a secure rabbinate in Warsaw. This lasted until the First World War. All the children came during the peripatetic years. Esther was the oldest — born in her grandfather's house on 31 March 1891 — and she suffered the most. Bathsheba was so disappointed in not having a son that she rejected her daughter. Esther spent the first years of her life with a wet-nurse, sleeping in a crib under a table. It is hard to condemn her subsequent jealousy of Joshua, born on 30 November 1893, also in Bilgoray. Bashevis arrived on 14 July 1904 in Leoncin. There were fifteen years between the births of Esther and Moshe.

The town of Leoncin was named in honour of the local squire, Leon Christowski, as was Jampol in Bashevis's *The Manor*. Like Jampol and Balut (in *The Brothers Ashkenazi*), Leoncin was built upon sand. This topographical detail assumes metaphorical status as the fate of Polish Jewry unfolds. The fact that Leoncin existed at all was an example of the insecurity of the Jews; it evolved because Squire Christowski took pity on some Jews expelled from their homes by the Russians in the chaos that followed the 1863 rebellion. Why the Singers went from Bilgoray to Leoncin was a tale Bathsheba never tired of retelling "with a great deal of bitterness".[1] The story must have made an impression because there are three published versions of it, each reflecting the character of its reporter.

Bathsheba was seventeen when she married Pinchos Mendel. She chose him above wealthier suitors because he was the most scholarly. However, it turned out that his wisdom was confined to the Talmud. "Beyond the realm of the Talmud", wrote Esther, "he was just a simpleton." "True, there were few to compare with him in learning," she added, "but he was unworldly, needed looking after like a child."[2] Bashevis also called him "unworldly",[3] but he meant it as a compliment. Joshua was blunter, regarding his father as obstinate.

Pinchos Mendel refused to take the Russian examination required by the occupying forces for all official rabbis. Esther recorded the flight from his Russian tutor's house with some sarcasm. Informed of a rumour that the tutor's wife was not wearing the prescribed wig, Pinchos Mendel for the first time "became a man of action — and he ran away". The same incident appeared in Joshua's memoirs, where the suspected breach of matronly modesty was measured against the responsibilities of a young husband and father. Joshua concluded that his father "hated responsibility of any kind". Avoiding also the strictures of his father-in-law, Pinchos Mendel returned to his parents "who made no demands upon him whatsoever", in effect deserting his wife and children — a fact noted by Esther, not one to miss a slight. Only Bashevis was forgiving (though being unborn at the time he had nothing to forgive); he sensed nobility in his father's refusal to conform to the demands of a rotten system, and courage in the way he clung to the old fashions despite the jeers of his in-laws, who went so far as to advise Bathsheba to divorce "this dreamer". Instead she persuaded Pinchos Mendel to look for a rabbinate of his own.

Contrary to everyone's expectations, he found a position at Leoncin, although (as Joshua pointed out) Leoncin was no prize. But even Joshua could not deny the talent that won his father the post. Pinchos Mendel passed through Leoncin as an itinerant preacher and so impressed the community with his sermon, a "blend of biting commentary, familiar interpretations of the Torah, and Hasidic miracle tales", that they invited him to remain as their rabbi. Joshua wrote that they were "enthralled", Esther called them "spellbound".

For all his lack of sophistication, Pinchos Mendel had considerable skills as a storyteller. "His words flow sweet as wine!" the women said, in Esther's book. "My father was a wonderful storyteller," said Bashevis during our conversation. "He never realized this, but he could tell a story; so could my mother." Maurice Carr, Esther's son, recollected how his grandfather ("the nearest thing to a saint") kept his fellow hasidim entertained with a story which lasted exactly the length of their train journey. "Somehow he managed to end just when we approached the station."[4] Bathsheba's sharp tongue and Pinchos Mendel's turn of phrase were a greater inspiration to Esther, Joshua and Bashevis than their piety; a piety which did not preclude the payment of a bribe to Leoncin's constabulary, to persuade them to overlook the fact that their new rabbi had not passed the official examination. Bathsheba was less accommodating; according to Esther she "never forgave him his escapade". Nor was she impressed with the *shtetl* of forty families, where only one house had a second floor, to which her husband led her. "Mother, who had grown up the daughter of a prominent rabbi in the province capital, felt debased by her husband's illicit, insignificant post," wrote Joshua in *Of a World That Is No More*. But Pinchos Mendel, "the eternal dreamer and *Luftmensch*", was delighted: " 'You see, with God's help it all turned out well after all,' he crowed with joy." Unlike Bashevis, Joshua only used the word "dreamer" pejoratively.

A whole chapter of Joshua's memoirs explores what he called "the mismatch between my mother and father". It was headed, "A tragedy, due to the fact that fate transposed genders in Heaven", meaning that it would have been better if his mother had been his father and his father had been his mother.

> Even externally each seemed better suited for the other's role. Father was short and round, with a soft, fine, delicate face; warm blue eyes; full rosy cheeks; a small, chiseled nose, and plump, feminine hands. If not for the great reddish-brown beard and corkscrew-like sidelocks, he would have resembled a woman. Mother, on the other hand, was tall and somewhat stooped, with large, piercing, cold-gray eyes, a sharp nose, and a jutting pointed chin like a man's.[5]

His father was "warm", "rosy", "soft"; his mother "cold", "grey", "sharp". Esther's description of Bathsheba picked out the same points:

> Pale, thin, and with those large grey eyes of hers, she looked like a Talmudist who spends his days and nights and years in study, rather than a woman. Even the black dress and velvet jacket she had on scarcely betrayed her.[6]

Needless to say, these physical signs were symptomatic of deeper divisions within their characters. This was how Joshua summed up his father:

> He was more a creature of the heart than of intellect, one who accepted life as it was and did not delve deeply into the way of things. In general, he was not inclined to overexert himself. Nor was he plagued by uncertainty. He believed in people and, even more, in God. His absolute faith in God's Torah and in saints was boundless. He never questioned the ways of the Lord, he nursed no resentments, he suffered no doubts.[7]

But Bathsheba was "an accomplished worrier, a fretter, a doubter; totally devoted to reason and logic; always thinking, probing,

pondering, and foreseeing. She brooded about people, about the state
of the world, about God and His mysterious ways. She was, in short,
the complete intellectual''.

The conflict between Pinchos Mendel and Bathsheba was
something more than a clash of personalities; it represented a division
within orthodox Judaism between the populist hasidim who believed
in miracles and danced to express their joy in God's creation, and the
more scholarly *misnagidim* exemplified by the rabbi of Bilgoray — "a
cold-blooded rationalist" Pinchos Mendel called him. Bashevis told
Commentary that his mother was a "little bit of a sceptic... especially
about the *zaddikim,* the 'wonder-rabbis'".

> My father always used to say that if you don't believe in the *zaddikim*
> today, tomorrow you won't believe in God. My mother would say, it's
> one thing to believe in God and another to believe in a man. My
> mother's point of view is also my point of view.[8]

It is surprising to see Bashevis siding so unequivocally with his
mother, even though his pen-name is derived from Bathsheba, for
hasidism is always an attractive option in his work, especially in an
untranslated novel, *Der Bal-Tshuve (The Penitent)*. Its hero, Joseph
Shapiro, is a successful businessman turned zealot. "If you do not
wish to be a Nazi," he fumes, "you must be the opposite of a Nazi... a
'Talmud Jew'."[9] This is the voice of Pinchos Mendel. Likewise, the
logic of his defence of the zaddikim is borrowed by Gimpel the Fool:
"Today it's your wife you don't believe; tomorrow it's God Himself
you won't take stock in."

Despite these arguments, Bathsheba refused to take stock in her
husband. Just how this fundamental difference in outlook affected
their relationship can be seen as the family moved from Leoncin to
Radzymin. The description comes from *Deborah,* wherein Pinchos
Mendel was known as Avram Ber, Bathsheba as Raizela, and Leoncin
as Jelhitz.

> Everything around him was so full of love and beauty. His feelings
> mastered him, and he began to sing joyfully: "How glorious and
> pleasant, most holy, are Thy...." He forgot that it was the season of
> *Sifra,* when music is forbidden, but Raizela immediately pulled him
> up. Reb Avram Ber broke off, the sudden interruption leaving a trace of
> sadness on his face.[10]

Nevertheless, Esther was sensitive enough to realize what this
relentless realism cost her mother.

> Raizela smiled a patronizing smile which seemed to say, "Heavens,
> what a terrible simpleton you are!" Nevertheless, it now dawned upon

her for the first time that her own sceptical outlook on life led to stagnation, to nothingness, and only such strong faith as animated Reb Avram Ber led to the highroad of life; it was only by utter simplicity and a childish belief in one's fellow beings that one could gain the whole world, with these qualities alone could one savour the true delights of life; indeed these qualities were in themselves the most beautiful thing that life had to offer, and a truly wise man was he who could accept this offering.[11]

The same attributes, especially "a childish belief in one's fellow beings", made Gimpel both a fool and a *mensh*. As a rabbi told Gimpel when he complained that his faith had made him a laughing stock: "It is written, better to be a fool all your days than for one hour to be evil. You are not a fool. They are the fools. For he who causes his neighbour to feel shame loses Paradise himself." What Bashevis did in "Gimpel the Fool" was to shift the responsibility from the believer to the scoffer; thus each time the faithful are made to look foolish the world is diminished. Consequently Bashevis felt his father's disappointment when a miracle was shown to have a rational explanation. If he did share his mother's point of view, he certainly looked more kindly upon his father that she ever did.

In My Father's Court was Bashevis's affectionate memoir of Pinchos Mendel's adventures as a rabbi in Warsaw. One chapter, "Why the Geese Shrieked", turned the dispute between his parents into a parable about growing up. A frightened woman brought two decapitated geese to the rabbi. When hurled together they shrieked. Bashevis was so terrified that he ran to his mother (rather than his father) for protection. Meanwhile Pinchos Mendel's eyes showed "a mixture of fear and vindication", vindication because the phenomenon demonstrated that there were "still mysterious forces at work in the world". But in Bathsheba's eyes there was "something like sadness, and also anger". She regarded the woman "with a certain resentment". The geese were a challenge; they confirmed Pinchos Mendel's mysticism and questioned Bathsheba's rationalism. When it seemed that he must triumph, her face grew "sullen, smaller, sharper. In her eyes could be seen indigation and also something like shame". Pinchos Mendel imagined that the shrieks came from the souls of unbelievers at the gates of hell, and he looked at Bathsheba as if to say: "You take after *them*." Then Bathsheba laughed, a laugh that made them all tremble. She asked the woman if the windpipes had been removed, was told they hadn't, and set to work extracting them. "On her face could be seen the wrath of the rationalist whom someone has tried to frighten in broad daylight." In Pinchos Mendel's heart was the knowledge that "logic, cold logic, was again tearing down faith,

mocking it, holding it up to ridicule and scorn". Bathsheba returned
the geese to the woman, who prepared to hurl them together again.

> If the geese shrieked, Mother would have lost all: her rationalist's
> daring, her skepticism which she had inherited from her intellectual
> father. And I? Although I was afraid, I prayed inwardly that the geese
> *would* shriek, shriek so loud that people in the street would hear and
> come running.[12]

Forced to choose between his parents, Bashevis picked his father
(despite what he told *Commentary*). He wanted the wonder of
childhood rather than the logic of the quotidian, but he got the latter.
Hidden in Bashevis's fiction is an attempt to reconcile his parents.
This is Gimpel's rational explanation of the miraculous:

> I wandered over the land, and good people did not neglect me. After
> many years I became old and white; I heard a great deal, many lies and
> falsehoods, but the longer I lived the more I understood that there were
> really no lies. Whatever doesn't really happen is dreamed at night. It
> happens to one if it doesn't happen to another, tomorrow if not today,
> or a century hence if not next year. What difference can it make? Often
> I heard tales of which I said, "Now this is a thing that cannot happen."
> But before a year had elapsed I heard that it actually had come to pass
> somewhere.[13]

Long after the incident described above, Bashevis was strolling with
his father past the empty religious bookstores on Franciszkanska
Street. He imagined what Pinchos Mendel, now the father of wordly
writers, must be thinking as he gazed into the deserted shops.

> The writers were a gang of clowns, lechers, scoundrels. What shame
> and mortification he felt for producing such offspring from his loins!
> Father put all the blame on Mother, the daughter of a *misnagid*, an anti-
> Hasid. It was she who had planted the seeds of doubt, of heresy, within
> us.[14]

For example, there was the occasion when certain predictions of the
Radzymin rabbi proved to be utterly wrong. His followers, including
Pinchos Mendel, promptly declared this to be a greater miracle than if
he had been right.

> "It's possible for a saint to be incapable of miracles."
> But my mother said, "How can a fool be a saint?"
> "Go on! Corrupt the children!" Father said.
> "I want my children to believe in God, not in an idiot," Mother
> replied.
> "First it will be the Radzymin Rabbi, tomorrow all Rabbis, and then,
> God forbid, the Baal Shem himself," Father cried.[15]

Pinchos Mendel's logic, expressing the progressive nature of doubt, reappears in Bashevis's fiction, where it frequently foretells the course of the action. For the moment it is sufficient to record Bashevis's agreement: "He was right."

> Even though my brother still dressed as a Hasid, he spent more and more time painting and reading wordly books, debating at length with Mother, telling her about Copernicus, Darwin, and Newton, of whom she had already read in Hebrew books. She had a predilection for philosophy and countered my brother's views with the kind of arguments religious philosophers still use.[16]

Pinchos Mendel's response was wholly emotional; he threw up his arms and screamed, "You unbeliever, you wicked person." "The fact that he screamed was a proof that he couldn't answer," said Bashevis.[17] Thus Pinchos Mendel was both wrong and right; his rabbis might have been fools, but it was philosophers, not rabbis, whose ideas created the modern world, this "slaughterhouse and brothel".

Nevertheless, Bashevis recognized the importance of truth, as pursued by Bathsheba. It was to her that Joshua turned before he was old enough to seek the answers himself. Observing that the windows of the tobacco shops in Leoncin "showed tomcats in lacquered boots smoking cigarettes in holders", he badgered his mother to explain "the connection between a cat wearing boots and smoking, for even then my passion for realism would not let me accept such an incongruity blindly".

At the age of three, Joshua was wrapped in a prayer shawl and harnessed to the yoke of the Torah. The word "yoke" gives a clear indication of Joshua's attitude to his religious education. His first teacher was a grotesque incompetent with sadistic inclinations, his successors were little better. On the first day, Joshua was led to the Torah and shown the aleph-bet. When he reached the final letter he was told to close his eyes. Opening them again he found raisins and almonds scattered over the grease-stained page, proof that the Torah was sweet. But Joshua the realist was not fooled. He tasted no sweetness when his teacher humiliated him, and he resisted the despised heder with all the determination of a three-year-old. In fact he formed a strong dislike for the Torah. This unequal tussle between the infant and his tyrannical master provided Joshua with a model for later fictional struggles; for example, in *The Family Carnovsky* when Jegor is exhibited naked before his school by its Nazi director as a member of a degenerate race. Unlike the unfortunate Jegor, Joshua refused to regard himself as a freak, he knew that the world "was no pit of iniquity totally riddled with the vanity of vanities but an incredibly

beautiful place abounding in indescribable joys''. So he waited until
his parents dozed off, ''then fled like a thief from the prison of the
Torah, the awe of God and of Jewishness''.

Instead of mixing with respectable boys from good hasidic homes,
Joshua befriended the sons of riff-raff. And in the synagogue, rather
than remain beside the eastern wall, reserved for community leaders,
where the Torah was discussed non-stop, he edged toward the western
wall. Here he heard talk of ''horses, cattle, fairs, fights, fires,
epidemics, highwaymen, thieves, soldiers, gypsies, and other such
fascinating subjects''. Sometimes there were beggars, ''men who had
roamed the world and could spin marvellous yarns'', and youths from
Warsaw employed in Leoncin as journeymen who ''told wondrous
stories about the capital city, where water could be drawn right out of
the walls, where lamps burned without naphtha, and other such
miraculous phenomena''. Apart from showing the birth of a rebellious
imagination, Joshua's behaviour in the synagogue anticipated his
political movement, always in the direction of the under-privileged.
Indeed, one of the few compliments he paid his father was to call him a
''man of the people who had compassion for the common man''. One
of these common men, an unemployed gentile, spread a story that a
Christian child had been lured to the bath-house and ritually
slaughtered, whereupon its blood had been collected in a pail, rushed
to the baker, and poured into the matzo mix. The fact that no child was
missing did not prevent the local villagers from taking the news
seriously enough to stone the Jews. Thus Joshua learned that stories
could be more than simple entertainment, they also had the power to
sway the masses; in other words, gullibility had a dangerous
underside. After the Radzymin rabbi's ''miracle'' when his supporters
turned defeat into victory by refusing to accept reality, Bashevis
remarked: ''Years later I observed that political groups were familiar
with the trick, as one could tell by the way they twisted facts and
corrupted logic.'' Learning from their mother (whose scepticism was
confirmed by history), both brothers grew sensitive to the dangers
inherent in irrational belief.

Like his brother, Bashevis began his religious instruction while still
an infant. He learned his aleph-bet at Radzymin, where the family
then lived. Unlike Joshua, he experienced ''the profound joy of
learning''. Even so, he was also tempted by the great outdoors, though
he was more inclined to metaphysical speculations than romping with
ruffians: ''I would gaze at the horizon. Was that the end of the world?
What happened there and what was beyond it? What were day and
night? Why did birds fly and worms crawl?'' Naturally it was his
mother he ''torments'' with these questions, but it was his father who

always replied, "That's how the Lord made it." This was insufficient for Bashevis, who had a passion for realism. He wanted to see God:

> He had created everything but could not be seen. One had to thank Him before eating a cookie, wear ritual fringes and sidelocks for Him. I pointed to a cloud and asked, "Is that Him?"
>
> Father became furious: "Idiot, that's a cloud. It absorbs water and pours out rain...."[18]

Bashevis's education continued in Warsaw. He must have had better luck with his teachers than Joshua:

> The heder, too often described as a place where innocent children suffered at the hands of a sloppy, ill-tempered teacher, was not quite that. What was wrong with society was wrong with the heder.[19]

Bashevis did not see heder as a metaphor for a totalitarian régime, he saw it as a microcosm of the world with miniature bullies, toadies, hypocrites, liars, moneylenders and victims. Therefore he was more inclined to accept the situation than to want to change it. He did not resist, rather he sought a role of his own. Even at that age, he claimed, he was aware how unusual he was; sometimes to the point of melodrama: "I'll go mad, I thought — there was too much happening in my head all the time. Shouldn't I jump from the balcony? Or spit down on the janitor's cap?" Eventually his skill as a raconteur won him a group of admirers. They gathered round as he repeated stories his brother had told his mother, underlining the genetic chain of influence. When Joshua and Bashevis described their schooldays they were also recreating their personalities in accordance with their self-images, showing how the child was father to the man.

No less her parent's daughter, Esther was excluded from a full education by her sex. Bashevis wrote of her:

> My brother Israel Joshua took after my mother's family, but Hinde Esther had inherited the Hasidic inspiration, the love of humanity, and the eccentric nature of Father's side.... She was a Hasid in skirts.... My father ignored her because she was a girl, and my mother could not understand her.[20]

Being too young to be of interest, Bashevis had no role in *Deborah*, unlike Joshua (who became Michael). "Michael and Deborah were never on very friendly terms", Esther wrote. Deborah (Esther) could not understand how her younger brother preferred playing to studying, "...as she poured out the tea she reflected that had she been a boy instead of a girl, she would not have found herself driven to commit such iniquities. She would have spent all her time in the study of the Talmud." When she overhead her father proudly say of

Michael, "One day he will be a brilliant Talmudist," she asked: "And
Father, what am I going to be one day?" Since he regarded this as a
non-question, he required prompting before replying, "What are *you*
going to be one day? Nothing, of course!" In Avram Ber's mind there
was only one ambition for a pious woman, "the bringing of happiness
into the home by ministering to her husband and bearing him
children". But Deborah had no intention of growing into such a
nobody.

> Amost every night, in bed, she firmly resolved to give up her duties of
> keeping house, and to become a student instead. Ever since childhood
> she had longed to receive an education, to cease being the nonentity of
> the family. She would learn things, gain understanding…she,
> Deborah — the girl who, as her father had once said, was to be a mere
> nobody when she grew up — would be a person of real consequence.
> She would make her own life.[21]

Despite these brave ambitions Deborah remained trapped by
housework, by "the usual drab routine", suffering constant
frustration, receiving daily reminders of her ignorance. Her father
disapproved of erudition in any woman, especially his wife, "and was
determined that this mistake should not be repeated in Deborah's
case". But instead of encouraging her daughter, Raizela perversely
belittled Deborah at every opportunity; for example, when Deborah
presented Raizela with the truth about the Radzymin rabbi she was
told to hold her tongue, even though Raizela had already called his
followers "feeble minded" and the zaddik himself "their golden calf".
Branding the zaddik a "downright liar", as Deborah had done, was
apparently going too far. As Bashevis noted, rather censoriously, "My
sister…kept…expressing opinions that she should have kept to
herself."

> "For goodness' sake, stop! You're an utter fool!" Raizela snapped back
> at her, having completely lost her patience. "No wonder it is written in
> the Talmud that *an ignoramus will ask questions for the mere sake of
> asking,*" she turned to Michael with a smile. Deborah did not
> understand this Hebrew quotation, but instinctively gathered the gist
> of it. She turned away shamefaced and with a vow that never again
> would she humbly serve the "great", only to be scoffed at, like those
> poor crowds that were struggling to see the *Tsadik*….[22]

What hurt Deborah more than anything was the conspiratorial smile
between mother and son that mocked their uneducated relative. This
was compounded when Bathsheba (in *Of a World That Is No More*)
echoed her husband's prophecies concerning his progeny:

> When my sister asked Mother what *she* should be when *she* grew up,

Mother answered her question with another: "What *can* a girl be?" My sister, jealous since childhood, couldn't accept the fact that her talents weren't appreciated. This was a source of constant friction between us.[23]

"In her jealousy of my brother Israel Joshua, she made up numerous accusations," wrote Bashevis, "but then, regretting what she had done, she would want to kiss him."

How was it that the same mother who poured scorn on the "miracle" of the Radzymin rabbi in front of her sons could scold her daughter for doing the same? It was as if, in this case, she was consciously refusing to take the role of liberator. Like her daughter she was confined by the traditional female role, but their common fate made them enemies instead of allies. Bathsheba's bitterness made Esther's aspirations distasteful to her, and she determined to stop her daughter turning into an over-educated housewife. To achieve this she curtailed her education, and whispered not a word against convention. To demonstrate how unfairly her mother treated her, Esther called upon the evidence of an impartial witness:

Mottel slipped into the kitchen where Deborah was sulking in a corner. Mottel knew the cause of her bitterness: he had overheard Raizela scold her without any justification whatever, whereas Michael, who had been playing truant, had been let off without so much as a word. Favouritism, thought Mottel, not without indignation.[24]

Actually, this is one of the few clumsy moments when autobiographical self-righteousness gives away the fictional disguise. Bashevis believed that his sister and mother were involved in a "Freudian drama". Esther accused her mother of not loving her, "which was untrue", added Bashevis while admitting that they were incompatible. Maurice Carr was not so sure:

Bathsheva's disappointment that her first-born was a girl, hardened into a lifelong bitter distaste (to which I can attest: On our 1926 trip to Poland, Bathsheva's first words were: "But Hindela, you're not as ugly as I thought you were!" After that she hardly spoke at all. As for Hindela's son, myself, she gave me one look and never again looked my way, let alone addressed me). Whether or not this unhappy relationship was the cause, my mother, who at the age of 12 became bloated with a mysterious, near-fatal sickness, suffered very poor health to the end.[25]

Against all the odds Esther became a writer. Indeed she was the first of the Singer siblings to show any flair for writing. Bashevis recalled that it was in the letters she sent to her future husband that "the first literary spark in our family became apparent".[26] "She wrote long, intelligent, even humorous letters, of which my father was unaware, but my mother was amazed that her daughter had acquired such command of words." She even wrote some stories at this time, according to her son, "but was persuaded by her parents to tear them up lest her luggage be checked at the border on her departure for Berlin and the Czarist customs officers or police suspect her manuscripts are 'revolutionary'".

Bathsheba's attitude toward Esther seems even more callous when it is compared to the way she was treated at her father's home in Bilgoray. "She was the only female in the family with intellectual tendencies, and Grandfather often decried the fact that she hadn't been born a man", wrote Joshua. "Mother was proud that her father discussed exalted matters with her...." Esther was more specific, "Raizela was the only person in the house he ever spoke to." Perhaps it was loneliness that turned Esther into a writer. Bashevis had no answer, just a question, "How did it come about?" Bashevis was asked flippantly if he became a writer as a result of Joshua dropping him on his head when still a baby (an incident described in *Of a World That Is No More*). "Well, you never know what nature does," he replied:

> I read about a case where a man got a blow on his head and suddenly became clairvoyant. So it's possible. But I would say that the genes play a bigger part. I've had many bumps on the head and somehow they didn't make me a genius. I'll try again.[27]

The most striking repository of these genes was Bathsheba's father, so it follows that a major influence resided in Bilgoray.

By all accounts, the rabbi of Bilgoray was an awe-inspiring character. "From the first time I met him, I was captivated by my grandfather's personality," wrote Joshua. "Although I naturally did not grasp its full impact at the time, nevertheless I felt its power."

> Grandfather was tall, with dark piercing eyes, a refined but grim face, a gray beard and earlocks, and a rangy physique. He was sharp of speech, taciturn, dignified. For some reason, I feared him immediately even as I loved him.[28]

Esther expressed similar sentiments in *Deborah:*

> He spent every moment of the day in his private study, poring over the Talmud and composing his books, and no one ever saw anything of him. On those rare occasions when he came out to stretch his limbs she simply longed to have a word with him, or at the very least to hear him speak (for, as it happened, she loved him passionately), but he had a strange incomprehensible language all of his own... which would quite overawe the love she bore him, so that in the end her respect for him would outweigh her love.[29]

By the time Bashevis visited Bilgoraỷ, his grandfather was dead and his Uncle Joseph the rabbi. Even so, the town itself, still bearing the mark of the deceased sage, exerted a fascination upon him, so that afterwards it became invested with symbolic power. Writing of Bilgoray in *In My Father's Court* he said, "In this world of old Jewishness I found a spiritual treasure trove. I had the chance to see our past as it really was. Time seemed to flow backwards. I lived Jewish history." Speaking to *Commentary* he added, "I could have written *The Family Moskat* (which takes place in Warsaw) without having lived in Bilgoray, but I could never have written *Satan in Goray* or some of my other stories without having been there." Bilgoray, of course, provided more than atmosphere. The words "spiritual treasure trove" are important. Treasure is the contemporary rediscovery of ancient valuables, an interpolation of the past into the present, a celebration of anachronism. Thus Bashevis can write about two periods simultaneously; of Bilgoray as the centre that holds the Jewish world together, a token of the spiritual possibilities of human nature, and of Bilgoray in its ruined state, a reminder of the destructive potential of that same human nature. The ambiguity goes deeper, however, for the imaginative recreation of Bilgoray is an inevitable precursor of its destruction. The very act which keeps Bilgoray alive — and which made Joshua and Bashevis writers rather than rabbis — is a symptom of the enlightenment that drained its unique vitality.

When Bathsheba took Joshua and Esther to Bilgoray they travelled toward the Austrian frontier by horse and cart, by ferry and by train. Joshua was obsessed by horses, to his mother's disgust, he would "gladly have given all the Gemaras in the world for one of the horse's whinnies". Among the horses that pulled them was an unfortunate creature called One-Eye, constantly reviled by its driver. "All of the world's catastrophies seemed to be heaped on One-Eye's swayed, lacerated back," commented Joshua. One-Eye became, in effect, the prototype of Joshua's sadder protagonists. At the end of *East of Eden* Nachman was cast into no man's land between Poland and Russia, discarded by the revolution he had lived for, with no company but a dying horse. "In that abandoned, exhausted, used-up animal, gasping in its death agony, he saw himself, his whole life." Bashevis was no less excited as he journied from Warsaw to Bilgoray, but his imagination soared too high to make social observation possible, "Like a king or a great wizard, I rode through the world...." And he conquered the world, transforming it into whatever took his fancy.

The sons of Jacob were herding sheep nearby. Before Joseph's stacks of grain, other stacks bowed down.... We saw sheep. The world seemed

like an open Pentateuch. The moon and the eleven stars came out,
bowing before Joseph, the future ruler of Egypt.[30]

Joseph was one of Bashevis's models. When he was telling stories to
his cronies at heder he imagined that he was Joseph and they were his
envious brothers forced to eat humble pie. On Joshua's trip they saw a
different Israel in the fields of Poland. Bathsheba wept as she said:

> "Once, before the Destruction of the Temple in the land of Israel, Jews
> tilled and sowed their own fields and women herded sheep.... Today
> the gentiles sit, each under his own grapevine and fig tree, while we
> suffer in exile, the objects of shame and contempt by other
> peoples...."[31]

While Bashevis gloried in the aristocracy of his imagination, Joshua
observed the world as a political machine.

He perceived that his grandfather's house had two spheres of
influence. "Between the courtroom and the kitchen was a vestibule in
which stood a large barrel of water, but this narrow passageway kept
the husband and wife further apart than would an ocean. Their two
domains were like two separate worlds." Into the courtroom went
litigants, visitors, travellers, all with stories to tell. And Joshua
listened, just as Bashevis did later in his father's court. While the men
went to the rabbi, the women went to the rebbetzin to pour out their
hearts. And Joshua heard it all. As well as grandparents, the house was
filled with uncles, aunts, cousins and more distant relations. Always
quick to nose out intrigue, Joshua was soon aware of the rivalry
between the rabbi's two sons, Joseph and Itche, and their wives, Sarah
and Rochele. Of the two Joshua preferred his Uncle Joseph, having
nothing but contempt for Rochele's father, a pious and erudite man
who set out to prove that everything in the world was forbidden. This
sage declared that it was a sin to pee in the snow on the Sabbath, "since
this could be compared to ploughing on the holy day". Despite this
innate scepticism Joshua, like Bashevis, succumbed to the magic of
the Sabbath in Bilgoray:

> I loved the Sabbaths in Bilgoraj. In this devout, old-fashioned
> community the sanctity of the holy day was felt starting Friday
> morning.... Grandmother put on a silk dress that shimmered with all
> the colors of the rainbow.... She also exchanged her week-day
> headcloth for a satin bonnet adorned with cherries, currants, grapes,
> and assorted fruit replete with stems and bows.... Grandfather came
> back from the bathhouse, his face flushed and glowing, his earlocks
> twice their normal length from the dampness.... His knee-length
> stockings were dazzling white, as was the shirt, especially against the
> blackness of his satin Sabbath gaberdine and the fur-edged cap.... The

old synagogue, with its supporting columns, brass chandeliers, and sconces, glowed in the candlelight.... And louder and more fervent than all was the voice of my grandfather. Although a *misnagid* and by nature taciturn, he was transported into rapture by the sanctity of the occasion.[32]

After the service there was a meal, to which the rabbi invited "the most bedraggled beggars, the most repulsive cripples, misfits and freaks whom no other householder would take into his home". Although the grotesques robbed Joshua of his appetite for "Grandmother's heavenly fish, soup, and chicken with carrots", he devoured their fantastic tales instead.

Joshua's grandmother also had a strong social conscience. Bilgoray's main industry was the making of horse-hair sieves. Many of the workers, who were paid by contractors, grew so poor they had to go begging from door to door for Sabbath food. His grandmother always had loaves ready for them, and hard words for the hasidim "who included in their ranks these contractors and some of the worst exploiters and bloodsuckers in town". Already sensitive to the cruelties of capitalism, Joshua witnessed what happened when these "humble and broken men" went to the rabbi to summon their employers to litigation. The town magnate was called Reb Joshua Maimon.

> The lawsuits were noisy affairs. The poor sievemakers wept, ranted, called for justice, fairness, and Jewishness.
> "Is it fair?" they lamented. "We have no strength left to work and we don't earn enough to feed our families!"
> "I pay my gentile workers even less," Reb Joshua observed calmly.
> Grandfather spoke about Jewishness. "Reb Joshua, the gentiles have their land to fall back on.... Gentiles don't eat kosher food, gentiles don't hire tutors for their children, gentiles work on the Sabbath.... Jews can't be likened to gentiles, beg the comparison...."
> "In business, Rabbi, you have to find every means of cutting costs," Reb Joshua explained, ignoring the workers' indignant outcries.[33]

Reb Joshua's cold logic reduced a worker to tears of frustration, whereupon the rabbi "sprang up and hugged him as he would a child". Stroking the man's sleeves of rags he whispered, "God is the Merciful Father." But Joshua didn't understand how a good God could sanction such injustice, could allow the poor to bear such suffering. He nagged his grandfather until the rabbi ran out of answers and sent him off to bed. Although Joshua rejected his grandfather's faith, he borrowed his principles when he judged his own creations in his fictional *beth din*. Every politician seemed wanting when compared to the rabbi of Bilgoray:

A kind of implacable force seemed to emanate from the tall, stern, imposing man who appeared to have been born for his role as shepherd of a community. He ruled the city with wisdom and justice, feared nothing and no one, did not let the smallest matter pass unnoticed, and granted immunity to no one, no matter how rich, pious, or powerful.[34]

And yet, the fact remained that he was unable to squeeze another kopeck out of Reb Joshua Maimon.

The visits of Joshua and Bashevis to Bilgoray were separated by the First World War, during the course of which there was no communication between Bilgoray and Warsaw. As a consequence of this, Bathsheba remained in ignorance of her father's death. Characteristically, Bashevis prefaced the dreadful revelation awaiting her with a premonition. But the rabbi's demise was only one of many:

> After a silence they began to tell her not only about her father but also about her mother and sister-in-law, Uncle Joseph's wife, Sarah. Grandfather had died in Lublin, Grandmother a few months later in Bilgoray. Sarah and a daughter, Ittele, had died of cholera, and two cousins, Ezikiel and Itta Deborah, the son of Uncle Itche and the daughter of Aunt Taube, had also died.[35]

The shock was an education for Bashevis, who was to use insecurity as a basis for narrative, turning a beautiful girl into a consumptive wreck within a few sentences. Thos who survived in his own family were well scattered by now.

> When my mother took me and my brother Moshe to Bilgoraj, my brother Joshua remained in Warsaw. He hadn't the slightest desire to bury himself away in such a Godforsaken hole as Bilgoraj. My father went back to Radzymin to help the Hasidic rabbi there compose his books.... Eventually, my brother went to Kiev, which the Germans had occupied, and he worked there in the local Yiddish press.... My sister Hindele had been living in Antwerp with her husband, and when the Germans invaded Belgium, the couple fled to England.[36]

Only Joshua would have called Bilgoray "Godforsaken". On the contrary, Bashevis would have us believe that Bilgoray and such *shtetlach* were the only places in the world not Godforsaken. And yet, while there, Bashevis began to educate himself in the matters of this world rather than the next.

Though outwardly normal, Bilgoray was marked for change, its "immutability was being penetrated from many sources"; by Zionists, Bolsheviks, Bundists and actors. Worst of all, there was a secular library. For Jews on the edge of emancipation, the library was a house of ecstatic liberation. It figures as such in almost every Yiddish writer's autobiography; the following passage comes from *My*

Memoirs by Isaac Leib Peretz:

> As I groped for the door, my hand trembled. Like a blind person, I felt for the keyhole. "I'll look in first," I said to myself. I saw only darkness, for the shutters were closed. However, through the cracks, beams of light filtered into the library, illuminating the books heaped on the floor. "The pillar of Smoke! The pillar of Fire! Both lead to the wilderness!" I turned the key, and the rusty lock emitted rasping sounds. My heart palpitated, yet I found the courage to open the door. I hastily threw the shutters wide open. I was in "their" academy — a storehouse of gentile learning.[37]

Bashevis himself used "entranced", "fascinated", "bewildered", "exalted", to describe his feelings after reading forbidden texts. "I borrowed a grammar and attacked it with incredible passion," he wrote, using the language of sexual assault. A poem resulted. And all Bilgoray claimed that the "Rabbi's grandson was absorbed in heretical literature".[38] The irresistible desire for knowledge began to destroy Bilgoray long before the anti-Semites finished the job.

The rabbi of Bilgoray was justified in banning theatrical troupes from his town, a tradition his son was unable to maintain. If Pinchos Mendel had managed to remove the artists from Leoncin, Joshua might not have been seduced by the world so easily. The artists arrived from Warsaw to decorate Squire Christowski's manor house and retouch the holy pictures in the church. What shocked the Jews of Leoncin most was the fact that these prettifiers of Jesus were fellow Jews. But Joshua, "possessed of an insatiable curiosity about everything and everybody", was delighted with the newcomers.

> I could gather more from one person than from a thousand holy books. I fled from these books and slaked my thirst for life among plants, animals, and people, particularly the common people whose lives seemed so round and complete.[39]

With the artists to distract them, the boys in heder stopped paying attention to their lessons. Despite parental warnings, Joshua sneaked over to the manor house and peeped at the painters through a hole in the fence. They wore conical hats, their clothes were multi-coloured from splashes of paint, they were a magical sight. One even kept pigeons beneath his coat. Even more marvellous were their creations:

> From their skillful fingers emerged a fantastic menagerie of animals such as my eyes had never beheld in life or in story books; also rivers, windmills, trees, shepherds, nymphs, and colourful birds that flew to settle on the walls and terraces.[40]

Joshua, who had wanted to draw ever since childhood, was

hypnotized, unable to take his eyes off "the geniuses who could paint such gorgeous pictures". But as ever authority intervened to ruin his pleasure, as Russian constables suddenly appeared to arrest the artists for having spoken ill of the Tsar. It was too late to save the Tsar, and too late to save Joshua.

> I choked back tears and for a long time gazed after the strangers who had disturbed my life in such a way that I would forever after be restless.[41]

Joshua's growing curiosity was further goaded by the arrival of a Litvak pupil named Sheike, a boy with an independent mind. His speciality was stories of the champions of Grodno, who were apt to make mincemeat of gentiles. Moreover, Sheike knew all about "Zionism, Socialism, about strikes and revolutions, about the assassination of policemen, officers, generals, and even emperors". Sheike left Joshua with a "nagging urge for something better, bigger, and more exciting than what I had".

Joshua's wish came true. In 1905 Russia went to war with Japan. At the same time word reached Leoncin of a pogrom in Bialystok. The report was filled with such terrible atrocities that Joshua actually turned on God, " 'It's God's fault!' I cried. 'He is evil, evil!' " When news of other massacres surfaced, the hasidim found a different interpretation; the end of days was at hand, the Messiah was on the way. Of this Pinchos Mendel had no doubt; the war between Russia and Japan was "clearly the conflict between Gog and Magog", a necessary portent. Other signs were the pogroms and revolutions, "omens signifying the suffering that everyone knew would presage the coming of the Messiah". Finally, passages in the Torah and "the Gemara and other holy books insinuated that the year 5666 would truly be the year of redemption". In the synagogue Pinchos Mendel announced, "Men, these are the true pangs that are a prelude to the coming of the Messiah.... With the help of God, we will be redeemed before the year is out!" Bathsheba, more at home with logic and scepticism than with cabbalistic divination, remained unmoved by her husband's proofs. She met his enthusiasm with "her level stare, the large gray eyes cooling his exuberance like a dash of ice water". Joshua, however, was thrilled by the promise of redemption, even though his idea of Paradise was rather more garish than his father's; instead of saints he would be surrounded by gentile slaves, food and wine. He listened avidly to the merchant's stories

> of street demonstrations and barricades; of men and women marching with red banners and singing songs defying the Tsar; of soldiers bayoneting people in the streets; of a girl in a red dress who led the

rebels; of Socialists who buried their dead wrapped not in shrouds but in red flags; of heretics who said that a human being didn't possess a soul but a kind of "electricity" that ceased functioning when the person died; of other heretics who said that the descendant of David, the son of Jesse, was not the Messiah but Dr Herzl, whose disciples would lead the Jews to the land of Israel....[42]

Pinchos Mendel was also looking forward to spending eternity in Israel, though he was uncertain of his transport; some authorities, for example, held that a great cloud would descend "which the Jews would board en masse and on which they would float off to Israel". While Joshua was enthralled by his father's exegesis, the details included above anticipated his interest in history, not as revelation, the mysterious working of divinity, but as a dialectical struggle between classes. As he was shortly to learn, history continued regardless of the Jews.

Rosh Hashana, the Jewish New Year, the appointed day, came and went without the Messiah appearing. Pinchos Mendel felt ashamed as if he had personally let down the community. His son was "enraged and embittered". There and then he "ceased to believe in the power of prayer and in the coming of the Messiah during my lifetime". Joshua's immediate response to this blow was to intone the name of the Angel of Fire, which his prayer book warned would lead to the destruction of the world.

> The fate of the world lay in my hands; I could either allow it to remain as it had for 5666 years and a day or I could destroy it in a flash. Until now, it had taken every bit of self-restraint not to speak the dreaded name.... But this year I had been so deeply disillusioned that I threw caution to the winds and, holding my breath, I uttered the forbidden name.[43]

Nothing happened, which shook his faith even further. Bashevis repeated some of the arguments his older brother had used against the Messiah,

> He said: How long should we wait for the Messiah when we've waited for him two thousand years and he didn't come? We may wait another two thousand years and he still will not come.[44]

But Pinchos Mendel's faith remained resolute, and in 1914 it seemed that his patience was about to be rewarded. "This was the war between Gog and Magog, Father said. And every day he discovered new omens proving that the Messiah was soon to come...." Pinchos Mendel's messianic vision of history and his son's apocalyptic revenge reverberated through Joshua's family sagas, as fictional fathers and sons advanced acrimoniously toward their Promised Lands, the one in

Paradise, the other in the Soviet Union. Both shared the same zeal, the same blindness to facts, the same fate. At the end of *The Family Moskat* Bashevis revealed their true Messiah. Hertz Yanover, heretic son of a Talmudic scholar, announced as the Nazis approached Warsaw, "The Messiah will come soon.... Death is the Messiah. That's the real truth." Far from being transported to Israel upon a cloud, the Jews were transformed into a puff of smoke.

Subsequently Bashevis softened this terrible image:

> Spinoza says in his *Ethics* that there is always something left from everything which has lived.... And so I believe too that the Jews of Poland have not completely disappeared.... You know the bodies of all these people might have died, but something — call it spirit, or whatever — is still somewhere in the universe. This is a mystical kind of feeling; but I feel there is truth in it, although there is no scientific evidence that it is so.[45]

At the same time he maintained:

> I'm a sceptic. I'm a sceptic about making a better world. When it comes to this business where you tell me that this-or-that régime, one sociological order or another, will bring happiness to people, I know that it will never work, call it by any name you want. People will remain people, and they have remained people under communism and all other kinds of isms. But I'm not a sceptic when it comes to belief in God. I do believe. I always did. That there is a plan, a consciousness behind creation, that it's not an accident.... But my brother, he was a sceptic. He said: maybe there was no plan, maybe there is no God, maybe there is no higher consciousness. In this respect we are different.[46]

Is it possible to be both a mystic and a sceptic? In the preface to *A Little Boy in Search of God* (subtitled "Mysticism in a Personal Light") Bashevis tried to marry the two: "In essence every mystic is a doubter. He is by nature a seeker. Mysticism and scepticism are not contradictory." Mysticism requires the faith possessed by Gimpel or Pinchos Mendel, but such faith can also be dangerous when exploited by an ideologue. In which case scepticism may be the best defence. But Bashevis shared Esther's view that total scepticism was sterile, that creativity demanded a sense of wonder. In "Gimpel the Fool" he attempted to reconcile the two by presenting falsehood as truth anticipated, a concept which works in the story but is less convincing outside. How can Gimpel ensure that his creative energies are not put to destructive ends? How does the mystic know when to be sceptical? What credulity needs is a constant check; not scepticism, but Judaism. Bashevis was sceptical of all man-made systems, but Judaism was divinely inspired. Surely, this was the answer; praise the transcendent imagination! But there was a flaw. Even if of extra-terrestial origin

Judaism functioned as part of human nature, which resisted its constraints. It was these struggles — between fathers and sons, mysticism and scepticism, religion and human nature — that provided the brothers with their material. They concentrated upon characters persuaded to act against their better natures by the dominant ideology. Bashevis unleashed the imagination, while Joshua suppressed the conscience. Bashevis's characters were beguiled into releasing the id from the constraints of their tradition, while Joshua's were fooled by charlatans. Bashevis took more risks, for he became implicated in the crimes he abhorred, at once a mystic and a sceptic, while Joshua was able to stand aside as a detached observer.

Bashevis wrote a story called "The Gentleman from Cracow". He claimed he was re-telling an old Frampol legend of how a gentleman came to Frampol from Cracow and led the entire community astray, save for the saintly Rabbi Ozer. The gentleman arrived in the middle of a drought when all were starving. "Just when all hope had been abandoned...a miracle occurred." In their despair the Jews of Frampol were prepared to believe in anyone, especially a gentleman who promised to end their troubles; how could they be expected to distinguish a miracle from temptation? They decided that the stranger was "clearly a gift from Heaven", and that it had been decreed above that "Frampol was not destined to vanish". But when the gentleman planned a ball, where he could examine all the beautiful daughters of Frampol and pick a bride, Rabbi Ozer made his first objection:

"What kind of charlatan is this?" he shouted. "Frampol is not Cracow. All we need is a ball! Heaven forbid that we bring down a plague, and innocent infants be made to pay for our frivolity."[47]

However, he was countered with unanswerable arguments; the gentleman's money will bring blessings to Frampol, the synagogue will be repaired, the sick healed. So the rabbi reluctantly gave his consent and the preparations began. Thoughts turned from higher things to concentrate upon the ball. Vanity became the ruling passion. And the gentleman's character developed in sympathy with this mood; his clothes became more showy, his appetite greater. The reader never has any more information about this man than was available to the people of Frampol, but we know they are being tested. In fact, only their rabbi stood between them and damnation.

Rabbi Ozer constantly warned his flock that they walked a downhill path led by the Evil One, but they paid no attention to him. Their minds and hearts were completely possessed by the ball, which would be held at the market place in the middle of the month, at the time of the full moon.[48]

The night of the ball began with a devilish sunset. "Like rivers of burning sulphur, fiery clouds streamed across the heavens, assuming the shapes of elephants, lions, snakes, and monsters." As a crimson comet fell from the sky the gentleman from Cracow began to address the throng:

> "Listen to me. I have wonderful things to tell you, but let no one be overcome by joy.... The Ruler of the Ten Lost Tribes of Israel knows of your miseries, and he has sent me to be your benefactor. But there is one condition. Tonight, every virgin must marry. I will provide a dowry of ten thousand ducats for each maiden, as well as a string of pearls that will hang to her knees."[49]

By now the people were too enraptured to even notice the devil's temptation, so the names of all the unmarried boys and girls were noted, tossed into skullcaps, and paired off. Thus Frampol fell. Satan was the tempter, and the agency he used was woman. "When the girls lifted their dresses to catch the gold coins...their legs and underclothing were exposed, which sent the men into paroxysms of lust." Pious men and women embraced without shame, "dancing and shouting as though possessed". The gentleman himself was paired with Hodle, daughter of Lipa the Ragpicker, outcast and harlot. As they danced a storm broke, and a single bolt of lightning struck the synagogue, the study house and the ritual bath. While the Jews cavorted with demons and witches, Frampol burned. And the gentleman was revealed as being "no longer the young man the villagers had welcomed, but a creature covered with scales...". Only Rabbi Ozer's house remained untouched among the general devastation.

> The town was unrecognizable. Where houses had been, only chimneys stood. Mounds of coal smouldered here and there.[50]

"Where are you, Jews, where are you?" called the rabbi. It is impossible to read these lines without thinking of the final fate of Frampol, as if this scene were a prophecy of the last catastrophe. But Bashevis relented; the Jews did not escape the Nazis, but he spared them damnation. In short, man is more dangerous that the devil.

Relentlessly chanting the Torah, Rabbi Ozer gradually won back his flock from Satan's spell. Naked they crawled from the swamp of slime, mud and ashes. Frampol was saved by the one man who adhered to the faith. But as the rabbi had foretold, it was the innocent was suffered, the unattended infants who perished in the fire. So Frampol learned its lesson, "A gold coin became an abomination...and even silver was looked at askance." However, the feeling remains that this conclusion was too easily reached, future safety too easily assured (from Satan, if not from man). Too much of the rabbi of Bilgoray, not enough of Pinchos Mendel, Rabbi Ozer was religion personified. What he lacked was the creative impulse. Even though Bashevis exposed the gentleman from Cracow in his true ugliness, and vividly demonstrated the inevitable consequence of flirting with him, he did not erase his initial attractiveness. Evil disguised as self-fulfilment continued to fascinate Bashevis. If all humanity's energy went into exorcizing evil, what would become of curiosity and a sense of wonder? A writer must take risks; the gentleman from Cracow gave more to Bashevis than Rabbi Ozer. "Old Jewishness" alone was insufficient to produce modern literature.

For all his faith, Pinchos Mendel fell into temporary despair after the Messiah's non-deliverance. It encouraged doubt and, worse, made the terrible occurrences of 1905 meaningless. "Even Father, incurable optimist that he was, could no longer subsist on faith and trust alone," wrote Joshua. So he decided to look for a better job, no easy matter for an unqualified rabbi. Now Pinchos Mendel was a frequent visitor to the court of the Radzymin rabbi, where he was welcomed as an honoured guest. Indeed, he had been presented with a fine rabbinical hat. Bathsheba was suspicious of such generosity, and wouldn't accept Pinchos Mendel's explanation that the gift was given because a rabbi should wear a special hat. "He didn't buy the hat for you but for himself," she maintained. "He wants to show the world that he has a rabbi among his followers...." In *Deborah*, Raizela offered Avram Ber a similar explanation, "The *Tsadik* of R—, you see, unlike most other *Tsadikim*, has very few learned *hassidim* among his followers, not to mention Rabbis, of course. Well, naturally, he likes to see a full-blown rabbi mingling with his crowd for once in a while.... Only that explains why he is so eager for your company...." "You're a sceptic! You're no better than your father!..." Avram Ber typically retorted. "I always said that your father made a very great mistake in giving you an education." But Bathsheba was correct, of course. The Radzymin rabbi proposed that Pinchos Mendel "study the codex with the students at the Yeshiva the rabbi had founded...edit the rabbi's writings and prepare his sayings and interpretations for publication...a handsome living." "Did the rabbi sign a contract with you?" asked Bathsheba. "God forbid, his word is good enough!" replied Pinchos Mendel. Despite her misgivings, Bathsheba agreed to the move. "Time proved Mother right," commented Joshua. "With her deep insight, she had detected a flaw in the saint's character. Later, Father was to pay dearly...." But for now his optimism had been restored.

Joshua never wrote directly of the period at Radzymin, though his

feelings can be deduced from the passion he poured into his anti-
hasidic novel *Yoshe Kalb,* in which Nyesheve and Rabbi Melech
represented Radzymin and its corrupt zaddik. As Bathsheba had
anticipated the real Radzymin rabbi (Reb Aaron Menachem Mendel)
quickly forgot his promises. He paid Pinchos Mendel no salary, but
doled out money at irregular intervals, and then only a pittance. While
he kept the Singers on the edge of destitution he lived like a lord.
Bashevis later noted,

> In Leoncin my sister and older brother had been pious, but the Rabbi's
> behavior had changed their attitude. My brother would imitate the
> Rabbi, shouting as he prayed, rolling his eyes as he dealt out food to the
> Hasidim. Father warned Mother that if she didn't stop abusing the
> Rabbi before the children they would proceed from doubting the Rabbi
> to doubting God. But Mother herself was the daughter of an opponent
> of Hasidism and had inherited some of her father's causticness. Even
> though Father resented the Rabbi, he felt that he had to defend him at
> home.[51]

However well-intentioned, it was actually Pinchos Mendel's refusal to
face facts that turned his progeny against religion. If he knew the rabbi
was a fraud, his support was a kind of hypocrisy. An absurd variation
upon his argument may be found in a satirical tale by Tashrak (pen
name of Israel Joseph Zevin) called "The Hole in the Beigel". The
story is narrated by a nincompoop, whose mind is over-exerted by his
rabbi's riddle, "What becomes of the hole in a Beigel, when one has
eaten the Beigel?" The questioned obsessed him until at last, in
America, he saw straight beigels without holes. But such an
innovation was not achieved without a civil war between the
conservatives and the reformers, "the Beigel-with-a-hole party and
the Beigel-without-a-hole party". The conservatives argued:

> "Our fathers' fathers baked Beigels with holes, the whole world eats
> Beigels with holes, and here comes a bold coxcomb of a fellow, upsets
> the order of the universe, and bakes Beigels *without* holes! Have you
> ever heard of such impertinence? It's just revolution! And if a person
> like this is allowed to go on, he will make an end to everything: today it's
> Beigels without holes, tomorrow it will be holes without Beigels!"

The reformers called such views old-fashioned and "contrary to the
spirit of the times". Open hostilities ensued.

> Children rose against their parents, wives against their husbands,
> engaged couples severed their ties, families were broken up, and still
> the battle raged — and all on account of the hole in a Beigel!

By stretching Pinchos Mendel's logic to its outer limits in such an absurd situation, Tashrak demonstrated the pettiness of such squabbles. Petty or not, Pinchos Mendel's unreasonableness had an unlooked for consequence; his children rose against their parents.

The arrival of the Singers at Radzymin (or R—) was recorded in *Deborah*. Michael (viz Joshua) was easily impressed, "Crumbs, what a town! What a town! Just like Jelhitz, and I don't think!" But Deborah was upset by the sight of a tramp, and experienced a prophetic sensation, "Such a wave of pity passed over her for the poor destitute white head of hair, that a pang of hate was born in her, hatred of the town where such a sight was possible." At first there seemed no cause for concern. Raizela continued to look "vexed and grieved" but "there was nothing she could find fault with", and every day Avram Ber returned from the yeshiva with fresh tidings of joy. However, this good fortune all depended upon the word of a single man, whose looks belied his holy reputation. When Deborah at last caught sight of the *zaddik* her remaining illusion went.

> The man frightened her by his very size. Never in all her life had she seen such a gigantic Jew. What a height! What a girth! And what a belly!... And his face was a shining red mass of flesh — utterly coarse! There was nothing holy about his appearance, in spite of the great length of beard. There was a crafty and self-satisfied twinkle in his luminous eyes. Deborah gaped. Could this really be the *Tsadik* himself? She compared him with the image of her grandfather, of her father. How utterly different![52]

All these hints of grossness were confirmed by the rabbi's subsequent behaviour. Owing Avram Ber months of unpaid wages he abandoned his duties to take the waters at a fashionable resort, accompanied by a retinue of servants. With no possibility of further income Raizela's purse became "positively consumptive". To make matters even worse, Avram Ber had no funds for feeding the students at the yeshiva. As the situation deteriorated so Michael's talent for mimicry (mentioned by Bashevis) grew keener; instead of attending the yeshiva to learn he went to entertain.

> Thanks to his gift of mockery, Michael became the most popular student in the *yeshiva*, though the youngest. "Come on, Michael, do your stuff! We're just about fed up to the neck!" his companions would demand entertainment, as if he were a professional clown.[53]

He also gave performances at home.

> Michael came home from the *yeshiva* every evening with a new store of jokes at the *Tsadik's* expense. These witticisms grew funnier and more biting as the plight of the students became worse. Michael was himself the author of many of them. He also gave imitations of the *Tsadik*

making a propoganda speech on behalf of the *yeshiva*, his voice quavering rapturously and his hands flung above his head in a frenzy of holiness.[54]

This is the earliest reference to Joshua as the author of anything, even if the pieces were only satirical sketches. It suggests that the genesis of his fiction was a reaction to a minor tyrant. Indeed, as a writer he was at his best when on the attack, a passionate enemy of oppression and injustice. Joshua's revenge upon the *zaddik* of Radzymin became complete when an adaptation of *Yoshe Kalb* was produced on the New York stage by Maurice Schwartz's Yiddish Art Theatre. The programme cover shows Maurice Schwartz as the grotesque rabbi of Nyseheve, and it can be imagined how much the audience laughed when Schwartz exaggerated the gestures once enacted by Joshua before his "hysterical" family.

The unhappy summer came to a dramatic end when the yeshiva burnt down. Bashevis remembered that his sister took him by the hand and moaned in a sing-song voice, "Where shall I take the children?" "There were many places to go, the town wasn't surrounded by flames," he added, "but my sister enjoyed the drama." Actually, the description of the fire in *Deborah* is ironic rather than melodramatic. Lunatic-like the rabbi dashed into the flames to rescue his valuables, a selfish act that was interpreted in a variety of favourable ways by his devoted followers. After the destruction of the yeshiva, Pinchos Mendel was virtually unemployed. He was forced to seek work elsewhere. A community in need of a rabbi invited him to become their *zaddik*. "*Tsadikim* are not appointed by their fellow men, but by God," he replied. But the equivocation of the tempter almost persuaded him until Raizela's cold-eyed sarcasm brought him to his senses.

> "Oh dear me, it's funny to hear you! You have only just entered the profession, and already you have all the cards up your sleeves. You're up to all the tricks of the trade.... To begin with you said that these *good people* wanted you as a *Tsadik*. Now your memory has failed you and you have changed it round to a 'spiritual leader.'... And now tell me, how can you complain about the *Tsadik* of R— if you're of the same kidney as he is?"[55]

As if in reward, Avram Ber's refusal was followed by another offer: to be a rabbi in Warsaw. Once again the family was filled with expectation at the prospect of a move, but the ambitions of Deborah and Michael were now more worldly as a result of the disappointments at R—. Michael, in particular, had grown "far too taciturn and grave for a boy of his age...and nature".

If ever he did crack a joke, it was so biting, so cynical, it made his companions wince. Quite suddenly he had grown into a man — a bitter man of fifteen.... He had reached the age of understanding — he could no longer pretend that life was a game. He had begun to think seriously of earning a living for himself, but did not know which way to turn. For his part, he would have become an apprentice to a tailor, or an errand boy, but at home he did not dare breathe any such suggestion. It would only have created a scandal.... Still, the desperate urge to do something remained, giving his early-matured brain no rest. His face had become pale and gloomy. Somehow he looked very much taller than he had done only a short while ago, and his habitual stoop had become very pronounced.[56]

Deborah left Radzymin in the same mood she arrived. The object of her pity at the exit was her admirer, Mottel, an orphan in the care of Avram Ber. He had participated in Deborah's discovery of forbidden delights. On the former journey from Jelhitz to R— he pressed so close that a "shiver ran through her and a sensation which she knew she ought to be ashamed of, to conceal". No less than her brothers, Esther was eager to be a student of love and literature, both as means of escape and self-realization. In R— Mottel lent Deborah a book which he "cautioned her to read in dead secret. She must never in all her life tell anyone about it, not in any circumstances divulge its source." Deborah and Mottel privately read Russian literature together. "Books took her out of herself. The drab surroundings became festive. She lived in a new and spiritual world." Unfortunately, it was when Esther attempted to take Deborah literally "out of herself" that the novel forfeited its originality. As the novel progressed from autobiographical adolescence to a "new and spiritual world" inhabited by alien characters, Esther lost control of her material and became dependent upon the imaginings of other writers. This spiritual emigration has a geographic correspondence in the novel; the move from R— to Warsaw. And it has a parallel in the transference of Deborah's affections from Mottel, left behind at Radzymin, to Simon, waiting in Warsaw.

Simon, the star of her father's yeshiva, was also the secret source of the books she had read with Mottel. He had come to Deborah's attention at the same time as the *zaddik*, a typical romantic hero:

Suddenly, as she stood musing over the *Tsadik*, vainly trying to recover from her amazement, she became aware of two blazing dark eyes fixed upon herself with a look that touched her to the quick; a tall and lean young man was approaching, clad or rather wrapped up in a long, shabby gaberdine encircled by a half-torn sash. He went by swiftly, seeming to float over the ground. His eyes were large and deep-set in a lean pale face all cheek-bones. In passing, the eyes gave her another flash, which stirred her to the depths, and then this young man too vanished in the doorway of the *yeshiva*.[57]

No hypocrite like the *zaddik,* Simon used his hasidic garb as a disguise to conceal his true revolutionary beliefs. It was these beliefs that brought them together again in Warsaw. Through a new acquaintance named Bailka, Deborah heard such stirring words as "association", "movement", "loyalty", "sacrifices", "comrades". She was warned that if she ever joined "the party" she must be brave, keep its secrets even if arrested. Deborah was bowled over. She swore to hold her tongue "even if it should mean torture and Siberia". She felt herself "on the threshold of a new life, a beautiful life". Having drunk in all of Bailka's words, Deborah next "consumed eagerly the contents of the booklet" she had been given to read.

> It was a small tract, which summoned her to a stupendous struggle against the enemy.... It described the fate of heroic men and women who would not acknowledge defeat.... She read on. Her heart bled. Her eyes flashed. Her cheeks burned. Her breath was hot. She was filled with passionate hatred of the enemy, an overwhelming longing for revenge, and with love and enthusiasm for those men and women who struggled and suffered so bitterly....[58]

Ten days later, tipsy with rhetoric, Deborah's name was enrolled on the list of members of the Socialist Party. A special meeting was arranged to honour one of its leaders, instantly recognizable to Deborah and reader alike because of his blazing eyes, the heat of which caused "a burning sensation" to "shoot through her breast". His touch was more super-charged than poor Mottel's, instead of a mere "shiver" she felt "the blood racing in her veins", "her flesh tingle", and was stirred to "the depths of her soul". As if in wish-fulfilment, these emotions were secretely reciprocated. But Simon could never reveal them to Deborah. He had been warned by his doctor to cut women out of his life. He wanted to keep Deborah safe from danger. But worst of all, he was convinced that Deborah didn't love him. A damp firebrand Simon might have been, but he was not without insights into the character of his beloved.

> Terrorism would sicken her. She loved humanity too indiscriminately. She was a reincarnation of Reb Avram Ber — in petticoats.... It would be a good thing if he could persuade Michael to join the party. That youngster had guts whereas Deborah was a waverer. It would probably be as easy to talk her into Zionism as it had been to convert her to Socialism. She was the sort of person who had to cling to something or other — anything would do, but, of course, a lover would be best of all! True, she had the makings of an idealist — an idealist without a definite ideal.[59]

These sentiments were really disguised self-criticism, of course. Esther knew herself and that the escape into romance was, literally, out of character. So Simon was banished for the sake of the novel, having had his blood-lust humanized by Deborah's influence. "Supposing we were to abandon terror as an instrument of class struggle...." Ironically, then, the love that Esther craved weakened her one real means of escape, her ability as a writer. Just as perversely, the mundanity of an arranged marriage brought back the inspiration to her fiction.

Like her fictional counterpart, Esther allowed herself to be married off. "The matchmaking episode is true to life," wrote her son.[60] How could a free-thinking socialist return so meekly to the era of matchmakers? There was only one explanation, which Esther gave. Deborah saw marriage as a means of escape. "So frantic was her impatience, so feverish her condition, that she failed to see any alternative to the dramatic gesture of giving herself away to a man whom she had never set eyes on.... She was conscious of only one thing: she must run away." At home Raizela chided her for "crying at one moment and bursting into song at the next". Deborah realized that "the family had come to look upon her as an hysterical, irrational creature". Bashevis certainly did. "She wasn't the kind of girl who could be married off easily," he wrote of his sister. To make things harder for the matchmaker, she had "acquired some modern ideas, and read Yiddish newspapers and books, longed for a romance, not an arranged marriage". Bashevis told how she became engaged to a diamond cutter from Antwerp (Berish in *Deborah*, Avraham Kreitman in life). Bashevis also noted Esther's emotional extremism; one moment she looked upon the marriage as an escape, the next as an exile. "You're sending me away because you hate me!" she accused Bathsheba. So Bathsheba offered to call off the wedding. Whereupon his sister cried, "No, I'd rather go into exile. I'll disappear. You won't know what happened to my remains...."

> Before Mother could answer, my sister laughed and fainted, but she always did so in such a way that she would not get hurt. She swooned, blinked, and smiled. Yet, even though she seemed to be pretending, it was all terribly real.[61]

Equally ambiguous was the psychosomatic illness Deborah developed just before the nuptials, as if her subconscious were giving her a last chance to change her mind. Whatever the cause, the pains around her heart were real enough, as was her nervous breakdown. A gentile doctor recommended a postponement, but the matchmaker insisted a *zaddik* would give better advice.

"So it had come to this, after all," thought Deborah en route to her bridegroom. "Somehow they had laid hands on her and were disposing of her just as they pleased, as if she were a corpse. And yet, here she was alive and in full possession of her senses." This was her real tragedy, of course, not the botched affair with Simon: a woman trapped between enlightenment and tradition. When the moment came, Esther lacked her brothers' ruthlessness, lacked sufficient courage in her convictions and her talent. Her marriage was a living death. Stuck with an incompetent husband ("My father was a *schlemiel,*" said Maurice Carr), surrounded by in-laws she could not abide, Deborah withdrew more and more until she began to lose possession of her senses and experienced "her first taste of madness, sheer madness". In the novel's final scene, set in the autumn of 1914, Berish broke the news of war to his wife. Deborah didn't respond. She was past caring. Bashevis remembered a golden chain his sister received from her future father-in-law. The same necklace made Deborah shiver "at the touch of the cold metal and the thought that the most vicious of dogs might safely be tied up with a chain such as this". *Deborah* reveals the miseries of an arranged marriage so powerfully that there seems a disingenuousness in Bashevis's dismissal of his sister's desire for romance, in his unwillingness to see the golden chain as a sinister thing. Especially since *In My Father's Court* ended with its author looking forward to "the turmoil that writers call 'love'...", a common enough thrill which his sister was denied. Esther's enlightenment diminished, because she hadn't the strength to snap the golden chain. The same tradition that nurtured her brothers, that gave them the intellectual and moral fortitude to reject it, simply smothered Esther.

Deep in Deborah's adolescence, Esther did not dwell upon Avram Ber's rabbinical duties in Warsaw. They were, however, the central concern of *In My Father's Court*.

> This book tells the story of a family and of a rabbinical court that were so close together it was hard to tell where one ended and the other began. The rabbinical court, the Beth Din, is an ancient institution among the Jews. It started when Jethro counselled Moses to "provide out of all the people able men, such as fear God, men of truth, hating covetousness...and let them judge the people at all seasons."... The Beth Din was a kind of blend of a court of law, synagogue, house of study, and, if you will, psychoanalyst's office where people of troubled spirit could come to unburden themselves.... The Beth Din could exist only among a people with a deep faith and humility, and it reached its apex among the Jews when they were completely bereft of worldly power and influence. The weapon of the judge was the handkerchief the litigants touched to signify their acceptance of the judgment.... At

times I think that the Beth Din is an infinitesimal example of the celestial council of justice, God's judgment, which the Jews regard as absolute mercy.[62]

Be that as it may, a painful irony is apparent by the end of the book. The fact that Pinchos Mendel was both father and rabbi, which initially made family and court inseparable, also hastened the disintegration of both. When Bashevis rejected his father's religious authority, he questioned his role as parent as well. Indeed, as the book progressed religion was replaced by philosophy, and Pinchos Mendel by Joshua. Finally, by welcoming "the turmoil that writers call 'love'", Bashevis was embracing his father's most seductive enemies. As if trying to mitigate his own guilt, Bashevis exposed his father's own love for books. During the First World War, at a time of great hardship, Pinchos Mendel received a sudden windfall. Instead of spending it all on necessities he decided to publish his book on the treaties of vows. Bashevis concluded:

> Now it seems to me that Father acted like any writer who wants to see his work in print. Of all the manuscripts he had written, only one thin volume had been published. According to Father, nothing was more estimable to God than the publication of a religious book, because it kindled the author's desire for the Torah and stimulated others to do the same.[63]

But these tracts were a world away from the books Bashevis read. The *haskalah,* the Jewish enlightenment, became an obsession. It was the threshold between the Jewish and gentile domains, wherein the choice between writer and rabbi must be made.

Joshua was the pioneer. "He was the big boy in the family and I was a baby," said Bashevis. "And since he was tall and, in my eyes, good-looking — also in the eyes of other people — and clever, I looked up to him more than to anybody else. Even more than to my parents. Parents are parents. My father was a rabbi, but here was a man." The opposition of "rabbi" and "man" is important, it anticipates a central conflict in Bashevis's work. In the Author's Note which accompanied the uncorrected proofs of *Old Love* he wrote, "The only hope of mankind is love in all its forms and manifestations — love of God being the source of all of them." But in the published version the sentence was amended to read, "The only hope of mankind is love in its various forms and manifestations — the source of them all being love of life...." This is the choice Bashevis had to make; between God and life, rabbi and man, father and father-figure. Bashevis recalled some of the arguments between Joshua and Pinchos Mendel. From the start he sided with his brother.

Logic spoke out of his mouth, you know; and I, a little boy, thought: he
is right. Although I would never have dared to say this, but I felt so....
Every word which he said was to me a bomb, a real spiritual kind of
explosion. And my parents were not really able to answer him.... And
later on my brother got the courage to take off his long robe, his *kapot*,
and to put on European clothes; and he looked so much nicer.[64]

"At the age of 18 I decided that I did not want to be a clergyman and I
gave up my theological studies," wrote Joshua laconically. "I wanted
to have a modern education and proceeded to acquire one by taking
casual lessons with inexpensive private tutors while earning my
livelihood by doing all kinds of odd jobs."[65] Lodging with another
family he would visit his parents clean-shaven and dressed in modern
clothes. When World War 1 began he was conscripted into the Tsar's
army. "Father was shamed and humiliated by him," wrote Bashevis,
"and occasionally so angered that he would order my brother out of
the house. But he didn't want his son to die at the front." So he tried to
persuade Joshua to wound himself. Joshua refused, saying that the
Jews had got enough cripples already. "The whole body of Jews is one
big hunchback..." he added. Bashevis commented,

> On the side of enlightenment, he spoke sharply and with great clarity,
> joking despite his dilemma. It was hard to know exactly where he stood.
> Although opposed to piety, he was aware of the faults of worldly
> existence. Hadn't worldliness itself caused the war? Inclined towards
> socialism, he was at the same time too skeptical to have that much faith
> in humanity. My father summed up my brother's point of view with,
> "Neither this world nor the world to come...."[66]

A fate which awaited many of Bashevis's own heroes, not to mention
those of Joshua.

Instead of maiming himself, Joshua deserted. After weeks on the
run he hid with an artist in Warsaw, "where he lived with a false
passport and painted — apparently unsuccessfully". Bashevis
brought him a basket of food from Bathsheba, and was astounded to
see "naked breasts on the figures of young and pretty girls". He
imagined the shuttle between father and brother as a metaphor for his
own writing.

> This was quite a change from my father's studio, but it seems to me that
> this pattern has become inherent to me. Even in my stories it is just one
> step from the study house to sexuality and back again. Both phases of
> human existence have continued to interest me.[67]

Bashevis described Joshua's painting as realistic:

> He did not make a man look as Miró, or Picasso, did when he drew a few

lines and said, it's a goat or a man. He tried to be as loyal, as faithful to
nature as he could be. But people have done it before him better, and he
decided that this is not his way. A man knows best what he can do and
what he cannot. He decided that his real power was in literature. He
used to read his stories to my mother and I listened. After I had learned
to read Yiddish well, he once put a story of his into a desk drawer. When
he left I opened the drawer and I read it. And what he wrote looked
beautiful to me.[68]

When Bashevis himself began writing his parents regarded it as a
tragedy.

They considered all the secular writers to be heretics, all unbelievers —
they really were too, most of them. To become a *literat* was to them
almost as bad as becoming a *meshumed,* one who forsakes the faith. My
father used to say that secular writers like Peretz were leading the Jews
to heresy. He said everything they wrote was against God. Even though
Peretz wrote in a religious vein, my father called his writing "sweetened
poison," but poison nevertheless. And from his point of view, he was
right. Everybody who read such books sooner or later became a worldly
man and forsook the traditions.[69]

Joshua entered his new career calmly, not so Bashevis. Having dealt
with his transition at length in *In My Father's Court,* he returned to it
in *A Little Boy in Search of God.* Here he described in feverish detail
the effect the new ideas had upon him.

I existed on several levels. I was a heder boy, yet I probed the eternal
questions.... I studied the cabala and I went down to play tag and hide-
and-seek with the boys in the courtyard.... I was aware of being quite
different from all the other boys, and I was deeply ashamed of this fact.
Simultaneously I read Dostoevski in Yiddish translation and penny
dreadfuls that I bought on Twarda Street for a kopeck. I suffered deep
crises, was subject to hallucinations. My dreams were filled with
demons, ghosts, devils, corpses.... In my fantasies or daydreams I
brought the Messiah or was myself the Messiah.[70]

Compare this to a much cooler sentence from *In My Father's Court*: "I
was at that time reading forbidden books and had developed a taste for
heresy; it was rather ridiculous, therefore, that I was attending heder
again." Either Bashevis was holding a lot back when he wrote *In My
Father's Court,* or he was recreating himself in the later book as his
own sorcerer's apprentice. And the more Bashevis began to dramatize
his enlightenment, the more he began to regret his lost tradition.

The figure of Pinchos Mendel haunts Bashevis's novels and stories,
pouring scorn upon the ideas his son once espoused. Even when
Joshua was explaining Darwin's theory of creation to Bashevis,
Pinchos Mendel was allowed the last word. "Can all the professors in

the world get together and create one mite?" Elsewhere, Bashevis
repeated this retort, "Blind forces couldn't create even one fly." He
added that while he basically agreed with the pessimistic view of
Malthus (discovered in a brochure brought home by Joshua) they
made him feel as though he were "swallowing poison". Not only did
Pinchos Mendel consider all literature as "sweetened poison", he also
believed that reading a newspaper was like "eating poison for
breakfast". When the narrator of "Brother Beetle" (one of Bashevis's
recent stories) was trapped on the rooftop of a former mistress by the
return of her crazy lover, he apologized to his parents "against whom I
had once rebelled and whom I was now disgracing". Naked, terrified
of perishing in such a preposterous way, he also asked God's
forgiveness. His folly was to set love of woman above devotion to God,
"instead of returning to His promised land with renewed will to study
the Torah and to heed His commandments, I had gone with a wanton
who had lost herself in the vanity of art". Released at last the narrator
removed himself from the scene. He walked until he was lost,
whereupon he asked (in English) an elderly passerby the way to his
hotel. "Speak Hebrew," replied the man, as righteous as the President
of the Friends of Yiddish. The narrator noted a "fatherly reproach in
his eyes…as if he knew me and had guessed my plight". But the
vanity of art was too seductive. Bathsheba once confessed to her
daughter that she had written an autobiography which she
subsequently considered profane and destroyed. Bashevis inherited
his mother's name, but not her piety.

Another recent story, "The Betrayer of Israel",[71] told of a little boy
who watched while his father, a rabbi, judged the case of a polygamist.
The rabbi accused the man of being a betrayer of Israel, but the little
boy turned out to be no less culpable. The boy was Bashevis himself,
of course, and by transforming the sordid tale into art he, too, became
a betrayer of Israel. Likewise, Philip Roth, in *The Ghost Writer*,
described how his alter ego, Nathan Zuckerman, turned a family
scandal into fiction, causing his "bewildered father" to think himself
and all Jewry "gratuitously disgraced and jeopardized by my
inexplicable betrayal". Both Bashevis and Roth make it apparent that
a Jewish writer given to expressing the unmentionable has to choose
between his talent and his people. Both authors chose their talent, and
thereby contributed to their fathers' deaths, or so their fiction would
have us believe. Such patricidal guilt is complicated by Jewish history,
in which the naive desire to murder the father was made hideously real
by the Nazis. So the surviving sons reincarnate their father again and
again, as a sort of adjudicator, as they wrestle with their talents to
produce works that will somehow differentiate them from the Nazis.

Their fiction becomes an attempt to assert a moral control over their imagination. Bashevis blamed his imaginative excesses upon a dybbuk, while Roth ascribed his to the id, but they were the true sources of their stories.

In order to justify the moral ambivalence inherent in his writing, Bashevis turned to the cabbalistic concept of *tzimtzum*. *Tzimtzum* states that

> God had to subdue His power and to dim His infinite light before He could create the Universe. Without this act creation would have been impossible because the light that emanates from God would have engulfed the Universe and caused it to disintegrate. Creation, like a painting by an artist, must have both lights and shadows. These shadows are the source of all evil and the powers that hold creation together. When God created the world He had to create evil.[72]

"In other words," Bashevis told Irving Howe, "the Cabala teaches us that Satan makes possible creation." "I feel sometimes I am half a devil myself," he added.[73] Half devil, half rabbi, Bashevis has himself fashioned a world out of the conflict. And *tzimtzum* is the secret signature in his books, it whispers hope when his narrative speaks only of despair. Consider, for example, the marriage of Gimpel the Fool to Elka the Whore.

After twenty years, "to make a long story short", Elka took sick. On her deathbed she confessed to Gimpel; he had been deceived, he was the father to none of his children. So strong had been Gimpel's belief, despite all the evidence otherwise, that the truth came literally as a blow, as if he had been "clouted on the head with a piece of wood". Having delivered her punchline Elka died, but even in death she registered her triumph, the success of her twenty-year fiction. "On her whitened lips there remained a smile." And looking at that smile Gimpel realized that deception was her only function, "I imagined that, dead as she was, she was saying, 'I deceived Gimpel. That was the meaning of my brief life.'" Elka used the same devices available to the storyteller when fooling Gimpel, indeed her lies gave the plot its structure. So Elka, the whore, became a metaphor for Bashevis, the writer. Even after death Elka's role was not over. When she was alive Gimpel became a thief, swiping things for her from the bakery. Now she was dead, and the bakery his, Gimpel was tempted by the devil to take his revenge upon Frampol. "'The whole world deceives you,' he said, 'and you ought to deceive the world in your turn.'" He added that the world to come was another fable Gimpel had swallowed whole. Gimpel succumbed and peed in the dough. But while the contaminated loaves were still baking Gimpel dozed and dreamed about Elka. He blamed her for his misdeed and began to cry. "'You

fool!' she said. 'You fool! Because I was false is everything false too? I
never deceived anyone but myself. I'm paying for it all, Gimpel. They
spare you nothing here.'" Sensing that his eternal life was in the
balance, Gimpel buried the loaves. Thereafter he left Frampol for
"the world" and a new life.

> Going from place to place, eating at strange tables, it often happens that
> I spin yarns — improbable things that could never have happened —
> about devils, magicians, windmills, and the like.[74]

Gimpel became a storyteller. This was the legitimate outcome of the
union.

Irving Howe thought "Gimpel the Fool" belonged to the Yiddish
tradition.

> The story has a feeling for the underdog, for social justice, and there is
> also in that story the figure of "the sacred fool" who has appeared in the
> writings of a good many Yiddish writers like Peretz and others.[75]

There are, indeed, similarities between Isaac Leib Peretz's "Bontsha
the Silent" and "Gimpel the Fool", beyond "the minimum of
schmaltz which some of our people demand" (Bashevis's concession
to Howe). "Bontsha the Silent" was the story of a pauper who passed
through this world unnoticed. When offered a reward for his
meekness in the hereafter he merely requested a hot buttered roll each
morning, shaming the assembled hosts with his modesty. Bontsha's
death was as hurried and undignified as his life.

> When Bontsha was brought to the hospital ten people were waiting for
> him to die and leave them his narrow little cot; when he was brought
> from the hospital to the morgue twenty were waiting to occupy his pall;
> when he was taken out of the morgue forty were waiting to lie where he
> would lie forever. Who knows how many are now waiting to snatch
> from him that bit of earth?[76]

Similarly, Gimpel knew that his only legacy would be his bed, "At the
door of the hovel where I lie there stands the plank on which the dead
are taken away.... Another *shnorrer* is waiting to inherit my bed of
straw." The difference was that while "Bontsha the Silent" used
pathos to highlight the injustices of this world, "Gimpel the Fool"
transcended the wickedness of the quotidian to offer a positive
synthesis of good and evil. Actually, Bashevis has specifically
dissociated himself from the so-called Yiddish tradition.

> When I began to write I already felt that this kind of tradition is not in
> my character. I am not a sentimental person by nature. By sentimental,
> I mean really sentimental, let's call it schmaltz as it should be called.
> Neither is it my nature to fight for social justice although I am for social

justice. But since I'm a pessimist and I believe that no matter what people are going to do it will always be wrong and there will never be any justice in the world, I have in my own way given up.[77]

Not only did Bashevis separate himself from his literary predecessors, he also put some distance between himself and his father-figure.

The only person I have a lot to thank for — from whom I learned a great deal — was my brother, I.J. Singer.... But even here I wouldn't say that I was my brother's disciple. I would almost say that I tried to create my own tradition, if one can use such words.[78]

In the early 1920s, after many vicissitudes, both brothers returned to Warsaw. Joshua had gone to live in Kiev at the war's end, inspired by the Russian Revolution, but his years there were a "period of continuous civil war and pogroms attended by starvation". Nevertheless, he did begin to write stories in his spare time. He also married Genia Kupfersteck, described by Bashevis as a "very good Jewish girl from Warsaw".

She came from the same kind of environment as we came, from a little town near Bilgoray called Krasnobrod. All I can say is she had all the charms of the good modest conservative Jewish girl who had one husband and one God. She was as similar to my mother as a girl could only be, and my brother married such a woman.[79]

Back in Warsaw, Joshua pursued his literary career and by 1923 was co-editor of a journal called *Literary Pages*. He immediately appointed his brother as proofreader, thereby rescuing him from the "half-bog, half-village" in Galicia where Pinchos Mendel was rabbi. Bashevis maintained that if his brother hadn't sent for him he would have submitted to an arranged marriage and become a storekeeper. In Warsaw he was more likely to become a materialist, a communist, or a Zionist. He lodged with Melech Ravich and met all the literary personalities. Even then he stood apart from all cliques, dismissing the *Literary Pages* as "radical, socialistic, half communistic, full of bad articles, poor poems, and false criticism" (though it is unlikely that he would have made such remarks in Joshua's presence). When Bashevis began an affair with an older woman named Gina Halbstark (a nom de plume) he was anxious to keep it secret from Joshua: "Most of all I was ashamed before my elder brother with his knowledge of life and sense of irony." The same pseudo-adolescent shyness kept him away when Joshua at last had enough money to set up a home of his own with his wife and children.

At Gina's house I was a mighty lover, but here I again became a child, a heder boy. This double role confused me.... In some book or magazine,

described the type of modern man...who must follow his own path and

I had stumbled upon a phrase: "split personality," and I applied this diagnosis to myself. This was precisely what I was — cloven, torn, perhaps a single body with many souls each pulling in a different direction. I lived like a libertine yet I didn't cease praying to God and asking for His mercy....[80]

Gina suited his split personality perfectly, behaving like "both a holy woman and a whore". Later, when Bashevis rented two apartments and led a genuine dual existence his only fear was that his brother should find out what he was doing. "He would have scolded me like a father."

CLOVEN

2
Reputations

JOSHUA MADE his reputation with a volume of short stories called *Pearls,* published in 1922. The collection brought him to the attention of Abe Cahan, editor of *Der Forverts* (the *Jewish Daily Forward*), the largest Yiddish newspaper in America, with a readership close to quarter of a million. Bashevis claimed that Cahan was "inspired" by his brother's writing. Certainly, he promptly invited Joshua to be his Polish correspondent, as well as offering to publish his fiction. Thus, at a single stroke, Joshua became an established writer. A secure income enabled him to set up the residence at 36 Leszno Street which Bashevis was so loath to visit. His good fortune did not excite universal rejoicing within the Yiddish intellectual community. "Literary and journalist Warsaw seethed over my brother's success," remarked Bashevis in *A Young Man in Search of Love.* This description was confirmed by a less partial commentator. Writing of Joshua in Yiddish literature, Charles Madison noted:

> Ever since he had become one of Cahan's retainers he was deprecated and impugned by fellow writers: communists considered him a turncoat because of his critical attitude toward the Soviet Union; others, living precariously, tended to be jealous of his secure financial position as a *Forverts* contributor.[1]

Maurice Carr has indicated how Joshua prepared his pieces for Cahan. "Joshua wasn't really a journalist," he said. "He wrote piquant articles for *Forverts.* He would write them in an hour once a week in a loft. He was a born writer and his words flowed freely. He wrote in a beautiful hand. Every so often he would turn back a few pages and make a correction. He would know at once what he wanted to change."[2] The link with *Der Forverts* proved to be permanent; first Joshua, then Bashevis was engaged by Cahan. Indeed, Bashevis continues to write for the newspaper to this day, long after Cahan's death in 1951.

As Madison suggested, the association with *Der Forverts* carried political implications. When the Bolsheviks took over the revolution

in Russia, Cahan supported them, until his on-the-spot
correspondents opened his eyes. Thereafter, *Der Forverts* became
sharply anti-communist, "the most important anti-Bolshevik
newspaper in America", Bashevis hyperbolically called it. The editors
of *Twentieth-Century Authors* added the following to Joshua's
autobiographical entry in the 1944 edition: "His Yiddish style has
often been compared with that of his friend and employer, Abraham
Cahan. Like Cahan, he has been violently opposed to the Soviet
régime." Of course, Joshua's opposition was verbal, never violent.
Such prophetic descriptions might have won him friends in the
United States, but his anti-Stalinism made him something of an
outcast among his peers in Warsaw. "The Yiddish movement was
then infiltrated by Communist fanaticism, and the fact that my
brother was the Warsaw correspondent of the *Jewish Daily Forward* in
New York, a newspaper known for its socialist orientation, only
increased the antagonism," remarked Bashevis in the memoir that re-
introduced *Yoshe Kalb*.[3] In 1926 Cahan sent Joshua to the Soviet
Union as a special correspondent, and his reports (collected and
published as *The New Russia* in 1927) turned the antagonism into
frank hostility. Nor did Joshua endear himself to his communist
critics with works such as *Earth Pain*, described by Charles Madison
as "a minor symbolic drama of the revolutionary period evidencing his
disillusionment with Bolshevism". Therefore, when he published his
first novel in 1927 it "incurred the wrath of noisy political factions".
Joshua was accused of not glorifying the masses, of not participating in
their class struggle. Although such politically motivated criticisms
may be discarded as worthless, it is not so easy to dismiss a similar
complaint when it comes from his sister. In her novel Esther made
Deborah chide Michael for mocking the masses who wait upon the
rabbi of R— (viz Radzymin).

> Deborah was angered by Michael's derision of the "mob". Ignorant
> and simple-minded, they were bamboozled, made nought of; but no
> one ever tried to enlighten them, no one ever ventured to expose the
> *Tsadik* and his confederates for what they were, and so the "mob"
> continued to lavish luxuries upon him in all innocence.[4]

Since *Steel and Iron* was constructed around two social experiments
the treatment of the mob was actually of crucial importance, and the
hero's reaction to it became a measure of his humanity.
   Bashevis criticized *Steel and Iron* on different grounds in the
introduction to *Yoshe Kalb:*

> As so often happens with young writers, my brother had tried in this
> first long effort to give his entire self. He thus described the type of

modern man…who must follow his own path and think his own thoughts. This genre of novel seldom succeeds, because the autobiographical and the fictional elements fuse with difficulty. The writer's intentions rarely fit neatly into his descriptions. Besides, it is enormously difficult technically to describe a skeptic, which my brother was to his very core.[5]

The autobiographical elements in *Steel and Iron* were based upon Joshua's wartime misadventures: first as a deserter from the Russian army, then as a virtual slave of the German occupying forces. "For a while, my brother Israel Joshua repaired a bridge for the Germans (later describing the experience in a novel)," wrote Bashevis.[6] In *Deborah* there was no real attempt to fuse autobiographical and fictional elements; what was not autobiography was simply wish-fulfilment. *Steel and Iron* was considerably more ambitious in the way it transformed autobiography into fiction; but the alchemy failed in the mis-match between its episodic structure and epic traditions. The consequence was a sense of expectations unfulfilled, as the history of Dr Grigory Davidovich Gertz exemplifies. His fictional career was as follows: mentioned in one chapter, described at great length in the next, thereafter of no significance. Even though the chapter in which his history was told, in the manner of the epic novel, had promised more. Perhaps Joshua wanted to demonstrate how individuals like his hero Benjamin Lerner were swallowed whole by history. But this does not dispel the dissatisfaction. Not until *The Brothers Ashkenazi* did Joshua manage to marry his subject-matter to the epic tradition, and produce a novel that moved to the rhythm of the expectations he created: introduction, description, action. By then, as Bashevis implied, he had abandoned the sceptical hero in favour of the monomaniac. Nevertheless, *Steel and Iron* is of significance as a political novel.

The first English translation, by Morris Kreitman (viz Maurice Carr), appeared in 1935 as *Blood Harvest*. In his introduction, Carr justified the change of title with a bombardment of seasonal imagery:

> *Blood Harvest* gives a series of powerfully drawn pictures of the "harvest" reaped by the warmongers in Eastern Europe during the latter years of the Great War — a ghastly crop of famine, fever, poverty, degradation and, finally, something which none of the master-harvesters had bargained for — the Russian revolution which, consummating the "harvest", forms a fitting, if at first glance somewhat sudden, close to this true-to-life book.[7]

Given the date of publication, it was not surprising that the translator chose to emphasize the novel's treatment of "two problems which have, unfortunately, become burning questions of the present day:

uncompromising Prussian militarism and its corollary, persecution of minorities". To remove any ambiguity concerning his target, Carr added that "the pictures given of Prussian ruthlessness and of the wretchedness to which this ruthlessness reduces minorities" were all the more valuable because they anticipated the Third Reich. In order to succeed in his task, outlined above, Joshua "had to change his 'peacetime' technique...and concern himself with mass rather than individual psychology". By choosing to see the wretchedness as an indictment of Prussian ruthlessness, Carr called this realistic, while the communists called it slanderous. There is no doubt that Joshua detested the Germans, but what of his depressing implication that the masses will only respond to Prussian ruthlessness and efficiency? Carr, understandably single-minded, did not consider that.

The 1969 version, translated by Joseph Singer, faced the question head-on. The jacket — which incorrectly claimed that the novel was previously unpublished in English — made the following statement:

> *Steel and Iron* is the story of Benjamin Lerner, a young Jewish infantryman in the Imperial Russian Army of 1915. Forced by circumstances to become a deserter and an outcast, he hides in Warsaw under a new name. He welcomes the arrival of the Jewish refugees who, uprooted from their provincial homes, are streaming into Poland: they are his people — martyred, long-suffering, but enduring.
>
> Lerner becomes sickened and shamed as he witnesses the refugees' abject acceptance of indignity and humiliation. A fighter himself, he joins with others to exert all his strength "in the lunatic conflict against steel, iron, stone and wood."[8]

By using such passive adjectives and nouns as "abject", "indignity", and "humiliation", the anonymous writer is all but blaming the refugees for their predicament. On the other hand, Lerner is a "fighter". The question becomes, are the masses redeemable? If so, by whom? The social experiments in *Steel and Iron* therefore concern the redemption of man by political means. There is no doubt that the raw material is unpromising. Consider, for example, the refugees referred to above. Their arrival in Warsaw as a line of wagons evoked in Lerner "strong feelings of pain and compassion", so much so that he was hypnotized by "a pair of brooding eyes".

> They burned with the accumulated anguish of generations, and Lerner no longer saw carts full of snotty children and grimy bedding but a procession of martyrs and saints who had been sanctified by their torture and privation.[9]

However, Joshua never allowed such facile myth-making to pass unchecked. Lerner was brought down to earth by a shove from a "desperate, sweaty man in flying gaberdines", and the "saintly procession again became a string of creaking wagons, cranky, small town Jews, and mangy nags with ragbound shanks". This scepticism, this refusal to accept the sentimental power of illusion, was what Lerner had to overcome in order to act. He had to cease regarding the refugees, workers and masses as political clichés and see them as individuals. Unfortunately the triumphant political movements are those which treat the individual as part of the whole. Just as Lerner had difficulty in separating the individual from the mass, so the individual was eager to shed the burden of self. In other words, to be successful Lerner had to return the individual to the mass. As he said to his lover, Gitta, during the second of the book's social experiments: "Keep at it... but not out of pity, out of a sense of duty. You'll see what a difference it'll make.... I speak from experience. Once the pity goes the disgust will soon follow. It worked for me, it'll work for you too."[10]

In the first chapter, appropriately called "In Harness", Benjamin Lerner is compared to a carthorse. Indeed, running to roll call, he paused, for the day was sweltering, and a "weary horse... its whole body covered with foam, stuck out a long, parched tongue and licked Lerner's sweaty shoulder to allay its thirst". Like One-Eye in *Of a World That Is No More,* this horse and his human counterpart do all the dirty work. Nor does their labour receive any recognition, as Lerner discovered when he missed roll call and wandered through Warsaw instead. He was shocked to observe how the city rolled on regardless of the war. He felt himself an alien being in an ordinary world, and the nine months at the front, "the fighting, the bleeding, the dysentery, the self-sacrifice, the lack of sleep, the hunger, cold, humiliation, and submission came into sudden, sharp focus as if to point up all their senselessness and futility". His humiliation was emphasized by another of Joshua's favourite images, when he had a vision of himself as "one who suddenly finds himself naked amongst well-dressed people". Final degradation comes when the simile is made real. For Lerner's sensation anticipated Gitta's fate. She ended up forcibly stripped and spread-eagled on the dirty couch of her German superior. The Germans claimed to be checking all Jewish women for signs of venereal disease, but that was window dressing. For Gitta's examination was painstakingly thorough.

> The manager let his eyes feast on the slim body pinned down like a butterfly by the coarse, red hands.
> "Exquisite!" he whispered.
> "Delicious," the young lieutenant agreed, wiping his hands on the bloody towel. Gitta fainted.[11]

Naked, defenceless, individuals have no hope of dignified survival in a
world of powerful beasts. When in uniform they are ignored, when
noticed they are violated. Either way, they are "things".

Gitta was Lerner's cousin. It was to her family's apartment that he
fled, having got rid of his harness and dropped his rifle in the Vistula.
His uncle, Reb Baruch Joseph, was a typically ill-tempered autocratic
patriarch. Once the owner of an estate near the Austrian border, he
had frittered away his fortune in crackpot schemes. When the
Cossacks arrived, they drove him out. In Warsaw, Baruch Joseph
dreamed up half-baked ideas to restore his finances, once his lands had
been restored. His latest brainwave was digging for peat. But such an
operation required a rich son-in-law. There was even a candidate,
Yekel Karlover. Unfortunately, Gitta despised him. And the arrival of
Lerner provided an even greater obstacle. Unable to ask Lerner to
leave, Joseph Baruch tried to drive him away by insulting his dead
father, a character with a passing resemblance to Pinchos Mendel:

> "You know, Benjamin, I never liked your father, may he forgive me
> these words. He was a damn fool.... Your father looked up to miracle
> workers and saints like a calf looks up to a cow. They took him for all he
> had...."[12]

But Lerner would not be provoked. For his own part, he was growing
restless. "Day by day he felt more constricted in the tiny alcove. The
whitewashed walls seemed to close in on him even more than had the
earthen walls of the bunker." It turned out that freedom from the
harness was impossible. He tried reading, but the "smooth white
pages seemed somehow strangely placid and incongruous with the
times, and the symmetrical Gothic characters hollow and inane".
How different from the comfort Calman Jacoby got from the Hebrew
texts he studied in his hut-like synagogue at the conclusion of
Bashevis's *The Manor*. Eventually, Baruch Joseph made Gitta cry
once too often, and Lerner stormed off. He found refuge in a studio
run by a sculptor called Rubinchik (named as Ostrzego in *In My
Father's Court*). The artists who gathered there formed a group known
as the Hares. Though they welcomed Lerner, he could not stand
them. They killed time by "drawing malicious caricatures of one
another...pointing out each other's weaknesses, and mimicking and
trying to provoke each other".

> After a long session of such character assassination the victim felt like
> some old whore who has been disembowelled on the autopsy table before
> unfeeling medical students.[13]

Another "thing". In short, they were little better than the Germans
who held Gitta's "trembling ankles and wrists". (No wonder Joshua's

writing made him enemies!). Simply to shake his lethargy Lerner tried
drilling the Hares, and he yelled at them like any sergeant. This
insignificant incident demonstrates the temptation to ape former
tormentors when with weaklings, and foreshadows Lerner's
predicament in more painful circumstances. When the Hares insulted
Gitta, Lerner departed, as he had left his uncle's home.

As soon as the German artillery could be heard in Warsaw the
Russians retreated. The Jews welcomed their conquerors: " *'Guten
morgen! Guten morgen!'* they called out. *'Morgen!'* the Germans
replied with indifference." At once they started rebuilding the bridges
the Russians had dynamited "in their inept fashion". Seen from a
distance there was something magnificent about the German effort:

> Coming out on a hill that overlooked the sprawling work area he had
> stopped to take in the impressive sight. Eddies of blue-black water
> swirled under the sunken bridge arch, waves broke against the
> protective walls, and sandbags were being piled up to dam the current
> upstream. Hundreds of men were crawling like insects by the cold light
> of the rising sun as misty vapors hid then revealed the wide panorama of
> motion.[14]

Lerner was enthralled. He imagined himself "directing all this furious
effort, serving as the nerve center through which it all had to pass".
But close-up the impression was very different, as Lerner discovered
to his cost. For the Germans who ran the operation were barely
human. Major Meyer, the commander, had a "shaved skull the colour
of raw meat". Without realizing what had happened Lerner, the
volunteer, was once again "in harness like a drayhorse". Though just
as downtrodden his fellow workers gave no support. They respected
him, but only because he had won a fist-fight. Soon Lerner began to
think that he was worse off than he had been at the front:

> There, at least, the men had been close to each other, united in a
> common struggle against the enemy, welded in a fear of some higher
> power. Here the workers existed in a kind of godless, fratricidal
> conspiracy in which the strong bullied the weak and the devious
> deceived the simple. And feeding upon and exploiting this divisiveness
> were the cynical, implacable Germans.[15]

The workers were divided into nationalities. Lerner, of course, was
with the Jews. Each worker was given a partner. Lerner was saddled
with a saintly Talmudist named Jehiel Mayer. "To the gentile
workers, Jehiel Mayer symbolized the Jew." But even among the Jews
the hasidim were despised for their unworldliness. And most
unworldly of all was Jehiel Mayer. Thus he became an object of
derision both to the anti-Semites and to the tougher Jews. Even

Lerner, his partner, failed him. He let out "all his rage and frustration on the sensitive young man". And so when Jehiel Mayer's legs were crushed by a falling girder, Lerner was filled with self-reproach "feeling as if somehow it were all his fault". He was unable to sleep, "haunted by Jehiel Mayer's eyes beseeching him: 'Tell me, why is it you all hate me so?...'" In fact, there was nothing Lerner could have done to save Jehiel Mayer, but he knew that in refusing to respond to him as an individual he had diminished his own humanity. He was morally to blame, since he set no better example than his fellows. Lerner had become just another worker and allowed Jehiel Mayer to become a "thing" to him.

As soon as this knowledge sank in, Lerner was given a chance to redeem himself. He was contacted by a fellow-deserter, now known as Sheepskin, a political activist. "He was drawn into the conspiracy much faster than he imagined. Somehow he and Sheepskin always managed to be in the same place." Lerner was told to talk to his co-workers, but he got nowhere. He complained to Sheepskin, "They're nothing but scum of the earth, the lowest cruds I ever did see." To which Sheepskin replied, "All masses are scum." Perhaps Joshua's communist critics read no further, for Lerner's attitude changed. At first Lerner remained sceptical, but he persisted with his persuasion and was rewarded.

> Slowly, so gradually that he himself wasn't aware of it, Lerner felt a change come over him. He lost his contempt and began to look at his co-workers as human beings with feelings, doubts, and frustrations.[16]

Now the men no longer scoffed when Lerner discussed the conditions on the bridge. They nodded in agreement. "'It's all the goddam Fritz's fault.... He sets Jew against gentile and scoops up the cream....'" Lerner, the revolutionary orator, was ecstatic. His former scepticism was transformed.

> As hopeless as he had felt before, he now believed that no goal was impossible, that victory would soon be complete. He grew fond of his fellow workers and felt a real concern for their futures. All his thoughts became centered on the bridge to the exclusion of everything else.[17]

Next Lerner was ordered by Sheepskin to fake an illness, so as to carry the revolutionary message to the Russian hospital orderlies and their doctor, the aforementioned Grigory Davidovich Gertz. But Grigory Davidovich had lost all "faith in the human animal". His journey had been the opposite of Lerner's; from ecstasy to scepticism. "His eyes looked out with skepticism from behind the polished glasses, with an ironic but crystal-clear awareness of the order of human existence." Instead of Marxism he followed the Jewish mystics, who said, "Do no evil, oppose no evil," sentiments Bashevis was later to attribute to Buddha, when he told Irving Howe:

> In a way, I'm not far from the Buddhist and the Indian way of thinking that the best thing you can do is run away from evil, not fight it, because the moment you begin to fight evil, you become a part of evil yourself.[18]

What wrought this change was a simple enough event. Whilst in exile Grigory Davidovich had become captivated by the peasants, so that "he came to love each one of them". And when his term of exile expired he remained with them. He even married a peasant girl. He forgot his Jewish roots. The simple existence of the peasants symbolized for him "the purity, the truth, and the nobility of mankind". But when war broke out Grigory Davidovich "watched with horror as his beloved peasants perpetrated the most terrible atrocities against Jewish men, brutally raped their wives and daughters, violated corpses, cut tongues, eyelids, breasts, and testicles from living victims".[19] He was devastated by the experience, and "new and strange feelings began to grow within him toward the humble, frightened Jews". As Lerner also found, he had an inescapable allegiance. While the massacres of other peoples had shocked him, he had felt no sense of identity with the victims. A prisoner of the Germans, Grigory Davidovich made one last effort to retain his world. He treated his orderlies as equals, but to no avail. "For all his sermons about love and fraternity they were unspeakably brutal to one another." This "unfailing goodness" drove Lerner wild, for he saw how efficient the hospital could be if Grigory Davidovich chose to use cruder methods. " 'Why the hell don't you crack down?' he would snap at the doctor. 'Scum like this respects only the knout, not sermons!' " So quickly had Lerner forgotten the revelation that the "worst thieves, bullies, and cut-throats to whom life meant less than a cigarette would sit like obedient children while he wrote letters home to their wives, mothers, or sweethearts". It was impossible to remain a constant optimist in such conditions; each new outrage led to more doubts. "Suppose everything for which he had sacrificed his life was a sham and a lie? . . ." wondered Grigory Davidovich. "Suppose man was inherently evil as his skeptical friends had insisted and no system could amend his innate cruelty and bestiality?" When Bashevis spoke about his brother's scepticism concerning social ideals he added, "He always used to say, it would all be very nice if there would be no human beings to practise these things." In a sense, *Steel and Iron* was Joshua's renunciation of optimism. For the terrible doubts of Grigory Davidovich clearly indicate the course of Lerner's own ideals. When Lerner first saw the doctor, the night of Jehiel

Mayer's accident, he felt "as if he had known him all his life". He was, so to speak, Lerner's future.

The insurrection, when it came, was an anti-climax. It started prematurely, after a drunken night on the town, the workers' sense of justice outraged by the fact that the Germans had bagged all the whores. Demands were made, the Germans opened fire, the workers charged, Lerner and Sheepskin kept running. And that was the unsatisfactory end to the first experiment in social engineering. Having stirred the men to the point of revolution, their leaders abandoned them. Again the opposing tendencies of the picaresque and epic traditions harmed the novel. Sheepskin's role was as an agent provocateur, first helping Lerner to desert, then drawing him into the revolt. Now, like Grigory Davidovich, his function was over but he left behind too many unfulfilled possibilities for the novel's good. His place was taken by Aaron Lvovich, a Jewish landowner from Russia with estates in Poland, trapped by the German advance. He had the idea of reviving his war-ravaged estates with the help of the Jewish refugees, thus simultaneously revitalizing their demoralized spirits. But the refugees did not trust him. They were persuaded by an agitator named Dushkin that Lvovich was a Haman bent on their destruction, and they refused to co-operate. Lvovich tried reason, but the Germans knew better, they rounded up their leaders. The refugees became compliant. In Warsaw Lvovich enlisted the aid of Lerner and Gitta. Lerner was on the run from the Germans, Gitta from her father. Yekel Karlover, her suitor, had attempted to turn himself into a Prussian,

> He even dressed like a German and strutted about in high yellow boots like any Junker. His breeches were light and fitted, his skull shaven at the temples and nape. He carried a riding crop which he remembered to periodically slap against his boots. He even acquired a shepherd dog to whom he spoke in German only: *"Hex, fass diesen Knochen. . . . Hex!"*[20]

He proposed to Gitta, she refused, Baruch Joseph threw her out. Together with Lerner she accompanied Aaron Lvovich (a more socially aware version of her own father) to his estate at Zaborowa. There the second of the book's social experiments began.

This time Lerner was the overseer. The decision how to treat the workers was his. Zaborowa must be restored; its dormitories rebuilt, its land made productive again. But the refugees took advantage of his leniency. "They only understand the whip," said Lvovich, repeating Lerner's advice to Grigory Davidovich. It was one thing to suggest such a solution, another to act upon it. And Lerner was no German. Nevertheless, he "adapted the methods he had learned from the

German overseers on the bridge".

> He laid out a specified amount of work for each man and announced: "Either this is done by noontime or no lunch." At first the men didn't take him seriously. "Words," they assured each other with a wink.
>   But when it came time to eat and their bowls weren't filled, they hurried off to complete the work, grumbling and cursing Lerner under their breaths.
>   "He's a Haman, that's what he is, an anti-Semite."[21]

And when some really complicated work was required Lvovich brought in German help; thus the watermill and the sawmill were repaired. For a while Zaborowa functioned as a productive part of the environment, a balance was achieved between supervisor, worker and nature. But the year was 1917. Aaron Lvovich abandoned his minor experiment for the greater one just beginning in Russia. Lerner, however, was more concerned with an outbreak of diphtheria on the estate that was filling the cemetery with children. When Lvovich proclaimed, "A whole new world is being built out there!" Lerner responded, "I care about people dying right here in Zaborowa!" Lvovich the idealist replied:

> "Who gives a crap about a few when millions are involved? God, the things I could be doing there now!" Aaron Lvovich said with passion. His eyes seemed to focus somewhere far away, envisioning the entire magnificent drama of revolution.[22]

Without Aaron Lvovich's protection, and with Lerner stricken with typhus, a new German manager was installed. He took the experiment at Zaborowa to its logical conclusion, and turned it into a replica of the work camp at the bridge. Hereafter Aaron Lvovich's careless monomania was to be Joshua's central concern. He lost interest in the humane sceptic as a fictional character. Hence Lerner's final appearance in *Steel and Iron,* as an insignificant soldier participating unwittingly in the Bolshevik coup, was entirely appropriate.

Joshua was deeply disturbed by the adverse response to *Steel and Iron.* Charles Madison attributed this over-sensitivity to Joshua's state of mind, which was "idealistically disillusioned and inwardly apprehensive". He quoted a friend of Joshua, N. Meisel, who found it "painful and regretful to see the self-torture of this erstwhile life-loving, joyous Singer". "In fact," wrote Bashevis in the introduction to *Yoshe Kalb,* "my brother *was* very downhearted, and had been for a long time." The reason for this unhappiness, according to Bashevis, was Joshua's inability to adjust to the Yiddish literary world of Warsaw. The maladjustment lasted into the 1930s. It may be that there is too much self-indentification in these diagnoses; for instance,

Bashevis adds in the introduction to *Yoshe Kalb* a sentence into which the powerful first person enters: "I saw with grief that he — as I, his younger brother — actually fit in nowhere." Whatever the cause, the effect was definite; Joshua took no part in cultural or literary activity for nearly five years. Indeed, he made a public declaration of the fact in a letter to several of Warsaw's Yiddish newspapers, declaring that he no longer thought of himself as a Yiddish writer. Bashevis thought this a "childish" action, as he remarked in the introduction to *Yoshe Kalb,* an adjective he repeated when asked his opinion of the letter.

> It was as if a man would decide: I'm not going to be myself anymore but am going to be another human being. He cannot make such a decision. A man cannot decide that he is going to be not himself ... although here there are a few thousand men who decided to become women. Anyhow it is easier for them to become women, or for a woman to become a man, than for my brother to become a German or a French writer. Yiddish was the language which he knew best; and Jewish life was the kind of life which he knew best. For him to say, I'm not going to be a Yiddish writer anymore was sheer nonsense, and he knew it. I told it to him, and all his friends told it to him. So when he was able to forget about this kind of childish promise and to come to work again he was happy.... So he went back to Yiddish literature, and this was the only way he could have functioned; what else could he have done? What he said about stopping to be a Yiddish writer was nothing but a kind of a protest. It's as sometimes people say, I'm ashamed to be a human being. But ashamed or not you still remain a human being.[23]

In Bashevis's judgement his brother was saved from despair by the magical potency of the fictional process; the only medicine he really required was the right story. Bashevis wrote that as soon as it turned up Joshua revived "not only spiritually but also physically. He began to look better; his blue eyes glowed with new interest and expectation".[24] This diagnosis seems to indicate that Bashevis imagines stories to exist in some cabbalistic fashion independent of the writer. Moreover, as with marriage partners, not every story is suitable for every writer; in fact, a writer must decide which stories are made for him alone. In an interview recorded in 1975 for the BBC's Radio Three, Bashevis described what he looked for in a story, and explained the intuitive process of knowing that it was meant for him.

> The first condition is I must have a story with a beginning, a middle and an end. In other words, I don't believe in this business which they call a slice of life where you sit down and just write. I must have a story. The second condition is that this yarn must interest me and create a passion for me to write it. Then there comes a third condition which is the most difficult condition. I must have the conviction or at least the illusion

that I am the only one who could write this story. If I suspect some of the other writers would be able to do it, this would mean to me that this is not really my story, it is not any more personal and I would not write it.[25]

Whence come the stories? "People love to tell their stories — when there is an ear which hears, someone who listens to them with a certain understanding," Bashevis said in *Encounter*. Many of his own stories being with the narrator buttonholed by an informant; for example, here are the opening lines of "Lost":

When I was counselling readers for the Yiddish newspaper where I worked, all kinds of people used to bring their problems to me: betrayed husbands and wives.... But one particular man came to me on Friday, late in the day, when I was ready to go home.[26]

Bashevis made it clear that he regarded stories as "the very essence of literature". "In other words," he said, "the story of your life is the very essence of your life. I'm always eager to hear stories because no matter how many stories I've heard they have never revealed all of life to me.... My interest is from the point of view of literature: actually, life itself. But being interested in other people is life."[27] Another interview, printed in *Tropic*, concluded with an aborted story. It demonstrates both how Bashevis is given "stories" as offerings, and how he has the judgement to reject the unsuitable. Plucking up her courage the interviewer told Bashevis a "true story". Boy wants girl, girl says no; at last boy flies away, girl wires plane to say she has changed her mind. Happy ending.

"This," says Singer, "is not a story. This is a happy event. If he had taken another plane, it would be a story. If she wired the plane but it was too late — he has changed his mind, maybe he has met another woman on the plane — it would be a story. This is nice but it is not a story."[28]

The other source of stories is Bashevis's own life. "As a matter of fact in all my writing I tell the story of my life, again and again..." Bashevis said.

Only the dilettantes try to be universal; a real writer knows that he's connected with a certain people, a certain time, a certain environment, and there he stays put, I would say, and he doesn't mind it because there is enough to investigate and to learn even from a small world, a limited environment.[29]

It was this small world which provided the unexpected source for *Yoshe Kalb*.

Having rejected his father's orthodoxy for the sake of

enlightenment, and begun his career as a writer with contemporary material, Joshua suddenly found inspiration in the archaic environment of small-town hasidism. What is more, Pinchos Mendel himself was the source of the story. Joshua recorded the fact in *Of a World That Is No More*:

> Among the many stories told that day was one Father told about a rabbi's son named Moshe Haim Kaminker, who deserted his wife, the Sieniawa rabbi's daughter. When the husband, Moshe, came back years later, the people accused him of being someone else, a beggar named Yoshe Kalb who had deserted his own wife, a woman of low origin. My father had personally known this man and he told the fantastic story in a most engaging way.[30]

Bashevis also recollected that his father "told this story not once but many times".

> Whenever there was talk about "disappearing" my father came up with it, and I remember I heard it myself maybe ten times; and I was every time as baffled as the first time because my father was a wonderful storyteller.... And the story in itself is really baffling. That a man should come up and say, I'm Yoshe Kalb, when others say he was not. Until today we don't know if he was or he wasn't. A story which is as dramatic as this had to be told in a dramatic way.[31]

The dramatic content of *Yoshe Kalb* had melodramatic consequences; it saved the lives of the Singer brothers. The success of the book led to Joshua's first visit to the United States, where he eventually settled with his family, afterwards sending for his younger brother, repeating the process that had taken Bashevis to Warsaw. "He didn't have to use much persuasion," Bashevis remarked.

Maurice Schwartz, the famous director of the Yiddish Art Theatre, whose production of *Yoshe Kalb* prompted Joshua's trip to New York, proclaimed: "Singer has had the courage to reveal to us artistically the truth about a mode of life which once was dominant, and which still possesses enough vitality to keep hundreds of thousands of Jews confined within narrow conceptions of this world and the other."[32] On the other hand, Charles Madison found the book blighted "with a kind of personal animosity" which blinded Joshua to the "genuine spiritual fervor germane to Hasidism", factors which "weaken an otherwise powerful love story and a fascinating account of Hasidic life of a century ago". There is no doubt that the corrupt genius at the centre of *Yoshe Kalb*, Rabbi Melech of Nyesheve, is a portrait of Joshua's first enemy, the rabbi of Radzymin. The descriptions of Rabbi Melech in *Yoshe Kalb* bear a marked resemblance to those of the Tsadik of R— in *Deborah*. According to Esther the Tsadik of R— was "gigantic", his face a "shining red mass of flesh" with eyes that had a "crafty and self-satisfied twinkle". His belly was prominent, indicating a worldly propensity to gluttony. Likewise, Rabbi Melech had a "bulging stomach". His eyes were "bulbous" and so lustful that they were always ready "to jump from their sockets". The well-being radiated by the Tsadik of R— became "furious health" in Rabbi Melech. Esther summed up the Tsadik of R—'s character with the words "utterly coarse". Since the subject matter of *Yoshe Kalb* was more sensational, sexuality being the motor of the plot, Rabbi Melech was labelled "sensuous". Needless to say, such a characteristic was inappropriate for a man who was head of a rabbinical court, whose followers came not only from Nyesheve but from many parts of Poland and Russia. *Yoshe Kalb* was not simply a blinkered attack on hasidism, but an indictment of a system of superstitious beliefs that conferred power on morally unqualified candidates. "The Rabbi can do no wrong" was the credo, and examples have already been presented to demonstrate how far his disciples would twist the truth to accord with their faith. Thus the court of Rabbi Melech, with its sycophants and servants, became a metaphor for all totalitarian systems. Its ruler was described as "nothing short of a monomaniac".

And his exercise of power was analagous to an absolute monarch or the dictator of a state with a single ideology. Rabbi Melech's *gabbai* (in effect, his prime minister) made this comparison explicit. "Israel Avigdor...knew that a Rabbinic court was — he spat out piously when he made the base comparison — like a royal court". In short, *Yoshe Kalb* was no less a political novel than *Steel and Iron*; the difference being that its politics were fully integrated within a powerful story. It is a novel of repression; intellectual and psychological repression are at the root of the tragedies, not sin.

The story of *Yoshe Kalb* definitely fulfils Bashevis's conditions (as told to the BBC): it has a beginning, a middle and an end, and it certainly excited a passion for Joshua to write it. Even the most difficult condition was met: the juxtaposition of Pinchos Mendel's anecdote with his own bitter recollections of Radzymin meant that Joshua was the only one who could write this story. As soon as Bashevis heard Joshua read the first chapters of *Yoshe Kalb* he knew that his brother had outgrown the prolonged post-publication depression occasioned by *Steel and Iron,* that he had become a different man. The chapters "were fiery chapters, fiery with action and folklore and tension". What added to the artistic excitement, Bashevis acknowledged, was the realization that Abe Cahan would publish it and he would get money for it. Indeed, *Yoshe Kalb* was serialized in *Forverts* early in 1932 and created "a furore in American

Jewry as well as in Polish Jewry". When Bashevis called *Yoshe Kalb*
fiery he was talking of the intensity of its prose, but the adjective can
also be used to describe the predominant imagery. The novel opens
with the marriage of Rabbi Melech's daughter, Serele, to Nahum, son
of the rabbi of Rachmanivke. It was a union of opposites. Nahum was
too young to marry. "He was frail and slender...nervous and
sensitive...sunk in mystic speculations." Serele, on the contrary,
"was a big, fleshy creature, with solid legs, a shock of red hair, strong
teeth and the fully developed breasts of a mature woman". The
Rachmanivke rabbi was also the exact opposite of the Nyesheve rabbi.
In the letters that passed between them his were "written in flawlessly
grammatical Hebrew, every phrase, every word, every quotation
classically exact", while Rabbi Melech's writing was "clumsily
formed...thick, ungainly, like himself, the words were misspelt,
distorted". And the contents matched the styles; Rabbi Melech was
anxious to complete the wedding preparations, while the
Rachmanivke rabbi was determined to delay as long as possible. But
the monomaniac won even though the Rachmanivke rabbi saw
through the haste of Rabbi Melech. He knew that Rabbi Melech was
in a hurry to marry off his daughter so that he could take a fourth
bride. He said of him, "The man is on fire!" He was referring to his
lust, of course. In fact, fire was going to destroy the court at Nyesheve,
both metaphorically and literally. Malkah, the object of Rabbi
Melech's lust, was "gunpowder" likely to "explode at any moment".
Her guardians named her "Spitfire". She was a rebel, driven by her
repressed sexual desires, the unconscious nemesis of Nyesheve. She
had good reason to despise the custodians of the cult of hasidic
wonder-rabbis, for they had rewritten her mother's history just as
efficiently as any school of Soviet historians. Malkah's mother,
married off no less unsuitably at the age of fourteen, finally ran away to
Budapest with a cavalry officer of the local garrison.

> The family cursed her and wiped her name from their records. Her
> husband, a sickly scion of a Rabbinic house, died of loneliness and
> humiliation. But no one outside the family knew the truth. It was given
> out that the Rabbi's wife was a very sick woman, and that she was living
> abroad in a sanitorium under the constant care of doctors.[33]

Malkah's rebellion began even before her wedding, when she refused
to have her hair cut on the customary day. And it continued thereafter.
As if in collusion with tormented Nahum, who was at first unable to
consummate his marriage, Malkah refused to let Rabbi Melech near
her on their wedding night. Naturally, Rabbi Melech concealed his
disgrace, though his actions clearly indicated some psychological

disturbance: He began to smoke one cigar after another. And every few minutes he commanded Israel Avigdor, "Fire!" And so the fuse was lit that would eventually crack "the walls of the stronghold of Nyesheve" and topple its ruler (*melech* being the Hebrew for "king").

When Nahum met his new mother-in-law, a "wild unconscious joy" lit their faces. Malkah was confused. "He was a man and yet a little boy...she wanted him, and she wanted a child too...."

> All the furious impulses of her nature, without discipline and without compromise, rose up in her. She bared her firm, shuddering breasts, and cupped both hands under it, so that she felt as if she were suckling a baby.[34]

"Restless with fever", Nahum substituted his wife. He caressed her "boldly and fiercely" and took her with a unique "outburst of passion". Serele, in her "bewildered gratitude", did not hear him "whisper once or twice a name that was not hers". As Joshua put it, Nahum had forgotten himself. Rabbi Melech, too, in the humiliation of Malkah's rejection "forgot who he was and where he was". Loss of self, as was clear in Pinchos Mendel's original anecdote, is a central theme; the philosophical core which is represented by the feverish and fiery imagery. So *Yoshe Kalb* was structured around Nahum's various identities; first as Nahum, then as Yoshe Kalb, and finally as no one. His tragedy was that he was never given the opportunity to find out for himself who he was. Each identity was imposed upon him, so that his genuine desires became transgressions, which can only be obtained by the extreme expedient of self-abandonment. Only when he was no one was Nahum at peace.

After his first encounter with Malkah, Nahum was unable to return to his former studies; he could only concentrate upon the cabbala in whose sexual imagery he conjured pictures of Malkah.

> Then Nahum's thoughts focused themselves definitely on Malkah. His body became rigid as he imagined himself kissing her, holding her body to his. He lifted his hands blindly, and only when his convulsive fingers closed on emptiness did he come to himself.[35]

And the self to which he returned was Nahum, the rabbinical student, husband of Serele, who knew that for merely thinking such things he was condemning himself to "fires which are named Death and Darkness and Curse and Abyss", the smallest of which "is sixty times hotter than the hottest fire on earth". On account of such fears Nahum resisted his inclinations, but like Joshua at cheder in Leoncin, his eyes strayed from the holy texts to the meadows beyond the windows, and he was enraptured by the "unutterable joy of nature". Nor could he control his dreams. So Nahum took the only course available to him, asceticism. He tortured his body. But again tempestuous circumstances almost robbed him of his will to resist. He took shelter from a storm in a blasted oak, only for a worse one to break out within, when Malkah suddenly appeared soaking wet. She clung to him in fear, as the lightning split the sky. But for Nahum the lightning was no aid to seduction, he saw "a second flash...which seemed to spring out of every corner of the sky" as "a whip of fire with a thousand lashes, the fire of God for the punishment of sinners". And he fled. But Malkah was not to be denied so easily; if the traditional background effects of the gothic seductress were useless against the superstitious power of Judaism she was a modern enough woman to create her own circumstances. So she set fire to the court itself. It happened one summer night, "when the excitement in the village was slowly waking her blood into a frenzy".

> At last, exhausted in body, but more restless than ever in mind, she turned back to the court.
>   When she entered she saw the lantern hanging on the wall of the big barn. Without knowing why, Malkah reached up and took the guttering candle out of the lamp. The door of the barn stood open...she crossed the threshold.... In this barn lay the Cossack uniforms which rotted from wedding to wedding; they lay in heaps, together with other rags, under a covering of straw.... In that pestilential uncleanness Malkah recognized, through her tense confusion, the whole horror of the Rabbinic court of Nyesheve.... With a gesture of loathing which shot through all her body, she flung the candle into a heap of straw in front of her.[36]

Thus started a fire with great implications, for Malkah had just undergone a mock wedding ceremony equally as empty as her own real one. She had "crossed the threshold" into a room where the guests were vacant uniforms, but instead of vows she had spat fire. What was burning was more than the court, it was the whole concept of arranged marriages. In effect, she had divorced both herself and Nahum from their spouses. She was a free woman, freed of all restraint, her instincts were released. She became "like an animal in rut", running about "wordless, panting, drunk". She was frantic, with one idea: to have Nahum. "Now! In this confusion! In this mad night!" And Nahum was helpless to resist her colossal will.

> She approached him swiftly and took one of his hands. In a tone of sure command, such as a mother might use to an obedient child, she said, "Come!"
>   He followed her![37]

And as they "became one" the sky took on "a fierier tinge from the blazing synagogue of Nyesheve". Malkah's fire lit up the heavens, and she cried aloud "in the first happiness of her life". But it was a pyrrhic victory; Malkah and Nahum were no more able to control the consequences of their passion than the Jews of Nyesheve were able to contain the fire. On seeing it their cry was not for water, but: "Jews! Save the scrolls of the Law!"

> But when these had been carried out of the synagogue, no one seemed to know what should be done next. These Jews were helpless. They were not accustomed to action of any kind.[38]

When Esther described the same fire in *Deborah* it only had anecdotal interest, now it was a full-blown symbol with a complexity of meanings. Its after-image haunted Nahum. Night after night he saw "the fires of hell, and they were like the fire which had destroyed the court of Nyesheve".

Unlike his betters at Nyesheve, Nahum could not sustain a double life. He was no hypocrite. He did not know what to do with the desire that had forced him to break the greatest taboo, and was prompting him to become a man utterly different from the Nahum everyone knew. His body had developed a will of its own. Thus Nahum began to see himself as not one person but two. He also imagined that he "was not Nahum at all, but another, a reincarnation which was taking on again its previous form". All the time "the two forces in him maintained constant war" and when they were evenly balanced he did not remember who he was. Malkah reminded him of one Nahum, Serele of another. But it was Malkah who was pregnant, and Malkah who died. But even in death she would not give up from her womb the second self she and Nahum had created, her happiness and her death. When she was buried Nahum disappeared. In pathetic parody of Malkah's great coup Serele tried to will him to return.

> Serele took a brick and placed it on the kitchen fire till it became red hot; then she muttered over it:
> "Stone, stone, as you glow with the heat of the fire, so let the heart of my husband glow with desire for me. Come, come, come!"
> Nahum did not come.[39]

And so Rabbi Melech pronounced his daughter an *agunah*, an abandoned wife. Nahum had divorced himself. He was no longer Nahum, but he must be someone.

He became Yoshe Kalb, Yoshe the loon. This happened in Bialogura. At first he had tried to be a blank, a nameless beggar. But soon someone asked what he was called, and after he had thought a moment he gave his name as Yoshe. However, a character was also required, so he became known as a loon, Yoshe the loon. Once again

Nahum (rather, Yoshe) had a personality imposed upon him, the ironic result of his attempt to be nothing. It was soon apparent that Bialogura was a perverse reflection of Nyesheve, and that everything that happened to Yoshe was an echo of a previous event. Thus he became the victim of a second arranged marriage, this time to Zivyah, half-wit daughter of Reb Kanah the beadle. Zivyah was a nightmarish combination of Serele and Malkah, tormenting Yoshe with her mindless animal sexuality as he tried to sleep. Likewise, Reb Kanah was the corrupt side of Rabbi Melech made visible, as he exploited Yoshe's mutability, offering nothing in return except a bed above his oven and his daughter. Yoshe made one half-hearted effort to leave. "Yoshe! Where are you going?" asked Kanah. "Into the world," replied Yoshe — a phrase Gimpel the Fool was to repeat, when he quit Frampol after the death of his faithless Elka. But for Yoshe there was no escape from Zivyah, just as Nahum was doomed to marry Serele and sin with Malkah. In fact, he resisted Zivyah, it was a nameless smuggler who impregnated her, but it made no difference. Fire trapped him for Malkah, the plague snared him for Zivyah.

The superstitious inhabitants of Bialogura became convinced that the plague was caused by the presence of a sinner in their midst, "they began to look for sins, each man watching his neighbour". They searched with the diligence of the secret police.

> A committee of wealthy Jews called in the chief attendant of the ritual baths, to ask him the names of the women who were remiss in their visits. Husbands were bidden to keep close watch on their wives, to see that their heads were properly covered and that no lock of hair stray out from under the cover and be seen over the ear or at the back of the neck.[40]

The rabbi, Reb Meir'l, while concerned, had found in an old book "a few words which indicated clearly that the Messiah was to appear this very year", so he saw the plague and rumours of war between Russia and Turkey as portents of the Messiah's imminent arrival (not unlike Joshua's father in 1905, some sixty years later). Indeed, he was half expecting the Messiah when the butchers appeared dragging Zivyah, five months pregnant. Yoshe was accused by Reb Kanah, but gave only enigmatic answers to the rabbis. "I do not know the truth.... I come from the world.... I am a stone." The rabbis were baffled, but nevertheless came to a conclusion that delighted all Bialogura. Yoshe must marry Zivyah with great pomp in the cemetery, thus the town would propitiate for the sin with a good deed. Actually, it was Nahum's ironic atonement; to marry a grotesque creature pregnant by another man instead of the beautiful Malkah for whose condition he was responsible. When Nahum married Zivyah he was dragged to the tomb, beneath which Zivyah had copulated, "as though mind and body were of two persons". "He let them do with him whatever they liked; but he himself was not a participant". That night Yoshe disappeared. And his wife was again told by her father that she was an *agunah* — an abandoned wife. It is worth noting that Gimpel's arranged marriage also took place in a graveyard, also to a slut impregnated by another. Yet while he and Yoshe were both regarded by their fellow citizens as simpletons their reactions were completely different. Unlike Yoshe, Gimpel stayed with his wife, and even accepted responsibility for the child's circumcision. "Shoulders are from God, and burdens too," was his response. He was the only true Jew in Frampol, the only one who believed with perfect faith and acted accordingly. Yoshe's only burden was his own sin, a rock in a sack which he carried over his shoulder. He was a victim of the very beliefs that gave Gimpel his strength, and each reflected the different characters of their creators.

Fifteen years later Nahum returned to Nyesheve. Once again Serele wore the garments of a wife. Here the enigmatic behaviour which had marked him as a sinner in Bialogura quickly won Nahum the reputation of a saint. "I tell you," said Rabbi Melech, "the man is not to be understood." No more a saint than a sinner Nahum remained aloof; however, this merely increased the ardour of his followers, who began to speak of him as the next rabbi of Nyesheve. Once more others were planning his future. But at the great Rosh Hashanah celebrations his two identities came face to face. He was recognized by Reb Shachnah, one of the rabbis of Bialogura, as Yoshe Kalb. Reb Shachnah's cry was prophetic, but it also echoed an actual event, "Jews! A fire burns in the court of Nyesheve! Yoshe the loon is living with the Rabbi's daughter!" So the fire ignited by Malkah was not yet burnt out, and it was left to Reb Shachnah, now "burning with the zeal of a prophet", to complete her revenge. "He traversed Jewry like a firebrand, leaving behind him a trail of smoke, unrest and dissension." Nahum or Yoshe? It was a question that divided families as efficiently as the civil war between the Beigel-with-a-hole party and the Beigel-without-a-hole party in Tashrak's story.

> Communities and groups excommunicated one another in solemn style. Matches were broken; parents recalled their married sons and daughters, and compelled them to divorce their partners. Nyesheve enthusiasts would not buy meat slaughtered by an enemy of Nyesheve, and vice versa. Such meat, each side argued, was undoubtedly unclean.[41]

Eventually, as a result of bloody disturbances, the civil authorities compelled the rabbinate to act, and the officially ordained rabbis took the opportunity to strike a blow against their unqualified hasidic rivals. Seventy rabbis — "the number which made up the Sanhedrin of old" — signed a proclamation which called upon Rabbi Melech to submit the case of his son-in-law to trial before a Tribunal of Holy Law. Rabbi Melech had no choice, even though the trial was a test of his authority. It was another battle between the *misnagidim* and the hasidim, the old arguments between Bathsheba and Pinchos Mendel acted out on a universal stage. The case went first one way, then the other, as Zivyah declared the defendant to be her Yoshe, and Serele maintained that he was her Nahum. All of his identities flashed before him; from his earliest days he repeated the sermon he had made at his wedding to Serele in a "far-off voice, which did not seem to issue from a living body". And still Nahum waited to be told who he was. Finally, the so-called Saint of Lizhane resolved the matter, by reviving one of Nahum's old schizophrenic fantasies.

> The Saint of Lizhane was shaking from head to foot.
> "You who are under judgement!" he cried. "Who are you? Answer!"
> "I do not know."
> "But I do know!" the Saint of Lizhane cried. "You are a reincarnation, the wandering soul of a dead man.... A dead soul! You wander from place to place, to mock the living, and you yourself do not know what you do.... You are Nahum and you are Yoshe; you are a scholar and you are an ignoramus; you appear suddenly in cities and you disappear suddenly from them; you wander in the cemeteries in search of your own kind...wherever you come you bring with you disaster, terror, pestilence; you unite yourself with women; you flee from them and you return. You know not what you do; there is no taste in your life or in your deeds, because you are nothing yourself, because — hear me! — you are a dead wanderer in the chaos of the world!"[42]

It was a masterpiece of misinterpretation. But it was sufficient to sway the assembly. Only Nahum's denial would suffice. "Nahum!" croaked Rabbi Melech. It was his last word. His reign was at an end, hereafter his court would be divided amongst his warring sons. And Nahum went into the world, neither as Nahum nor Yoshe, but as no one. His own man at last. Bashevis's novel *The Estate* ended with the words: "His intimates went out to telegraph the Jewish settlements that Jochanan, the Rabbi of Marshinov, had died." It signalled the end of an era, the passing of the last saint. Similarly, Joshua wrote toward the end of *Yoshe Kalb*: "All day long the news was passed from point to point: the Rabbi of Nyesheve was dead." But all that had ended, in Joshua's view, was an age of superstition and repression. Unfortunately, nothing better was to succeed it.

With happy foresight Joshua described, during the course of the novel, how some ushers, expelled from one of the large Hebrew schools in Lemberg "for indecent relations with a cleaning-woman", turned the story of Yoshe into a play, "having nothing better to do".

> One of them had written a comedy entitled "The Saint of Nyesheve, or, Yoshe the Loon and His Two Wives," and the unemployed ushers tried it out in a low tavern frequented by servant girls, wagoners, shoemakers, bakers' assistants and the like. The play, in which the Rabbi of Nyesheve, Yoshe the loon, Serele the Rabbi's daughter, and other leading figures were represented in the flesh, was a great success, and the ushers decided to tour the provinces.[43]

Thanks to the vanity of a Yiddish translator named Maximilian Hurwitz, who wrote synopses for the English-speaking audience of the Yiddish Art Theatre, many national libraries own souvenir programmes of Maurice Schwartz's production of *Yoshe Kalb.* It is stuffed with splendid photographs of Maurice Schwartz and others in full costume, contemporary reviews and newspaper articles, including one from the *Forverts* which purported to give the genesis of the production:

> Even before the serial publication of the novel was completed, opinions were voiced that it contained material for a powerful drama. Maurice Schwartz was then in Europe, and in New York theatre circles, as well as in the literary circles, it was said that Schwartz was sure to come back with a contract or verbal understanding to dramatize the novel. And so it turned out. As soon as Schwartz heard about the novel and read parts of it, he put aside all his other plans for the season and began to prepare "Yoshe Kalb" for his return to his former Art Theatre.

Maurice Schwartz also returned with Joshua. "In the summer of 1932 I landed on the shores of the United States for the first time," wrote Joshua. "I came to New York for a three months visit in connection with a stage version of my novel, *Yoshe Kalb,* which was produced by Maurice Schwartz at the Yiddish Art Theatre in the fall of that year."[44] Even in these simple sentences there was an echo in the words, "landed on the shores", of Columbus's great adventure. "He was really dazzled by America," said Bashevis. America took to him, also. The article from *Forverts* (begun above) concluded:

> With this evening and with Singer's departure there will come to a close a remarkable chapter in the history of Yiddish literature and the Yiddish drama.... In the few short months that Singer has spent among us in New York he has gained the friendship and respect of the writing fraternity. The great success, the hymns of praise, and the honor meted out to him have not turned his head. He has behaved throughout his stay with admirable modesty and sociability, which one

does not often encounter in artists under similar circumstances.

Unhappily, Joshua has not recorded his opinion of the production. However, Bashevis was not so reticent. "Well, Maurice Schwartz, of course," he said.

> Maurice Schwartz was by nature a kitsch director or drama-maker. He wanted everything to be like a super-colossal Hollywood production. Although he never had any chance to work in Hollywood, he was a Hollywood man. So he made it more sensational than my brother wanted it to be.[45]

Hints of what Bashevis meant can be found in Maurice Schwartz's own essay in the programme. He described dramatic scenes that are not in the novel; for example:

> Nahum...succumbs to the strength of Malkah's inflamed passion and great love for the young man with the black eyes, by whom she would like to have a child and then die. She sets fire to the court. She calls upon thunder and lightning to send down a fire that shall devour them both.

Against this feeling must be put the opinion of Abe Cahan who, while noting that those who have read the novel "cannot help comparing it to the play", exclaimed that the play *Yoshe Kalb* was "composed and directed in a truly wonderful way", and was among "the most remarkable in the literature of the Yiddish stage". Moreover, it received flattering reviews from both the Yiddish and the English press, and on 22 February 1933 Maurice Schwartz was awarded the Rabbi Beer Manischewitz Memorial Award for Distinguished Service "for the outstanding contribution of the year to the Jewish theatre in America, 'Yoshe Kalb'". Perhaps the review that best conveys the atmosphere of the play was Brooks Atkinson's piece for the *New York Times*. He began by comparing the "lassitude and fever" of the Yiddish theatre against the "bloodless" offerings of the "Anglo-Saxon stage".

> Although the Yiddish stage is beset by many business problems, it is not afflicted with sophisticated realism. It can still indulge itself honestly in the grease paint theatre.... During the last few weeks Mr Schwartz and his capacious company have been acting a Jewish legend entitled "Yoshe Kalb".... Far from being a naturalistic episode in the lives of hard-headed moderns, it is a genuine story with flavor and compass and kaleidoscopic colors.... Nor is the acting in the three-piece suit dimension.... His actors who still know how to wear the dressing-room beard, are an uncommonly picturesque collection. You must hunt far through the neat diocese of the Anglo-Saxon theatre before you will find such racy make-ups.... Made up in this headline

style and romantically bedizened, the actors attack their drama with perfervid conviction.... While the Anglo-Saxon stage is playing with attitudes and bright remarks, the Yiddish stage can still tell a full story and invigorate the scenes with pictorial figures, and since audiences believe in it, they can respond uncritically. Whether business is good or business is bad, Mr Schwartz's theatre is alive.[46]

However far removed from sophisticated realism the play was, the novel remains a sophisticated piece of literature. As Bashevis remarked in the introduction, "the novel is still a source of enjoyment and learning for many lovers of literature", indeed, of all his brother's novels it is the one to which he feels closest. His enthusiasm may seem rather surprising, given the anti-hasidic nature of *Yoshe Kalb*, but Bashevis explained it this way:

> *Yoshe Kalb* contains a lot of the mysticism. Except that my brother took mysticism not with one grain of salt but with many. Which I don't do, because to me the mystic is not someone to make fun of or to mock. I feel sometimes that if he would have lived longer he might have become a mystic himself; maybe yes, maybe no.[47]

In fact there are certain similarities between *Yoshe Kalb* and Bashevis's first novel, *Satan in Goray*, which was published in 1935. Though Bashevis was anxious to point out how strange Joshua found the book:

> When I published *Satan in Goray* he was still alive of course; and he read it and was astonished that his brother could go so far away from him. At the same time it wasn't *so* far away from him because he also knew all these things. But it was good that we were not alike; it would have been a tragedy, at least for me, if I were to write just like my brother.[48]

Both *Yoshe Kalb* and *Satan in Goray* are about the destruction of Jewish communities by outside forces. Of course these forces could not have been successful without the co-operation of the inhabitants — at which point the brothers differ. Joshua was more inclined to find fault with the prevailing system of belief, while Bashevis blamed the frailty of human nature. Whereas Rabbi Melech of Nyesheve was corrupt, Rabbi Benish Ashkenazi of Goray was a righteous man. His failure was his inability to stand up to the representatives of evil. He cracked, not the principles of Judaism. Actually, Bashevis proposed strict adherence to religious beliefs as the only panacea against evil inclination, the very thing that prevented Nahum establishing his own identity as a modern man. At the same time, Bashevis, himself a modern man, knew that he was one of the agents of destruction; therefore the dybbuk which invaded Rechele at the conclusion of the

novel is a metaphor for the novelist. It represented the triumph of
fiction, which is stronger than Bashevis's misgivings. This self-
consciousness is missing from Joshua's work, which is at its fiercest
when ripping apart a foe worthy of his personal animosity. He lacked
his brother's introspection, his accusations fly outward. The leading
ladies of both *Yoshe Kalb* and *Satan in Goray* suffer extremely
unpleasant deaths; the one caused by the delivery of a child, the other
by the devilry of a dybbuk. The different treatment of these two
women within the texts exemplifies the divergent sensibilities of
Joshua and Bashevis.

"Malkah is sane but greedy for life, for enjoyment," said Bashevis,
"while Rechele is a nervous wreck with a kind of sexiness which
hysterical, neurotic women sometimes suppress in themselves."[49] He
thought that Malkah and Rechele were probably inspired by his sister
Esther. In the case of Rechele this is obvious, but Malkah seems to
derive more from literary precedents than life itself. Perhaps this is
why her fate seems less cold-blooded; it was conventional in a way that
Rechele's was not, her death being uniquely cruel. One final
similarity: both were raised as orphans, though neither was, and both
were consequently brought into the communities they were to ravage.
Malkah was a rebel, she resisted repression, she would not accept the
misinformation fed to her by her uncle and aunt. But Rechele was a
victim; her imagination was warped by the hideous profession of her
uncle, and the terrifying stories of his grotesque mother-in-law. Her
uncle, Reb Zeydel Ber, was a slaughterer.

> Once Rechele saw two blood-smeared butcher boys skin a goat and let it
> lie there with eyeballs protruding in amazement and white teeth
> projecting in a kind of death-smile.[50]

But if anything, Granny, his mother-in-law, tormented Rechele even
more with her monologues.

> As they lay under the feather bed, in the pitch dark, the old woman
> would tell Rechele stories of wild beasts and goblins; of robbers that
> lived in caves with witches; of man-eaters that roasted children on spits;
> and of a wild one-eyed monster that stalked about with a fir tree in its
> hand looking for a lost princess. Sometimes from her sleep Granny
> would cry out wildly and incoherently. The roots of Rechele's hair
> would tingle with terror, and, her whole body a-quiver, she would wake
> up the old woman with the cry: "Granny? What are you saying?
> Granny?
>   "Granny, I'm afraid!"[51]

What Rechele could not see, but only imagine, became more
horrifying than the dreadful sights that surrounded her. Against the

latter she could close her eyes. Consequently, Granny was able to torment Rechele, even after her death. So much so that, left alone in the house on the night before Yom Kippur, the frenzy of Rechele's imagination brought about a paralytic fit.

> She fell asleep and in her dreams Granny came to her.... Rechele's whole body shuddered. She awoke, drenched with sweat.... The pots on the oven and on the benches moved and were suspended in air. The candle box turned around and did a jig. There was a scarlet glow on the walls. Everything seethed, burst, crackled, as though the whole house were aflame.... Late that night, when Uncle came home, he found Rechele lying with her knees pulled up to her chest, her eyes glazed and her teeth clenched.[52]

Thenceforth Rechele was one apart, her imagination cursed with the terrible ability to anticipate reality so that all her worst fears could come true. Later, when she read, "the pages turned of their own accord". In her own way she had become as unsuitable a bride as Malkah. "Nobody wants me!" Rechele said. "Unless Satan will have me!" Prophetic words!

Like Nahum, Rechele became the battleground for a dispute between "the sacred and the profane". The sacred was all face, the profane had no true shape.

> The Face swayed in prayer; it spoke with zeal, like Rabbi Benish in the old days, chanting the holy writ; it raised questions of Torah and resolved them; it told pious tales to strengthen the faith and vanquish disbelief.[53]

But the profane was stronger, until in the shape of a bearded figure "hairy and naked, wet and stinking, with long monkey hands and open maw" it actually defiled her. Thereafter Satan made nightly visits to Rechele, and she was "ravished...so many times that she was powerless to move", also she suffered "extraordinary tortures". She swelled, vomited reptiles, barked like a dog, mooed like a cow. But these are trivialities compared to her final indignity.

Describing this, Bashevis abandoned the swift narration of the rest of the novel and adopted the objective style of an inquisitorial recorder, as if he were seeking a witness to vouch for the logical momentum of the novel, as if he were recoiling from the sadist his art had forced him to become. In one of his more recent stories, "One Night in Brazil", it was made clear to the narrator that "a dybbuk sits inside of you". This is the demanding dybbuk that compels a writer to make choices for the sake of the story which may go against his natural inclination. Thus Rechele suffered not for some higher moral purpose, but for the amoral satisfaction of art. Malkah's death in childbirth was rapid; however agonizing for her, it was relatively painless for the reader.

> On the coldest night of that year, which fell, strangely, just when spring was due, Malkah, the wife of Rabbi Melech, was taken with violent labor pains, and could not bring forth her child. A sleigh with three fast horses was sent to the nearest town, to bring the old doctor who had always attended the wives of the Rabbi. But though he came in all haste, he arrived too late. Malkah died, together with her unborn child.[54]

Her death is shockingly sudden, but neither compulsive nor repulsive. It is a literary death; she has served her purpose, she has only one more function. After her death, as has been described, she continued to refuse to give up her unborn child, despite the ministrations of a midwife and the commands of a Tribunal of Rabbis. Rechele's death was a perverse variant of this episode; instead of a dead child she had a dybbuk in her womb. And it was the dybbuk that was the author of her fatal humiliation. It first revealed its presence when Rechele "lay with parted legs like a woman in labor on the stool". Thereafter she was its puppet.

> And for spite the spirit flung her bonnet to the earth and uncovered her body, and she spread her legs to show her nakedness and to bring men into thoughts of transgression: And she passed water and befouled the holy place and her breasts became as hard as stones and her belly bulged so that ten men could not depress it: Her left leg she twisted around her neck and the right she stuck out stiff as a board and her tongue lolled like a hanged man's (God preserve us): In this state she lay and her cries went up to very Heaven and the earth was split by her cries: And she vomited blood and filth and it dripped from her nostrils and from her eyes and she broke wind.... And many righteous women did testify that a stink issued from *that same place* for the spirit dwelt in there *(vid. sup.)*: and she also made such lewd gesticulations as cannot be put down in writing.... And all this to the accompaniment of thunder and lightning, so that many of the congregation were struck with terror and their knees knocked and they cried: Woe unto us, For the profane doth triumph over the sacred (which God forbid).[55]

Why such detail? Because Bashevis had written a book about the potentiality of the human imagination, and its vulnerability to evil. Rechele had tried to imagine the Messiah, to give birth through her mind, therefore Bashevis was compelled to produce a series of images to demonstrate that such ambitions could only be the devil's temptation. Finally, the dybbuk was driven out by blasts from the ram's horn, and emerged as a "flash of fire from *that same place*", the place of defilement. Three days later Rechele died. Like Malkah she had been killed by the destructive impulses she fostered; nor did their wombs deliver anything living. Their ends were final. Sarah, the heroine of Bashevis's *The Slave,* was another who died as a result of childbirth. In order to conceal the fact that she once was a Christian named Wanda, Sarah was compelled to pass herself off as a mute. But her painful labour loosened her tongue, she shouted out in Yiddish and Polish. At once the people cried: "That's a dybbuk speaking." But in this novel Bashevis seemed to have relaxed the severity of his judgement; religion was not absolute piety but the relation between man and his fellows. Moreover, though Sarah did die a child was born; the lust between her and Jacob, the slave, had been transformed through suffering into love and a positive hope for the future. Though both *Satan in Goray* and *The Slave* are set in the same period of Polish history, the middle of the seventeenth century after the Chmelnicki revolt, their composition was separated by Hitler's holocaust. History outran Bashevis's worst fears.

Satan in Goray begins as if it were a folk tale or legend. Chmelnicki is called wicked and Goray is described as being "in the midst of the hills at the end of the world". But instead of opening with "once upon a time" the novel starts explicitly, "In the year 1648". Thus Bashevis establishes immediately his mode of working; a juxtaposition of the fantastic and the factual, which culminates in the eye-witness account already quoted. Certainly Goray's destruction was real, with its murders and rapes. The Cossacks "violated women and afterward ripped open their bellies and sewed cats inside". This is what Goray looked like after the event:

> Goray...was completely deserted...the prayer house and the study house were filled with dung left by the horses that the soldiers had stabled there. Most of the houses had been leveled by fire. For weeks after the razing of Goray, corpses lay neglected in every street, with no one to bury them. Savage dogs tugged at dismembered limbs, and vultures and crows fed on human flesh. The handful who survived left the town and wandered away. It seemed as though Goray had been erased forever.[56]

When Bashevis wrote about the devastation of Josefov in *The Slave,* also at the hands of Chmelnicki, there was an added resonance in the words, "the whole of Poland had become one vast cemetery". After the twentieth-century catastrophe Bashevis saw its seventeenth-century counterpart as a recurrent motif in Jewish history, hence *The Slave* encompassed all times, from biblical to contemporary. Consequently, *The Slave* has great depth, but *Satan in Goray* has the heartless exuberance of a folk tale to add to the bite of fact. Thanks to the vocabulary of such tales, Bashevis was able to introduce talk of "the end of days" without any fuss. For the Jews, in order to justify their sufferings, saw Chmelnicki's massacres as "the birth pangs of the Messiah". And a man, Sabbatai Zevi, arose to fulfil those expectations. Rabbi Meir'l's brief daydream became the central theme of *Satan in Goray*, as the survivors await the day of judgement.

Goray's chief opponent to Sabbatai Zevi was Rabbi Benish Ashkenazi; so long as he retained his powers the messianic fervour could be controlled. But the massacres had weakened his resolve, "had re-awakened in him the old paradoxes regarding faith, predestination and freedom of will, and the suffering of the virtuous". Moreover, his own household was engaged in an interminable family quarrel that had been smouldering for years. This concerned his two sons and their wives. Bashevis had already said that he couldn't have written *Satan in Goray* without visiting Bilgoray, and it is plain that Rabbi Benish was based upon his grandfather, the rabbi of Bilgoray. Likewise, Ozer and Levi, Rabbi Benish's sons, were modelled after Bashevis's uncles, Joseph and Itche. Joshua said of them, in *Of a World That Is No More*, that they were "constantly at odds and embroiled in a fierce competition". Bashevis wrote that Ozer "always held a piece of chalk between his fingers with which he perpetually marked calculations on every closet and table that he passed", while Joseph (as noted by Joshua) was a skilled mathematician who "always carried a piece of chalk with which he scribbled mathematical problems on walls, tables, and benches". And Levi, like Itche, was spoilt by his mother who "sent delicacies to him...stuffing and pampering him". Now Rabbi Benish could barely keep the peace in his own family, let alone in Goray. It was different in the old days when he "reigned in Goray like a king". But even then he feared that Polish Jewry was taking the wrong path. "They delved too deeply into things that were meant to be hidden, they drank too little from the clear waters of the holy teachings." What he feared was the cabbala, which he considered contradictory and lewd, which contained texts that could easily be exploited by Sabbatai Zevi's followers. Indeed, when Rechele collapsed in the prayer-house after prophetic utterances she was carried through the crowd "as though she were the sacred Torah". "Some even touched her with their fingertips as she passed and bore their fingers to their lips, as when a scroll is taken from the Ark." She had become the embodiment of this cabbalistic concept:

> So it is with the Torah, which discloses her innermost secrets only to them who love her. She knows that whosoever is wise in heart hovers near the gates of her dwelling place day after day. What does she do? From her palace, she shows her face to him, and gives him a signal of love, and forthwith retreats back to her hiding place. Only he alone catches her message, and is drawn to her with his whole heart and soul,

and with all of his being. In this manner, the Torah, for a moment, discloses himself in love to her lovers, so as to rouse them to renewed love.[57]

What the cabbala encouraged was materialism, the transformation of an abstract idea into an image, the reduction of divine mysteries into human relationships. The danger came when it was taken literally. But instead of speaking out, Rabbi Benish had heeded the verse in Amos, "Therefore the prudent doth keep silence in such a time." Now he hadn't the strength.

Strangers kept arriving in Goray with wonderful tidings concerning Sabbatai Zevi. A Jew from the Yemen informed the congregation that the "Great Fish that lurks in the river Nile has succumbed at the hands of Sabbatai Zevi.... The lion that dwelleth on high will descend from Heaven, in his mouth a seven-headed scorpion.... With fire issuing from his nostrils, he will carry the Messiah into Jerusalem.... In Miron a fiery column has been seen stretching from earth to heaven.... The full name of God and of Sabbatai Zevi were scratched on it in black.... The women who divine by consulting drops of oil have seen the crown of King David on Sabbatai Zevi's head." And why shouldn't he be believed? After all the impossible horrors they had witnessed with their own eyes, such miracles were not so unbelievable. But only Rabbi Benish knew what the others would have to learn; which is "the moral of this tale".

> Let none attempt to force the Lord: To end our
> pain within the world: The Messiah will come
> in God's own time: And free men of despair
> and crime: Then death will put away
> his sword: And Satan die abjured,
> abhorred: Lilith will vanish
> with the night: The exile
> end and all be light:
> Amen selah:
> Concluded and done.[58]

He banished the Yemenite. But the contamination had taken root in Goray, Reb Mordecai Joseph, a cabbalist, cried, "Benish, the dog, denies the Messiah!" One of Rabbi Benish's students protested, "Sabbatai Zevi is a false Messiah!" He was beaten senseless. The hysterical procession towards Satanism had begun.

Another disciple, Reb Itche Mates, arrived. And he was entertained in Rabbi Benish's own house by Levi, the rabbi's son, a secret supporter of the sect. Although Itche Mates could divulge "mysteries of mysteries" he was a fanatic with "dead eyes". His trade was as a peddler and a scribe, and while in Goray he checked the mezuzahs on the doorposts. That was how he met Rechele, whose mezuzah had the word for God completely erased. When she cried that only Satan would take her, he decided that he had been sent by heaven to save her. So he proposed marriage. At the same time Rabbi Benish received a letter which warned him that Itche Mates was a forger and seducer.

> In every town he comes to he speaks upon the heart of some woman to join him in the bond of matrimony, but his purpose is to make her unclean and to give her a bad name. For after the marriage his wives all move away from him, because of his ugly ways; from too much magic working, he has himself been caught in the web, and no longer has the strength to act the man's part.[59]

Indeed, after seven days of celibate marriage Itche Mates "was examined by the men for signs of maleness". Rabbi Benish was further informed that followers of Sabbatai Zevi consumed alive "all who dare cast the slightest doubt on their depraved belief", and that men of wisdom and understanding were afraid to open their mouths. Thus it becomes clear, from this language, that the moral is directed against all false messianism, including the political kind where the means attempt to force the end, and which in its supreme self-righteousness regards any dissenting viewpoint as unholy. And so Rabbi Benish made his final attempt to stamp out the Sabbataian heresy in Goray, he prepared for war. He warned his congregation against false messiahs, he pointed out that it was a sin "to try to hasten the end of days", he branded Itche Mates a foolish zealot. But his melancholy mood would not leave him, and it was rumoured in Goray that he was preparing for his end. His defeat came on the night Rechele was betrothed to Itche Mates. Word reached Rabbi Benish that profanations were occurring; men were dancing with women in a frenzy sparked off by Itche Mates's own hysterical behaviour. Like the Rabbi of Bilgoray, as described by Joshua, Rabbi Benish stormed off toward Rechele's house to drive this evil out of his town. But Rabbi Benish never arrived.

> Casting a terrified glance over his shoulder, Rabbi Benish realized that evil was abroad and tried to return to his house.... Suddenly the storm seized him, bore him aloft for a short distance, as on wings, and then cast him down with such violence that in the turmoil he could hear his bones shatter. With the last vestige of his consciousness he was still able to think: "The End".[60]

Reb Mordecai Joseph crowed, "The demons have him now — may his name perish." In his agony Rabbi Benish cried out, "Take me away to Lublin. For God's sake! I do not want to lie in the graveyard in Goray." As he left, a woman screamed, "Holy Rabbi, why do you forsake us? Rabbi! Holy Rabbi!"

Levi became the new Rabbi of Goray. He sanctified the marriage of
Rechele to Reb Itche Mates. But the real power had been usurped by a
new arrival, Reb Gedaliya, who appeared in Goray bearing amazing
news of Sabbatai Zevi. He informed the bewildered citizens that
Sabbatai Zevi, already revealed as the Messiah, "had departed for
Stamboul to claim the crown of the Sultan who ruled the land of
Israel". His victory astounded the world, so Reb Gedaliya said.

> The people of Judea were now in high repute. Princes and kings came to
> honor them and prostrated themselves before them. Earth and Heaven
> would rejoice on the day that Sabbatai Zevi arrived in Stamboul. All the
> Jews would certainly celebrate the Feast of Weeks in the Land of Israel.
> The Holy Temple would be restored, the Tables of the Law returned to
> the Holy Ark, and a High Priest would enter the Holy of Holies.
> Sabbatai Zevi, the redeemer, would reign throughout the world.[61]

Like Rabbi Melech, Reb Gedaliya was a sensuous man, "with a great
belly".

> His coat was of beaver and covered with silk, and the hat he wore was
> sable. His black, broad, fan-shaped beard hung down to his waist, his
> curly hair fell over his shoulders.[62]

He was also a ritual slaughterer, an occupation which Bashevis places
not much higher than murderer; there is a clear connection in *Satan in
Goray* between the atrocities perpetrated by Chmelnicki's warriors
and the work of butchers, represented by Reb Gedaliya and Reb
Zeydel Ber. Thus when meat became available in Goray again for the
first time since 1648, the year of the massacre, it was clear that Goray
had fallen prey to temptation. "Even the old conservative citizens of
Goray, the opponents of Sabbatai Zevi, did not openly step forth
against Reb Gedaliya; because they too relished a spoonful of broth
and a bit of meat, they pretended neither to see nor hear." This new
mood of well-being did not accord with Reb Itche Mates's ascetic
melancholy; and just as Reb Gedaliya was already the true leader of
Goray, so he also became the personification of the Sabbatai Zevi sect.
Passover, the festival that celebrates the ending of the slavery in
Egypt, became a joyous anticipation of the new salvation in Reb
Gedaliya's hands. His sermon encouraged the pleasures of the flesh,
and spoke of sexual union as a metaphor for holy unity.

> He demonstrated by means of cabala that all the laws in the Torah and
> the Shulchan Aruch referred to the commandment to be fruitful and
> multiply; and that, when the end of days was come, not only would
> Rabbi Gershom's ban on polygamy become null and void, but all the
> strict "Thou shalt nots", as well. Every pious woman would then be as

fair as Abigail, and there would be no monthly flow of blood at all; for impure blood comes from the Evil One. Men would be permitted to know strange women. Such encounters might even be considered a religious duty; for each time a man and a woman unite they form a mystical combination and promote a union between the Holy One, blessed be He, and the Divine Presence.[63]

Bashevis noted that the women's gallery was much fuller than in former years: "It was well known that the women looked on Reb Gedaliya with sympathetic eyes." Nor did Reb Gedaliya forget his duties as ritual slaughterer: "From early morning until late at night he stood before a blood-filled pit and, with his long butcher's knife, tirelessly cut into warm, distended necks, slaughtering innumerable calves and sheep, hens, geese, and ducks." At his Seder he extended the limits of his licence, the women sat with the menfolk, and more than the prescribed four goblets of wine were drunk. Sabbatai Zevi's heresy had been established as Goray's only ideology; his opponents "were silenced...others out of fear of persecution said nothing".

The same gradual corruption that overtook the inhabitants of Frampol in "The Gentleman from Cracow" had clearly taken hold in Goray. Indeed, the two works, the story and the novel, are closely related in more ways than this. Most major characters in the story have a counterpart in the novel; Reb Gedaliya is obviously a variant upon the Gentleman himself, corrupting with golden words and meat instead of money and food; Rabbi Benish is a somewhat frailer version of Rabbi Ozer, and Rechele is no less unfortunate than Hodle. As the Gentleman from Cracow picked Hodle for his bride, so Reb Gedaliya chose Rechele, notwithstanding the fact that she was already married. Shortly after Reb Gedaliya's Seder, Rechele had a vision, during which the Angel Sandalfon informed her that "perfect and full redemption will come at the new year". Moreover, the Angel spoke of Reb Gedaliya as a saintly man, and said that "the worlds on high do tremble at the unions he doth form". As ordered, Rechele repeated these prophecies in the prayer house. Whereupon she fainted. Dressed in her Sabbath finery, veiled, limp in Reb Gedaliya's arms, she was transformed into the living Torah. And in the rapturous aftermath of this revelation the curtain of the Ark "was hung on poles as a kind of canopy and borne aloft over the heads of Reb Gedaliya and Rechele". It is a parody of a marriage, sanctified by mass hysteria. Thereafter Reb Mordecai Joseph and Reb Itche Mates went off to spread the news far and wide, while Reb Gedaliya "settled Rechele in his house...although she was a matron". Here she was set up as a prophetess.

He had a room painted white for her, and he hung the walls with guardian amulets, and placed a Holy Ark and Torah there. Rechele was dressed in white satin; her face was hidden by a veil. During the week she could be seen by no one except Chinkele the Pious who served her. But on the Sabbath ten women from the sect gathered in her room to make a prayer quorum, as though they were men — for thus Reb Gedaliya had bidden.[64]

During the nights Rechele was visted by more than angels.

Reb Gedaliya would enter naked, a thick growth of hair covering his body like a fur coat, wearing only a skull cap, and with a wax candle in his left hand. He would lift the white silk gown that covered Rechele's body, kiss her feet, and waken her. "Rechele, it is midnight. The heavens are parting. The Divine Parents are coupling face to face. Rechele, be of good cheer. This is the hour of union."[65]

As the profane demon who later raped Rechele said, there was nothing he could do to her that hadn't already been done. Slowly Reb Gedaliya relaxed more and more of the injunctions in the scriptures. "Now the affairs of Goray town were managed by Reb Gedaliya. His new rulings disagreed with the practices cited in the Shulchan Aruch, but the few learned men who remained pretended neither to see nor hear what was happening, for the common people believed in Reb Gedaliya." He even led parties of youths to the river so that they could surprise women bathing. No one dared speak against him in public, the only words against him were rumours spread by hidden foes. Thus Goray was altered, so that no one recognized it any longer. On the surface all was joy, but the narrator confirmed the terrible rumours, "evil often transpired secretly".

A severe drought only increased the hysterical expectation of the Jews; the peasants, blaming the Jews, began sharpening their knives, as in Chemelnicki's days. Nevertheless, Goray was elated, there was plenty of meat, abundant marriages, and the Messiah was expected three days before Rosh Hashana. As the appointed month approached the faith of the people of Goray grew stronger. And they stopped work, because it seemed useless to complete anything. This is just how Joshua described Leoncin, in *Of a World That Is No More*, as they also prepared for the Messiah's coming on Rosh Hashana. Day after day people checked the clear skies for a sign of the cloud that was to transport all the Jews to Jerusalem, but Rosh Hashana came without a sight of it, and "never before had there been such weeping as this year at the Penitential Prayers" in Goray. But even in the face of this overwhelming disappointment Reb Gedaliya was as brazen as any commissar explaining away the failure of the latest five-year plan.

He swore a mighty oath that Sabbatai Zevi was the true Messiah of the

God of Jacob; he made the Jews put away their sadness and gird themselves with trust and joy; he said that the Four Matriarchs had visited Rechele at night to solace her, and they had reported that Satan had leveled a bitter accusation in Heaven against those who wavered in their faith; as a consequence, the end of days had been postponed until such time as the wrath of God should be placated.[66]

With such political arguments Reb Gedaliya comforted his followers, but no sooner were they reassured than the prayer house was rocked to its foundations, both literally and metaphorically. First there was an earthquake which caused a fault in the prayer house wall, extending from the roof to the foundation so that it was rumoured to be unsafe to worship there, then Reb Mordecai Joseph and Reb Itche Mates returned with the shattering news that Sabbatai Zevi had been converted to Islam. Still Reb Gedaliya conceded nothing; he met Reb Mordecai Joseph's accusation that he was an adulterer who worshipped an idolator with the words, "Jews, he is blaspheming!... He is cursing the Messiah of the Lord of Hosts!"

> "This dog barks lies and deceit. Not Sabbatai Zevi, but Sabbatai Zevi's shadow was converted. There is an explicit passage in the Zohar! The Messiah has ascended to Heaven! He will soon descend and redeem us. Here are letters to prove it! From all the holy men!"[67]

Vanquished, Reb Mordecai Joseph at last grasped what had happened in Goray, "Jews, help! The Evil One triumphs! Woe...!"

The Jews, as often happened, were divided. First there was the division between the still faithful followers of Sabbatai Zevi and their opponents, then there was a further sub-division among Sabbatai Zevi's own supporters, already prefigured in the distinction between the ascetic Reb Itche Mates and the sensual Reb Gedaliya. There were those who believed that the Messiah would only come when all were virtuous, and there were those who maintained that the generation welcoming the Messiah must be utterly sinful. As for Goray, Reb Gedaliya and Levi were still leaders of the town. They excommunicated their opponents, burned books, had Reb Mordecai Joseph attacked, and compelled Reb Itche Mates to divorce Rechele. Whereupon Gedaliya married her, without waiting the legal ninety days, "thus openly demonstrating his contempt for the Talmud".

> From that time on, Goray indulged in every kind of license, becoming more corrupt each day. Assured that every transgression was a rung in the ladder of self-purification and spiritual elevation, the people of Goray sank to the forty-nine Gates of Impurity. Only a few individuals did not join in but stood apart watching Satan dance in the streets.[68]

But just as Rechele had consecrated Reb Gedaliya with her prophecy, so she ruined him with her dybbuk, so that he was "afraid of people and the mockery in their glances". Only after her terrible death was his true nature revealed.

> And Gedaliya became an apostate (God save us) and rose to high position among the idolators and a troubler of Jews: And some folk say that Gedaliya was none other than Samael himself and that all his deeds were nought but seduction.[69]

Satan in Goray presented Bashevis with a paradox that would subsequently trouble his fictional alter egos rather than their author. But in his first novel it is the writer who must face up to the fact that his methods are exactly those which lead Rechele to destruction. Throughout the novel there is a tension between restraint and licence; for example, in the conflict between the Talmud, which teaches by reason and example, and the cabbala, which seeks knowledge through intuition and poetic imagery. These, in turn, lead to the disciplined mind and the unrestrained imagination. But, as a writer, Bashevis must depend upon the unrestrained imagination; in short, he has to use the same devices to ensnare his reader that the disciples of Sabbatai Zevi use to enrapture their hearers; creating artefacts out of air both must rely upon the splendour of their imagery. Hence, Bashevis's last-chapter attempt to turn *Satan in Goray* into an exemplary story with a moral. But this cannot undo what has already been written; like it or not, Bashevis is imaginatively on the side of Reb Gedaliya. However, this does not nullify the dangers Bashevis perceives in the attempt to force imagination into reality or ideals into facts. Language has magic possibilities, ideals can bring about wonderful changes; but both can be infernally misused. Just look around you.

When *Satan in Goray* was published in Warsaw, Joshua had already permanently settled in the United States with his wife and child. Bashevis knew that his situation in Poland was very precarious, and he began to dream the emigrant's eternal dream.

> America was considered "the Golden Land", and my brother whom I loved was there. So the moment my brother left I had only one idea; to come to America, the sooner the better. When my brother sent me an affidavit this was for me the greatest happiness.[70]

But once in America, Bashevis experienced the same sort of crisis that had afflicted Joshua after the publication of *Steel and Iron*. At the same time Joshua was working on his masterpiece, *The Brothers Ashkenazi*.

3
Poland

GOLDENEH MEDINA has two meanings in Yiddish: Golden Land and Fool's Paradise. And for as long as Joshua lived it seemed that he had found the Golden Land while his brother was lost in a Fool's Paradise, a thought not contradicted by the title of Bashevis's latest volume of memoirs, *Lost in America.* Nevertheless, America never dominated the imagination of the Singer brothers, as it had the generation of immigrants that preceded them. Neither attempted to emulate their benefactor, Abe Cahan, and produce an equivalent of *The Rise of David Levinsky,* his novel about the metamorphosis of a Russian student of the Talmud into a Manhattan clothing manufacturer worth millions. Cahan and his contemporaries, the prophets of Americanization, paradoxically found themselves writing books that spelled out what was lost in the translation from Yiddish to American, from religion to secularization. They found themselves describing the ambitious immigrants as actors, alienated from their real feelings by the English language. But their most potent episodes — the learning of English, the shedding of the capote, the shaving of the beard and earlocks — did not have the same meaning for the Singers. For them such acts were not associated with the new life in America, but with the *haskalah* and their own literary apprenticeship in Warsaw; they had not betrayed their father in some distant land, but before his eyes. Furthermore, Yiddish was no echo of a lost culture but their *mamaloshen,* the language of their days and dreams. In such circumstances it could never become a token of spiritual ascendancy. Likewise, the Singers were well aware that the autonomous Jewish culture of the *shtetlach* had been crumbling since Napoleonic times, and that immigration was a sympton of that disintegration rather than a cause. Consequently, when they came to plan novels on the scale of *The Rise of David Levinsky* they turned to Poland for material rather than America. No less than Cahan they did write novels of transition, but their transition was one of traumatic change within a small world rather than one marked by geographical transformation. Their characters were spiritual emigrants from an ancient to a modern world. Gentile Poland was their equivalent of America.

"My brother influenced me mightily," said Bashevis. He went on to specify the nature of that influence:

> When I began to write myself my brother encouraged me and gave me certain rules for writing. He said: when you write tell a story, and don't try to explain the story. If you say that a boy fell in love with a girl you don't have to explain to the reader why a boy falls in love, the reader knows just as much about love as you do or more so. You tell him the story and the explanations and interpretations he will make himself, or critics will do it for him. He had two words which he used: *images* and *sayings*. Sayings were for him essays, interpretations. He called sayings, *zugerts*. It means you just talk, you just say things. You don't paint a picture, or bring out an image. He said, leave the *zugerts* to the others. You tell them a story. Because you may know stories which they don't know — but you don't know more about life than they do.[1]

In fact, the pupil kept more rigorously to these rules than the teacher. For in his ambition to encompass the roots and fruits of the class struggle within the Jewish community of Lodz in the fictional history of *The Brothers Ashkenazi,* Joshua frequently froze the action between incitement and reaction to include "sayings". A brief example will suffice: Martin Kuchinsky, a blood-thirsty Polish revolutionary whose motto was "Something hot, and dripping", accused Felix Feldblum, his co-conspirator, of sounding "more like a sermon delivered in a synagogue". But before Felix was allowed to respond, Joshua inserted several paragraphs in which Felix's discovery of anti-Semitism among his fellow revolutionaries and within the Polish working class was described, thus adding an historical dimension to Felix's personal distress. It becomes clear, in reading *The Brothers Ashkenazi,* that Joshua aimed to marry individual motivation with historical inevitability, which required several sayings on the course of Polish history and the class struggle. And it is this deviation from the lesson he taught his younger brother which reveals most fully the differences between Joshua and Bashevis, both as writers and as chroniclers. Although *The Manor* covered a specific period — "the epoch between the Polish insurrection of 1863 and the end of the nineteenth century" — its characters were less impelled by temporal forces than by corporeal desires, and their doubts were not so much related to the contemporary historical process as to some universal code, as the title of the novel implies.

While Bashevis used the manor of Count Jampolski, into which Calman Jacoby moved, to demonstrate the snares of vanity and sophistication, Joshua presented the palace of the Huntze family, which Max Ashkenazi finally inhabited, as a soul-destroying symbol of imperial history, forever inimical to the Jews. Surrounded by the regalia of the Polish aristocracy Max Ashkenazi fancied that he was King of Lodz. But in reality he was no more King of Lodz than was the hump-backed Jewish tailor, mockingly enthroned by the anti-Semitic mob, King of Poland. After the crowd had spent its anger on the Jews and order had been restored by the Cossacks, the tailor was brought before the Governor, doing his best to suppress a smile, who said, "I understand you proclaimed yourself King of Poland." History had worse humiliations in store for Max Ashkenazi. Unlike Max Ashkenazi, Calman knew from the first that he had fallen into a trap: "Yes, Count Jampolski in his old age had divorced himself from all luxuries while Calman, the Jew, had taken up residence in a palace, amid gold, silver, porcelains, lackeys, and servants." Nonetheless, he could not resist Clara's demands for opulence. The final reference for Joshua was history, whereas for Bashevis it was religion; Max Ashkenazi ignored the lessons of the former, Calman the teachings of the latter. Both brothers punished their characters accordingly. However, since it is impossible to write about the Jews (and both Ashkenazi and Jacoby, as names, refer to a people as well as a family) without mentioning their religion, and equally impossible to write about them without confronting their history, these co-ordinates are not mutually exclusive. Indeed, one character almost crossed over from *The Estate* into *The Brothers Ashkenazi;* but unfortunately Zina was arrested before she could reach Lodz with her cache of arms for the revolutionaries.

The chief consequence of Bashevis's strict adherence to his brother's axioms is an all-pervading sense of insecurity. Because Bashevis avoided explaining why a boy falls in love, as well as eschewing any overt political commentary, his novels have a breathless, restless quality. His readers are kept in a constant state of anticipation, heightened by the fact that accurate prediction becomes an impossibility. His characters are never given fixed temperaments; their moods constantly shift with events. A certain substantiality is perhaps lost; as Dan Jacobson has remarked, you do not feel of them as you do of Joshua's characters who "seem to block out the sun".[2] Moreover, should such a character be faced with an important choice, an exercise in free will, Bashevis will admit the agonies of indecision only to end the scene before the consequences are revealed; these are typically disclosed much later, reported by a messenger in the manner of Greek tragedy. In fact this evasiveness has a purpose; it reflects the utter futility of endeavour and achievement, and reminds us that all worldly pleasure and success is temporary. Thus Bashevis's treatment of character reflects the modern conception of the fragmented personality, the loss of certainty in the self as portrayed in the great nineteenth-century novels and in those of his brother. And if neither human nature nor time itself can offer sufficiently firm foundations for the construction of a life, the Jews of Poland were more insecure than most. Hence Bashevis's treatment of chronology corresponds with his treatment of character; both are relative to circumstances, leaving his characters unfixed both by time and temperament, and subject to the most alarming changes. The fate of Shaindel makes this point perfectly.

Shaindel was the most beautiful and lively of Calman Jacoby's four daughters; while still a child, during the festival of Simhath Torah, she crowned herself with a melon and cried, "I am the queen of Jampol." But her destiny was no more regal than that of Max Ashkenazi or the hump-backed tailor. Though her marriage promised much she lost touch with her former vitality, grew prematurely aged, and finally became mad; and at each stage of this decline, with cruel precision, Bashevis reintroduces that first image of her. Standing over her grave on the day of her funeral, her husband Ezriel Babad once more brought to mind that Simhath Torah when she had called herself the queen of Jampol: "It seemed only yesterday that it had all happened. But in this time Shaindel had managed to bear children, to become insane, to spend years in an asylum, and to die." The reader is as bewildered as Ezriel; a potential heroine reduced to dust; what went wrong, how did it happen? These are the unanswerable questions which Bashevis poses. By adhering to Joshua's rules, Bashevis has fashioned his fictional technique into a metaphor for the fate of the Polish Jews. *The Manor* and *The Estate* are therefore predictions of their doom. In the final analysis there can be no explanation of the holocaust. As Bashevis put it in *The Estate*:

> These Jews in the House of Prayer deserved destruction for many offences: for being capitalists (wasn't that a joke?), they were strangers (merely eight hundred years in Poland). What were they not? Chauvinists, reactionaries, petty bourgeois, fanatics, jargonists, barbarians. Every "ism" spelled doom for them. But their real crime was that they tried to lead sanctified lives, without wars, without adultery, without mockery or rebellion.[3]

The Manor opens with the Polish rebellion of 1863, but there are no explanations as to its cause and its outcome is conveyed in a single word: "unsuccessful". Of more interest to Bashevis was the effect upon Jampol of the sight of Count Leon Jampolski being led through his own town in chains by the Russians. The Jews, who lived in an area of Jampol called The Sands, were astonished at the bearing of the Count, who walked as jauntily "as though he were going to a party" rather than to Siberia. Subsequently it was announced that Count Jampolski's estates had been confiscated. The Jews shrugged their shoulders: "such was the way of the Gentile, where might was right". Later, when Calman Jacoby in his turn left the manor the Jews of Jampol shrugged their shoulders once again: "Calman had made his bed, let him sleep in it." But Calman's problem was that he had been sleeping in the Count's bed, not his own: "Calman lived in the manor house, occupying the Count's bedroom and sleeping in his bed." In the Countess's bed was Clara, Calman's second wife. Zelda, Calman's first wife, was "not always up to his carnal demands"; Clara, unlike pious Zelda, was wanton. Clara had "black burning eyes" and "a beauty mark on her left cheek". When the Count returned from exile he was accompanied by a woman, though his wife was still living; she also was "a brunette with black eyes, dazzling teeth, and a beauty spot on her left cheek". In effect, Calman had been transformed by wealth and lust into a parody of Count Jampolski.

His metamorphosis began when, taking advantage of the confiscation, he bid for the lease of the manor. Calman's behaviour before the new Russian overlord was in spectacular contrast to the Count's: he prostrated himself before the new master "to kiss his gleaming boots and plead for mercy". Thus Bashevis introduces abiding images of the Polish aristocracy and the Polish Jews; the one proud, immutable, the other wretched, mutable. While the adaptability of the Jews enabled them to usurp the property of the fallen aristocracy, it left them prey to the same vices that corrupted the former nobility. Even pious Calman, who seemed so resolute in the face of temptation, was eventually snared. At first he allowed the Countess to remain in the manor and moved his family into a cottage formerly inhabited by a blacksmith, from which he barred all modern conveniences, fearing that "such luxuries, merely decorative at first, would soon become indispensable". But the requirements of the business began to erode Calman's position; he had to travel on horseback, for which his long gaberdine was unsuitable, so he had to put on the short jacket of the heretic. Worse, he had to employ Lithuanian Jews who spoke Russian. "These strangers, who were beardless and wore Gentile clothes, considered themselves enlightened, but the town found them heretical." Before long Calman admitted to himself that he had become "the captive and not the master of his fortune", and it is clear that Bashevis means worldly success to involve spiritual decline. The only day he felt free of its yoke was the Sabbath: "Fortunately the Almighty, blessed be His name, had given the Jews the Sabbath." This distinction between the gentile world of the senses and the Jewish world of the spirit forms the major tension of the book, and prophesies its conclusion. Just as the gentile world was represented by the manor, so the Jewish world was represented by the rabbinical court at Marshinov.

Unenlightened Marshinov is a symbol of the pure Jewish spirit, and the hasidim who cluster around the rabbi represent the body of the religion. As Bashevis observed in *The Slave*, "Because of such men...God had preserved the Jews." And they, in turn, preserved the Jewish people through the *galut* by their contrariness, by forcing themselves to go against human nature. The hasidim of Marshinov were not like those castigated by Joshua in *Yoshe Kalb*; hypocrites, concerned with form rather than content. Strict observance was not enough for Marshinov; more important was *kavanah*, intense concentration, which blotted out everything except love of God. In his essay "The Spirit of Hasidism" Bashevis wrote:

> *Simcha shel Mitzvah*, the joy inherent in religious observance, is the very core of Hasidism. Baruch Spinoza, the seventeenth-century pantheist, had preached a love of God founded on reason, *Amor dei Intellectualis*. The Hasidim, by contrast, taught that God must be loved, above all, with the heart.[4]

This is the hasidic answer to human nature run riot, a passionate heart bounded by rigid control. They may dwell in Marshinov, but their domain is the next world. Even when the old rabbi died and his eldest son, Reb Shimmon, attempted to usurp his power (a situation Joshua would have called typical), he was thwarted by the congregation who demanded his saintly grandson, Jochanan, as their new rabbi. Jochanan was in the mould of the great hasidic rabbi, Nachman of Bratislav, described thus in the same essay by Bashevis:

> Reb Nachman, who was less than forty years old when he died...united in his personality extraordinary erudition, impassioned love of God, and a quality that might be characterized as holy hysteria.[5]

It seems that "a mediocre writer of plays and novels in Russia", Israel Axenfeld, "ridiculed the teachings of Reb Nachman...and satirized him cruelly". Axenfeld, on the contrary, "preached logic, good grammar, modern hygiene and, above all, the importance of being practical and worldly". Other disciples of the *haskalah*, the enlightenment, disdained Yiddish as "jargon" and "attacked the folk beliefs of the east European Jews and their tales of demons, evil spirits, dybbuks, transmigrations of the soul, and miracle-working saints". They urged their fellow Jews "to adopt modern dress, and to put an end to the...filth, the isolation and such old-fashioned practices as marrying off their young children". Likewise Wallenberg, the apostate, at their first meeting, advised Ezriel to desert the Jews: "It is

absurd to live in Poland and jabber away in a German jargon, and it is
even more ridiculous to live in the second half of the nineteenth
century and behave as if you belonged to antiquity.'' Bashevis is
clearly more sympathetic towards Reb Nachman than Axenfeld, and
more drawn to Jochanan than Wallenberg, but he is surely too
enlightened to be in favour of filth and arranged marriages. One of the
excitements of Bashevis is that he baffles such easy assumptions.

Jochanan, the new rabbi of Marshinov, was Calman's son-in-law,
being married to his youngest daughter Tsipele. In conspicuous
contrast to the mutual attraction of Shaindel and Ezriel, and the
passionate romance of Miriam Lieba and Lucian, this arranged match
was a success; Tsipele did not deteriorate and die in a sanatorium like
Shaindel and Miriam Lieba but grew ''comelier, more Jewish''. In
one of Bashevis's stories, ''Her Son'', a character remarks:

> Those romantic loves that the poets laud with such lofty phrases
> actually ruin lives. Our pious grandparents considered what we call
> love a crime, and that's what it is. If this kind of love were truly virtue,
> modern man wouldn't deify it so. It is the very opposite of free will —
> the most extreme form of hypnosis and fatalism. Our God-fearing
> mothers and fathers lived a decent life without this slavery, and believe
> me, they were more ready to do things for each other than the people
> who are involved in love affairs.[6]

The story is based upon the matrimonial fates of Calman and his four
daughters, and it does seem that Bashevis endorses this anti-romantic
point of view; an extraordinary position for a writer who is such a
modernist, such a master of ''erotic-mystic'' fiction. But it is also true
that *The Manor* and *The Estate* draw their vitality not from the pious
Zeldas but from the wanton likes of Clara. How to explain this
contradiction?

When Bashevis criticized the *haskalah* propagandists he was also
criticizing himself, as he tacitly acknowledged in the following passage
from an essay entitled ''The Spirit of Jewishness'':

> The Emancipation created a new type of Jew, one who could renounce
> the laws of his religion yet remain a Jew; or at least not go all the way
> toward conversion. This so-called worldly Jew was a riddle both to
> himself and to the Christian world.... The ultraorthodox Jews have
> unofficially excommunicated the modern Jew.... To them, we are all
> branches broken off from the Jewish trunk. They are convinced that
> our future is the obliteration of our Jewishness. They, few as they are,
> will maintain the yoke of our religion. They, the extremists, will be
> there to receive the Messiah.[7]

The unexpected introduction of the personal pronoun in the fourth sentence exposes Bashevis's allegiance to the enlightenment, but equally revealing is the phrase "a riddle...to himself". As a writer Bashevis is attracted to the passionate, but as a Jew he cannot shut his eyes to the possible consequences of such passion. This dilemma found its fictional dimension in the character of Ezriel Babad, who was torn between Warsaw and Marshinov, and at home in neither. He was a riddle to himself and a mess of contradictions; although his career as a doctor qualified him to cure neurasthenics he was no less distracted than his patients. Although he wanted to be healer his search for knowledge and self-fulfilment caused him to betray both his father and his wife Shaindel. Just as Ezriel was, in part, a fictional portrait of Bashevis himself, so his father, Reb Menachem Mendel, was based upon Bashevis's own father Pinchos Mendel, both men ending as poor rabbis in Warsaw's Krochmalna Street. In tormenting Ezriel Babad to the point of breakdown Bashevis was repaying a debt; he was proclaiming the unanswerable wisdom of his father. When Mirale, Ezriel's free-thinking sister, visited Krochmalna Street, Reb Menachem Mendel attacked the ideas of her friends thus:

> The body is everything to them. If, as they say, there is no God, then it doesn't matter what one does. At first we are tempted by some minor sin, but as soon as that is committed, the will lures us into more serious evil. Without law and a judge to administer the law, there is no reason why one should restrain oneself. Why not give in to evil completely?[8]

To which Mirale replied: "Because one is a human being." An answer the rabbi treated with contempt: "Animals kill only for food; murderers enjoy killing." Bashevis likewise places humans lower than animals; for evidence he has the holocaust, the supreme example of the destructive power of unrestrained human nature. However, even as he grants the need to struggle against human nature, he cannot deny that this same nature has a creative as well as a destructive side.

Its destructive power gives the narrative its structure. At the beginning of *The Manor* the Babad and Jacoby families are intact, the Jewish community of Jampol well-ordered, by the end of *The Estate* the families have disintegrated and Jampol is disorganized. Only Marshinov remains untouched, awaiting its final destruction. In the two books he described what happened when the restraints placed upon the Jews (both by themselves and the anti-Semites) were lifted in the wake of the 1863 rebellion. And he was as merciless as a scientist who raises a stone to see how the creatures beneath respond to light. He drove his characters relentlessly from sin to sin, sparing them no consequence, demonstrating that Jews when permitted have the universal response to temptation: they succumb. This is the conclusion the logic of his story forces upon him; and it is at the heart of his equivocation. It is why he can say that hasidism is based "on a profound religious logic and a historic reason". It keeps the Jews pure. But human nature is also a creative force that Bashevis cannot ignore, for it is the source of his stories. That is why Clara will always outshine Zelda. That is why Israel Axenfeld receives such harsh treatment. All propogandists want to impose their own pattern upon society, as a consequence of which they lose touch with "the juices that nourish creativity". Bashevis continued:

> The true artist is never inspired by sociology or politics.... Throughout the ages, genuine art has been confined to only two themes — love and religion.... The genuine artist still draws his inspiration from the eternal truths of the relationship between man and woman, and between man and his creator.[9]

But in order to tell the story the writer needs an Eve or a Clara, or an Elka, which brings us back to *tzimtzum*.

Evil is not a metaphysical concept for Bashevis; for him it is a real presence in the world. Hence the importance of Marshinov, as the repository of good. Joshua has no such Manichean view of the universe: why blame the devil when man is a more obvious culprit? Hence in *The Brothers Ashkenazi* religion was not a saving grace, but a repressive system of rules and regulations that squeezed the humanity from its adherents. Like Calman, Abraham Hirsh Ashkenazi had a favourite rabbi. His rabbi lived in Vorka, some way from Lodz. But Vorka was no Marshinov, and by attending the Passover service in order to present the rabbi with a silver goblet, Abraham Hirsh deserted his wife on the point of childbirth. For Abraham Hirsh the goblet became an object of worship that superseded religion: "As often as he saw it he thought of it standing, lustrous and prominent on the long table at which the Rabbi and his followers were seated: *his* goblet, Reb Abraham Hirsh's goblet, *his* gift to the Rabbi." This reverence of object, and with it self-regard, blinded him to his true duty, which was to remain with his wife. The rabbi said: "Abraham Hirsh, your generations will be rich men." This prophecy terrified Abraham Hirsh, for he valued piety above wealth, and his fears were well-founded: the prophecy came true, the twins who were born in his absence became rich and impious. Indeed, the older, Simcha Meyer (later Max), worshipped gold in the same way his father had adored God.

This transference of religious fervour into secular energy was common to Max Ashkenazi's generation. As Max dedicated himself to capitalism, so Nissan Eibeschutz found truth in communism. Nissan was the son of an ultra-pious teacher and rabbinical scholar, Reb Noske, who prayed while his family starved. Reb Noske was as much a portrait of the Singer paterfamilias as was Menachem Mendel; but while Bashevis acknowledged the wisdom of the man, Joshua clarified the practical consequences of his other-worldliness. Indeed, Nissan hated him on account of it, and rejected everything he held sacred, but he had his father's obsessive nature. As if to rub in the irony of Nissan's inheritance Joshua compared his devotion to revolutionary texts with his father's love of Talmudic commentaries. Nissan abandoned synagogue to "attend services of another kind", greeted the revolution "with a joy...almost blinding in its intensity", and turned up at Max's Russian factory "with a grey little Jewish beard and with whiskers which suggested the earlocks of a pietist". Jewishness therefore became not so much belief in God as the single-minded pursuit of an obsession, as though lack of moderation were a birthright. In effect, it remained the controlling feature of their lives. But in *The Brothers Ashkenazi* all fanaticism, religious or political, however well-intentioned its genesis, leads inevitably to an inhuman régime; be it the rabbi in Vorka, or the dictatorship of the proletariat in Moscow. Bashevis might imagine that the heads of the hasidim touched the heavens, but Joshua saw that their feet stood in filth. By the end of *The Brothers Ashkenazi* the Jews were torn between a religion that had lost its humanity and a country that had no place for them. Though driven by their Jewishness they had no destination. Not even a Marshinov.

Calman's heart drew him to Marshinov, but his affairs took him to Warsaw; for example, he had to find a husband for his oldest daughter Jochebed. Although only eighteen she was already known as the young spinster, a rebuke to a man who had "inherited from his forebears the principle that the sooner one's daughters are married off, the better". Just as Sholem Aleichem used Tevyeh's four daughters to dramatize the fate of the Jews in a chaotic Poland, so Bashevis utilized the marriages of Jochebed, Shaindel and Miriam Lieba to demonstrate the dangers inherent in contact with the gentiles. In recognition of his new status Calman arranged a match between Jochebed and Mayer Joel, son of a wealthy Warsaw merchant, despite the uneasy awareness that his future in-laws exuded an air of cosmopolitan vanity. Mayer Joel handed Calman a letter to deliver to Jochebed "which he had copied word for word from a manual of model letters". This may lack sincerity, but it was less dangerous than the Polish novels Calman brought back for Miriam Lieba. In doing so, Bashevis suggested how the contamination of urban life entered Jampol. Furthermore he was ensuring that Calman's marriage plans for Miriam Lieba would go disastrously awry; in short, he was unconsciously encouraging her along the road to apostasy. Jochanan, grandson of the rabbi of Marshinov, was proposed as a groom for Miriam Lieba. In accordance with modern trends Calman decided to ask Miriam Lieba's opinion before agreeing to the match. He invited Jochanan and his mother to the wedding of Shaindel and Ezriel, to which he also asked Count Jampolski and his family. Thus Calman became her matchmaker after all, for Miriam Lieba turned her back on Jochanan, the devout Jew, and danced off with Countess Helena, through whom she met Lucian. A similar situation developed in *The Brothers Ashkenazi* when Dinah Alter, whose head, like Miriam Lieba's, "had become filled with romantic stories about kings and knights and heroes", was matched with Max Ashkenazi. The weedy scholarly Max in no way represented her desired partner, "who would carry her off in the night, as heroines were carried off in the stories she had read". But Reb Chaim Alter, unlike Calman, gave his daughter no choice. Dinah's will was broken after eight days of resistance and she submissively married Max. But her marriage was as much a disaster as Miriam Lieba's. The implication is clear; had Dinah been allowed to marry the man of her choice, the older brother, Yakob, she would have had a greater chance of happiness. It seems that the sceptic was more in favour of love than the mystic; Dinah's tragedy stemmed from her thwarted desire, Miriam Lieba's came from its realization.

Unfortunately for Miriam Lieba, Lucian was both psychotic and anti-Semitic. "Jacoby, eh?" he mused on hearing Miriam Lieba's family name. "That means Jacob — Jacob's grandchildren. The Jacob who cheated Esau out of his birthright." But Miriam Lieba was blinded by her imagination, to her Lucian appeared "in an ethereal light, like the visions of saints described in books by Christian mystics". Against this any Jewish suitor would appear ordinary. Her passion was further inflamed by a novel Helena lent her:

> Suddenly she herself was in Paris. She sat in a carriage and Lucian embraced her — simultaneously she was in a carriage, a boudoir, a salon. She was wearing an evening gown, and carried a fan. He wanted to kiss her, but she averted her face. "No, Lucian, I am promised to a storekeeper in Lublin."[10]

Miriam Lieba's time of decision came during Purim. Purim is a time of joy, a celebration of the deliverance of the Jews from the hands of Haman. But Miriam Lieba refused to participate in the festivities, handing the part of Queen Esther to Tsipele, just as previously she had handed her Jochanan. Instead she removed himself from her family and wandered beneath the moon, whereupon Lucian suddenly appeared as if risen from the ground. His fingers, which gripped her wrist, were bony like a skeleton's. He asked Miriam Lieba to run away with him. A battle commenced within her. She imagined her future as a Jewish bride, and considered the alternative:

> They'd shave her head, fit her with a wig, insist that she attend the ritual bath. She'd bear children, wrangle with her mother-in-law, grow old before her time. The life of the Jews was narrow and stagnant. Her mother had had nothing. Jochebed had nothing. The world outside was huge, brilliant. If she went, she would become a countess and have Lucian; she would reside in Paris among its rich boulevards and amorous women.[11]

This is precognition, for Miriam Lieba did indeed live in Paris with Lucian; but the irony is cruel, instead of luxury she lived in poverty, a victim of misery, alcholism and consumption. When she said, "Yes, I'll go away with him. I'll convert," her voice seemed to come "from deep within her, as if it had been lying in wait in some demonic spiderweb". In abandoning her family and her religion for Lucian and Christianity, Miriam Lieba was giving herself to death and the devil. Having made her fateful decision Miriam Lieba was whisked out of sight, not to reappear until Justina Malewska, Wallenberg's daughter, dramatically informed Ezriel Babad: "She's become a laundress to keep from starving." This information does more than keep the reader informed, it re-establishes a link between Ezriel and the Wallenbergs. Thus Miriam Lieba's plight was instrumental in wrecking Shaindel's marriage, for through this reconnection Ezriel met Olga Bielikov, his second wife. As if conscious of this Miriam Lieba cried out to Ezriel when he visited her in the sanatorium, "Don't betray Shaindel!" From which it may be deduced that Reb Menachem Mendel was no more successful than Calman in protecting his offspring from outside influences. In *The Estate* Ezriel summarized their histories:

> What had become of his parents' progeny? Their daughter was an exile in Siberia. One grandson lay in an Evangelical cemetery. Another was a settler somewhere in Palestine. Ezriel lived with a convert.[12]

Like Gimpel, Reb Menachem Mendel knew that curiosity was dangerous, like Gimpel he believed in faith for its own sake:

> Reb Mendel knew the ways of temptation. One began with questions, then one adopted modern styles of dress, and next there was loss of faith, even apostasy. Consequently, Reb Menachem Mendel had accepted with alacrity the rabbinate at Jampol. Enlightened individuals could not possibly inhabit so small a community.[13]

But even in Jampol, more so after the 1863 rebellion, there was no escape from the enlightenment. It followed inevitably in the train of Calman's success. However, even without prompting, Ezriel was capable of asking awkward questions: "What was there before the universe? Does a goat have a soul? Was Adam a Jew? Did Eve wear a bonnet?" And such questions, as the rabbi foresaw, led to a more serious doubt. Later Ezriel asked Calman: "Who saw God give Moses the Torah on Mount Sinai? The Jews have their Torah, and the Christians have something else. If their religion can be false, so can ours." By the time of his engagement to Shaindel, Ezriel was already expressing rationalist views: "Science concerns itself only with the visible, the things that can be weighed and measured.... The truth is all I care about." Consequently the subsequent trip to Marshinov with Calman left him unmoved; his rationalism found no echo in the holy joy of the hasidim. The confusion he felt was dramatized when he was unable to find the way back to his lodgings; as Bashevis put it, "Ezriel had lost his way." Much unhappiness ensued before Ezriel also conceded that he had lost his way. In *The Estate* he was forced to the conclusion that "among the rationalists, one found the most irrational people. They could not explain why they did things, involved themselves in tragic love affairs, risked unnecessary torments". It was to the arguments of the rationalists that the rabbi of Marshinov addressed his Pentecost discourse. He took as his text a passage in the Talmud which stated that "even before the people knew the nature of the Ten Commandments, they were prepared to obey them". The rabbi maintained that divine ordinances must be accepted on faith, "for if you argue and think about anything long enough, doubt is sure to arise", and doubt is a prelude to rejection. But only in the fulfilment of holy duties should action precede thought:

> In secular matters and those pertaining to the flesh, it is the opposite course one must follow; one must consider and deliberate first, and only then perform one's duty. It is the evil-doer who first inflicts harms and then asks questions. For wickedness awakens endless questions in man. All doubts vanish in the performance of virtuous deeds. Yet how can one recognise the true spirit of virtue? The answer is: through joy. The man who injures someone is disturbed and full of conflicts. But a good deed is succeeded by inner happiness. For a man who is uplifted, all questions are resolved.[14]

But these assurances were not sufficient for Ezriel, he observed: "The writers of the Torah completely ignored human emotions, man's nervous system." However, when Ezriel, now a doctor dealing with nervous disorders, returned to Marshinov towards the end of *The Estate* he admitted that he could detect no signs of melancholia, so prevalent in the outside world. He now saw the wisdom of the rabbi's sermon. But even though it was clear to him that happiness could only be found in Marshinov he was unable to abandon his rationalism completely. "He argued with himself that a materialistic existence was bad and that religion was a remedy for all ills. But could he believe as these men did that every law, every custom had come down from Mount Sinai?" Though it was Simhath Torah, Ezriel still could not accept the Torah wholeheartedly. He is last heard of en route to Israel, still trying to find the way. The basic problem remained unresolved; it was, as Ezriel remarked on the night of Miriam Lieba's elopement, "that love obeys no laws". And however much Bashevis may punish Miriam Lieba for her sins, he cannot eradicate the self, even for the sake of Judaism.

Miriam Lieba's flight marked the beginning of the break-up of Calman's family. Within two years Tsipele and Jochanan were in Marshinov, Jochebed and Mayer Joel were in a home of their own, and Zelda was dead. Only Shaindel remained in the house while Ezriel studied in Warsaw. Now a widower, Calman was the prey of matchmakers and vulnerable to Clara. Despite his prayers "that the Lord deliver him from temptation", and a warning letter from Jochanan, Calman succumbed. The wedding was a grand affair, so ostentatious that Calman feared he might be eating forbidden food. He sensed that some of the guests were treating the whole thing as nothing more than a Purim prank. But it was no more a prank than was Miriam Lieba's elopement with Lucian, and its consequences were not much better. Before long Calman knew he had committed a grave error. Indeed, Clara was soon unfaithful. Visiting Warsaw she met a young free-thinking comrade of Mirale, Alexander Zipkin, and that same night an affair began, as if in confirmation of Reb Menachem Mendel's warning that "one is easily trapped by the words of heretics. Who are these contemporary philosophers? A pack of murderers and lechers". Needless to say, such lechery could not make Clara happy; on the contrary she dreamt of her own death. Nevertheless, Zipkin was installed in the manor as a tutor to Clara and Calman's son, but the peasants knew his true occupation, "a young stallion is better than an old nag". Finally Calman could blind himself to the truth no longer, being no Gimpel. He dismissed Zipkin, then quit the manor for Marshinov, abandoning vanities to go back to the Jews. He was deliberately rejecting the world: "Let everything at the manor fall apart; he had been working for the devil anyway." So like Count Jampolski before him he passed through Jampol on his way into an exile which was also a return.

The world did indeed seem to be in the hands of the devil; like the manor it was falling apart. At Christmas Lucian became a murderer.

Alexander II was killed by a bomb. There were pogroms in Warsaw. Some Jewish radicals turned from the anti-Semitic workers in disgust, others became more revolutionary seeing the turmoil as the birth pains of the new epoch. Similarly, in Marshinov Jochanan believed he was witnessing the throes "preceding the arrival of the Messiah". Just as the old hassid in Bashevis's story "Grandfather and Grandson" on hearing of the bloody deeds of the Jewish revolutionaries concluded, "The Redemption must be near!" echoing Pinchos Mendel himself. The similarity of historical outlook between the ultraorthodox and the Jewish revolutionaries is made explicit in *The Brothers Ashkenazi*. After the May riots, which he helped initiate, had turned into pogroms, Nissan was confronted with the possibility that Schopenhauer might be right, that human beings were just loathsome animals. But despite the empirical evidence to the contrary his faith triumphed, like his father he refused to abandon hope: "The stern old moralist and pietist had learned to look beyond all sufferings, all set-backs and moral lapses, to the grand dénouement of the messianic deliverance. Though it might be delayed through thousands of years, it was bound to come…so now his son remembered that, whatever might be the delay, the revolution was bound to come…." Both saw the world as a diabolical, self-destructive place; the difference was that the revolutionaries saw it as their role to hasten the promised end. For the enlightenment fed the illusion that Jews could enter history as innovators. "We Jews must not interfere. Whoever rules will persecute Jews," said the grandfather to the grandson in Bashevis's story. The grandson did not listen and was killed.

Bashevis's messiahs are doomed to end up as patients of Ezriel or megalomaniacs or dead. Man is not destined to do good deeds in this world. Ezriel, on his way to see Mirale, now a political exile on the run, passed a yeshiva and was tempted to hide himself within. "If religion was opium, as they say — it was the opiate most suited to the Jewish soul. Jews had been dreaming over the pages of the Torah for two thousand years — these were noble dreams at least, not bloody nightmares…." Judaism may well preach patience, but its history encourages messianism.

In Bashevis's work, logic finally breaks down against human nature. Although Ezriel could resist Wallenberg's arguments to convert, he could do nothing to fight against the flesh of Olga Bielikov, who had herself "converted a little". When Olga told Ezriel that there could be nothing between them he replied, "Logically, you're right." But he knew that logic could do nothing against the "turmoil in his marrow, blood, stomach, sex organs", that a mere letter from Olga had started. If it were only the brain, logic might triumph, "but every part of the human body reacted to symbols". Thus the Polish language itself spread corruption, only Hebrew was untainted by modern ideas: "The Hebrew letters were steeped in holiness, in eternity." If Ezriel had been a rabbi instead of a doctor, had ignored man's nervous system like the Talmud, he would perhaps have been happier. In *The Manor* and *The Estate* the doctors are all supported by women who are left behind as their husbands progress. For, being modern men, they become ashamed of their ignorant wives and become infatuated with more advanced women. "Although Shaindel knew nothing about Olga, she spoke of another woman whom Ezriel would marry after Shaindel's death. Ezriel was amazed. There was a force of logic in all her madness. Through what power had she surmised that her rival was a modern educated woman?" And in turn the brains of these modern men become "a little insane asylum" of their own. Modernity may have equipped such men to deal with the vicissitudes of contemporary history, but it has left them vulnerable to the more sulphurous parts of human nature which only religion can control. They ignore magic at their peril. To survive it is necessary to fight human nature. At the end of *The Manor* Calman sits alone in a small synagogue he has constructed for himself. Only here with his Hebrew books is he safe from temptation and wickedness: "Among these shelves of sacred books, Calman felt protected. Over each volume hovered the soul of its author. In this place, God watched over him."

If *The Manor* dealt with cosmopolitan temptations, the house itself being a metaphor for the world, then *The Estate* described the fate that awaited the inheritors of that world. A decrepit theatre director surveyed his lot: "What's left of my life but reviews? I have pasted everything in a scrapbook and that is, so to say, my estate. A writer leaves behind books, a painter — pictures. What remains of us? Time devours us like a wolf." Without religion, or even any moral code, the younger generation, already sickened by the world's sweets, embraced nihilism. Lucian put it this way: "I have but one ambition: to live in the present. After I die, they can throw me to the dogs." Later he shot himself. His despair found an echo in the words of Sasha, Calman and Clara's son, who boasted at the end: "I'm not afraid. I'm not afraid of anything. When I saw them put my mother into the grave, I decided that this world is nothing but a plague and we're all a bunch of worms. I'm ready to put a bullet through my skull. That's the truth." Ezriel had returned to Jampol in search of Sasha, now master of the manor house, to seek his help in securing the release of Zina, arrested en route to Lodz. It was as though the old aristocracy had returned to claim its own, for Sasha was more like Lucian than any Jew. So powerful was the thrall of the manor that in a single generation it would reproduce the characteristics of its prototypical owner even out of such unpromising material as the Jacoby family. Sasha had been corrupted by the example of Clara who also exclaimed: "If man was no better than a dog, let him be forgotten." But he could only understand her fate superficially, for he had not been equipped to grasp her deeper torment. Such a detail as this would pass unnoticed by him: "As hour after hour went by, the corpse became less and less Clara. The nose grew longer and acquired a Semitic curve, as if during her lifetime Clara had been able to keep it in check." The struggle that Ezriel acknowledged is a stranger to him: "The simultaneous existence within one of both an evil spirit and a good one, as described in the Holy Books, was apparently a profound psychological truth." The strength Sasha lacked is of course Judaism, which at least would ensure that his wickedness would not be enjoyed. Unlike his father he had no alternative vision to guide him to salvation, no Marshinov. Finally conscious of this, Ezriel escorted his own son Misha to Marshinov. "Ezriel reminded himself of a saying in *The Best of Pearls*: 'The children are the secrets in the hearts of their parents.' The children testified to the hypocrisy of their fathers...." His demand was simple: "Rabbi, I brought him here. I want him to become a Jew." In a way Ezriel was repeating the action of his own father when he went to Jampol to protect his children from the enlightenment. Like Calman, at the end of *The Manor*, Ezriel had come to recognize the validity of Marshinov: "But could their behaviour serve as an example for others?" he asked himself.

> Yes, it was possible. Humanity could abolish warfare, divide the land so that there would be enough for everyone. Each group could have its language, its culture, its traditions. But one thing all would have to have in common: a belief in one God and in free will; a discipline that would transform all man's deeds into serving God and helping one another.[15]

But unlike *The Manor*, *The Estate* cannot be concluded on such an optimistic note; Marshinov has been rendered obsolete by history. Therefore the novel ends with the words: "His intimates went out to telegraph the Jewish settlements that Jochanan, the Rabbi of Marshinov, had died." What is more, he was without a successor; for Zadok, his son, was a free-thinker. But even so the mores of the manor were not wholly triumphant. The world of *The Estate* is wider than that of *The Manor* for it includes places where the spirit of Judaism may yet survive. In *The Brothers Ashkenazi*, Palestine is portrayed as a passing dream, a possibility for the future; in *The Estate* it is a necessity, alone ensuring the survival of the Jews. This of course reflects the different dates of composition; by the time Bashevis came to write *The Manor* and *The Estate* sand was covering the traces of Poland's Jewry.

The Estate opens with a death; that of Daniel Kaminer, Clara's father. His removal established Sasha as a rival to Mayer Joel; this competition between Calman's son and his son-in-law nicely reflects the split that had already occurred in the larger Jewish community. Polish Jewry was further fragmented as the new generation began to leave for America and Palestine. And this crack-up of a culture was given a further physical manifestation in Shaindel's breakdown, which occurred as a direct result of her son Joziek's emigration to Palestine. At first these distant places appeared only at second-hand, described in letters received by those characters still in Warsaw. But eventually, via the agency of Clara who went to New York in search of Zipkin, the novel also crossed the Atlantic. On arrival in that hitherto legendary land, Clara guessed that "if there was a life after death it would be like this — different and yet the same". What made it the same, of course, was the universality of human nature: "It's the same world and the same people," Clara told Zipkin. Like Ezriel, Zipkin had become a doctor with the support of his wife; and as with Ezriel he too felt confined by her parochialism. Bashevis further emphasized their parallel fates. In Poland, Ezriel and Olga had their illicit night in a country hotel; in America, Zipkin and Clara spent a "honeymoon" week in a secluded cottage. Ezriel told Shaindel that he was visiting Miriam Lieba, which precluded her accompanying him, Zipkin told his wife that he must also visit a former patient who would see no one but him. Clara had been driven into taking a lover by romantic folly, Olga also was steered by romantic fiction: "The heroines of the French novels that Olga read did not permit obstacles to keep them from rendezvous in cheap hotels or in the Bois de Boulogne." There is no doubt that, in the opinion of Bashevis, such books are "sweetened poison". They are the propaganda of a sick world, and are equally potent in Poland or America. They reduce man's estate to dirty sheets and spoiled offspring.

Although Ezriel was first attracted to Olga thanks to her simplicity of dress amid the ostentation of the other guests at Wallenberg's party, she also began to yearn for finery. After Shaindel was committed to an asylum Olga took charge of Ezriel's career, until Ezriel was forced to admit "that it was Olga who had brought him a wealthy practice, secured him from need, and helped him gain a reputation". Thus he found himself as much in debt to the modern woman as he was to his old-fashioned wife, and as much circumscribed by Olga's desires as he was by Shaindel's superstitions. Just as Shaindel did not like to mix with the enlightened, so Olga was disturbed by any sign of Jewishness.

She was made uncomfortable whenever Zadok visited his uncle to discuss some new philosophical problem he had encountered, for they disported themselves as if they were yeshiva students. Olga did not like to be reminded of her origins, nor did she like the way Ezriel was unbalanced by their disputes. She was determined to free her children from the handicaps of Judaism so that they could progress in Polish society. Visiting a Jewish village she was shocked by its primitiveness: "So this is the Judaism for which Ezriel yearns. He came from this and wishes to return to it! 'But it's not for me!' Olga said to herself. 'Not for me or my children.' " In fact a considerably worse fate was in store for her daughter, Natasha.

Wallenberg died leaving Olga enough money to purchase a country estate from a dissolute aristocrat. Like Jampolski's manor this Topolka serves as a metaphor of a corrupt and corrupting world. Before long Olga was so dazzled by vanity that her desires reflected those of the rotten Polish aristocracy. She planned a great ball, which happened to coincide with the fast of the Ninth of Ab, which commemorates the destruction of the temple of Jerusalem. While the Jews prepared a meal of bread, ashes and a hard-boiled egg, Olga's kitchens were working non-stop cooking ducks and geese, and outdoors on a spit a whole pig was roasting. However, just before the meal, a boat full of guests spilt into the Vistula; all were saved but the brush with death prompted a Bacchanalia. Olga danced with an officer, happy to be with someone so self-confident: "it was relaxing to dance again, to allow herself to be led by someone who knew exactly how to conduct himself". So unlike Ezriel with his doubts, his guilts, his indecision, and his Jewishness. But it was a wicked world into which the officer would lead her, as Natasha learnt. She eloped with a lieutenant named Fyodor she met at the ball. Naturally Fyodor betrayed Natasha and she ended up in the home of a wealthy merchant, already the father of married daughters, who had an Asiatic name. At seventeen, "pregnant with a bastard", she was doomed to "become the stepmother of two women older than herself". This disaster destroyed Olga. And Ezriel's second household began to disintegrate as Olga fell prey to superstition:

> Ezriel made fun of all this nonsense, but something of what she said remained with him. He observed, as he had many times before, that latent madness in the human brain always showed up in a crisis. Primeval fears had not vanished. There existed in everyone a hidden desire to worship idols, to perform black magic. The Book of Deuteronomy constantly warned against such dark propensities. Whoever its author was, he apparently knew that fatalism was the most profound malady of the soul.[16]

The Estate demonstrates that the rules of society conceal the most primitive desires, and that any dreams will be devoured and the dreamer cast into the pit. Olga believed in Polish society and destroyed her daughter as a result, and even Ezriel "daydreamed about going to Russia with Olga, or of settling with her in France, or in America, where one could live freely, without bearing the burden of generations". But there is no such thing as living freely. Freedom without responsibility is anarchy, according to Bashevis. And free-will is not a carte-blanche for pleasure; the self must not only act in its own interest. Therefore the "burden of generations" becomes more than a curse, a godsend to anti-Semites; it is also a training to combat selfishness and wickedness. Gimpel said, "Shoulders are from God, and burdens too." Whatever material progress has been made, human nature remains unchanged. And only those who are perverse enough to counter human nature have any hope of establishing a community of good citizens. Thus part of the burden is the need to look from this world to the next: to spurn the seductive promises of manors and estates in favour of more abstract benefits. Consequently, Bashevis does not concentrate upon a single event as if it were unique, for example the 1863 rebellion; rather he sees history as a series of infinite repetitions. Because he discounts any theory of historical progression it is natural that his two constant points of reference, the Bible and the holocaust, should co-exist with the present time in all his fiction as visible or invisible commentaries, thus turning nineteenth-century Poland into a universal metaphor.

While Bashevis concerns himself less with the minutiae of a period than with those problems which are eternal, Joshua always has contemporary history as the sub-text of his story. Joshua does not deem it sufficient to blame all wickedness upon the evil side of human nature; rather he seeks the causes in politics, economics and history. There is a sense of progression, both in terms of character and history, which at once makes his work seem more opaque but less modern than his brother's. History is organic, fed by greed. And Lodz was its mutant offspring, finding its true unnatural role as the factories switched to steam power. "The chimneys of Lodz clustered like the trees of a forest, but they blossomed in smoke and poisoned the air." Later, Lodz was described as a "hoggish gourmandizer", as if the city itself were responsible for its slump; a monster prepared to devour its creators. He is not so much concerned with the freedom given to the self, but with the possibilities of economic and political advancement history suddenly afforded the Jews; which, in effect, gave them an alternative persona; thus Simcha Meyer became Max and Jacob Bunim became Yakob. Nevertheless, he shared Bashevis's attitude to

the role of the Jews in this history. It was, simply, that they don't
belong; a change of name can alter neither character nor the fact that
one was born a Jew. Even Yakob, who looked like a modern European,
died because he was recognized as a Jew. So *The Brothers Ashkenazi,*
like *The Manor* and *The Estate,* reached the same conclusion as the
grandfather who said: "We Jews must not interfere. Whoever rules
will persecute Jews." The novel ends with this terrible vision:

> A thick mist had descended from the skies over Lodz. A wind rose and
> blew the dust of the cemetery in the eyes of the mourners. Heavily and
> slowly, like the rolling mists above them, they turned back to the
> desolate and alien city.
> "Sand," they muttered, covering their eyes with their hands.
> "Everything we have built was built on sand."[17]

This was not only symbolically but also literally true, for the Jewish
suburb of Balut was built upon a sandy field. The land was purchased
by Reb Solomon David Preiss under false pretences from
impoverished Polish nobles in the aftermath of the 1863 rebellion.
When the Canarski brothers discovered Reb Solomon's true purpose
they tried to retrieve their land in the courts, only to discover that
money was more potent in the eyes of justice than breeding. The
triumphant Jews proclaimed that no law would ever be able to destroy
their presence; but they were wrong, for they had not reckoned with
the court of history.

In *The Brothers Ashkenazi* history is a juggernaut, best represented
by the advance of the Germans into Poland. The novel opens with a
declaration of its epic intentions, even though the pioneers it follows
are not Jews but Germans, en route to Poland in the wake of the
Napoleonic wars. And what role did the Jews play in this march of
history? As ever they were spectators, "gathered with wide-open eyes
to observe the interminable line of carriages moving ceaselessly
forward". A century later, history was repeated as another invading
German army rolled into Poland and once again the Jews "gazed with
astonishment in their black eyes at the newcomers". This, as Saul
Bellow has pointed out, is the traditional role of the Jews. *The Brothers
Ashkenazi,* like *The Manor* and *The Estate,* shows what happens to
those Jews who seize their chance and break with this tradition;
however, the power of this initial image already suggests their fate. At
the beginning of *The Manor* the Jews are also spectators at the
banishment of Count Jampolski, an image which is likewise repeated
when Calman leaves The Sands. These coincidences reveal
similarities, but their presentation highlights the differences. In
Bashevis there is a suspicion that the whole of world history is an
illusion projected by the devil, while God's light was dimmed, an

impression sustained by his fictional technique, to which the only antidote seems to be a consistent code of ethics; be it Gimpel's gullibility or Rabbi Jochanan's hasidism. In *The Manor* and *The Estate* this goodness is passive, in "Gimpel the Fool" it becomes more active when Gimpel enters the world to become a storyteller. This self-conscious valuation of the writer's role finds a grander echo in Bashevis's Nobel lecture:

> The pessimism of the creative person is not decadence, but a mighty passion for the redemption of man.... Strange as these words may sound, I often play with the idea that when all the social theories collapse and wars and revolutions leave humanity in utter gloom, the poet — whom Plato banned from his Republic — may rise up to save us all.[18]

It may be dangerous to combat evil in the world, but it is necessary to confront it in fiction. Hence Bashevis's characters provide the centre around which history revolves. In *The Brothers Ashkenazi*, scenes are constructed in the opposite order; familiar characters are gradually revealed to be participants in historical events. For example in the ferment after the assassination of Assistant Police Commissioner Jurgoff, Nissan is eventually discovered behind the barricades waiting, along with thousands of others. This presents Joshua with a problem of balance unknown to Bashevis; on the one hand his story concerns a group of individuals, on the other it follows an historical process which involves classes not individuals. Whereas Bashevis seems to have successfully given his "sayings" fictional life, Joshua sometimes seems to smother his characters with "sayings".

When Max Ashkenazi cut the salary of his weavers to maximize his profits, a strike resulted. It was led by Tevyeh, a long-time socialist, and Nissan. Nissan already had personal reasons for disliking Max, but now that conflict became as much political as personal. During a protest meeting held in a synagogue, Joshua took the opportunity to insert a few "sayings" on the dreadful living conditions of the weavers. This is unnecessary in terms of dramatic development, but vital as an explication of the class struggle. Political motivation gives the novel an authority of tone, but it also weakens the spontaneity of the action since it is predictable that Max will always act as a capitalist and Nissan as a socialist. They have been trapped by history. This leads to a paradox already encountered by Benjamin Lerner in *Steel and Iron*; while Joshua's message is anti-totalitarian, his method tends to the classification of the individual. Nonetheless, *The Brothers Ashkenazi* has a dynamism that finally synthesizes the separate personal and political aspects. The dynamo being Judaism. If the battle between Max and Nissan represents the political tension of the novel, then the rivalry between Max and his brother adds the personal dimension. And it was with Yakob's final triumph that Joshua most dramatically resolved his paradox.

Jacob Bunim tactfully waited for the death of his father before going to "the extreme of un-Jewishness", but thereafter he became Yakob the brilliant European. And unlike his brother he looked the part. Indeed, he was able to bluff his way into Russia to rescue Max from a Soviet prison, only to come to grief on the border of his Polish homeland, his cosmopolitan appearance notwithstanding. A gendarme of the new Polish republic greeted them with the words: "Well, where do you two Sheenies come from?" And in that single moment all Yakob's years of good living vanished. Nor are his papers of any use, because he was a "Sheeny". But what made him a type in the eyes of the anti-Semite suddenly made him an individual in the eyes of the reader. When the gendarme was replaced by a lieutenant Yakob cried: "My brother and I are manufacturers of Lodz. We own houses there. We place ourselves under your protection." Unfortunately, the officer was a greater sadist than the gendarme, who had merely ordered them to strip. He forced Max to yell: "To hell with all the Yids!" But even then Max's humiliation was not over: "Now you can give us a little dance, Mr Manufacturer and house-owner of Lodz. A little dance and song, to entertain our soldier-boys here." So Max danced till he dropped. But Yakob was made of sterner stuff. Naked, without pretensions, his true character was revealed. He slapped the officer and was shot dead. Judaism therefore both saved him as an individual and caused his extinction. Likewise, Judaism disbarred ultimate absorption into any mass movement. In the end Nissan was broken, humiliated and astounded by the revolution he had helped initiate. And Felix Feldblum, who was convinced that his constituency was amongst the gentile workers, was last seen in Lemberg horrified by the pogrom he had witnessed, perpetrated by this same revolutionary material — among the mourners "stalked one figure in a light-blue uniform — Felix Feldblum, officer in the Polish Legion, fighter for the freedom of Poland, one-time believer in her Messianic future". Yakob's death was watched by "the naked figure of Jesus". Alongside the crucifix were a Polish eagle, portraits of generals, and innumerable Polish flags. Symbols that spell danger for Jews. The world is no illusion, what is illusory is the belief that Jews have any secure place in it.

Max came to this realization only when it was too late. In his eagerness to enter the European order Max was prepared to act with total ruthlessness. Having already possessed the daughter of Chaim Alter he took the opportunity to possess the man himself, made bankrupt by the wedding preparations. Max purchased a share of his father-in-law's crippled weaving factory, thus in one move becoming partner both to the daughter and the father, adding Ashkenazi to her name and that of the factory. His campaign to conquer Lodz began. The first casualty was his own father, who seeing the rabbi of Vorka's prophecy fulfilled broke with his son for abandoning religious study in favour of business. Since Alter's motto had always been, "The less you bother with figures, the better off you are", it did not take long for the more meticulous Max to gain absolute control of the factory. He overcame his first major crisis, the strike led by Tevyeh and Nissan, by the simple expedient of arranging for the police to arrest the two trouble-makers. But even now Max's Napoleonic visions would not let him rest; moreover, he was goaded by the easy triumphs of his brother who was just as successful without even trying. Unlike Max he was blessed with charm and luck. In order to satisfy his ambition Max turned his attention to the Huntze family, the major manufacturers in Lodz. His father was the firm's general agent with splendid offices in once-forbidden Vilki, and it was this position Max conspired to usurp with the help of Huntze's disaffected sons.

Heinz Huntze was a self-made man, but despite his wealth he retained his working-class manners, much to the embarrassment of his children. His daughters were able to dispense with their common surname by marrying worthless aristocrats, who returned the compliment by marrying the girls for their money. Cheated of such an expedient Heinz's three sons attempted to persuade the old man to purchase a baronetcy. Sensing an opportunity, Max decided to lend the sons enough to purchase the title themselves. In order to gain acceptance as their secret court Jew, Max trimmed his beard until "it was the beard of a heathen or an apostate", and cut off the greater part of his earlocks. All this made him no less of a Jew in the eyes of the Huntze brothers, but they took his money anyway. Whereupon Max prepared himself for his great coup, gradually acquiring more and more of the Huntze stock as security for loans. The unwelcome baronetcy ruined Heinz Huntze; like Calman and Ezriel Babad he found that the necessary ostentation ate into his moral and financial resources. He turned his house into a palace and the effort killed him. This palace, however, remained as a symbol of the new order, matching the parasitic desires of the brothers. They reconstituted the hierarchy of the factory, and the first to go was Abraham Hirsch Ashkenazi, replaced by his son. As a symbol of his allegiance to the new men Max displayed the company logo his father would not countenance: two naked Germans with fig-leaf and spear. Furthermore, he cast off his Jewish clothes, removed his beard

altogether and "never again used Yiddish, except when counting
money and adding columns of figures". Finally, he changed his name
from Simcha Meyer to Max, a move which he regarded as his "final
break...with the old life...the modernization of his name symbolized
the interment of the one-time Chasidic Jew and the birth of the
liberated European". The words "interment" and "birth" convey the
significance of this event. Certainly Abraham Hirsh hereafter
considered Simcha Meyer as dead, and recited the appropriate
prayers. Max, of course, revelled in the change. He was a man fit to
breathe the poisoned atmosphere of Lodz. But so great were the
appetites of this new Max, that like a "hoggish gourmandizer" he
would even consume his creator, leaving only a regal shell. This is
what Abraham Hirsh felt his son had already become, and what Max
thought he wanted to be. But both father and son were wrong. Max
could not be King of Lodz because he was a Jew, destined always to
look like a misplaced pedlar.

As fast as Max rose, Yakob kept overtaking him. Soon after Max
became general agent for the Huntze factory, Yakob was appointed
general agent by their chief rival Maximilian Flederbaum; worse, he
opened an even more opulent office across the street so that Max had
to order curtains for the windows of his office. Subsequently Yakob
discarded his ailing wife and took up with Flederbaum's daughter
Yanka, who appointed him director of her father's factory. This was
more than Max could stand. He also decided to divorce the wife he had
taken against her will, in order to marry a Russian widow with enough
funds to finance his take-over of the Huntze factory. But even as he
was making these plans his own daughter Gertrude, a replica of her
father in her obstinacy, was pursuing her uncle. So that Max's
triumph in winning control of the Huntze factory was matched by
Gertrude's victory over Yakob. As Max and the widow Marguiles
moved into the Huntze palace, Gertrude and Yakob were on their
honeymoon. But there was no happiness for Max in his second
marriage. When he divorced Dinah "there was a realization of a
certain emptiness of which he would never rid himself, and he felt as
though he were standing above an abyss into which something
precious had slipped out of his hands...." Now in the palace that
emptiness was made real, he was lost amongst the vastness of the
house, and he looked "smaller than ever in the midst of this
grandeur". And at night he climbed into bed "like a man mounting a
scaffold rather than a bridegroom approaching a bride". Such was the
private life of the self-proclaimed King of Lodz. As if to reassure
himself of the validity of his achievement he left the palace untouched,
even retaining the baronial coat of arms, and the decorations which

were "fantastically un-Jewish". These reminded Max of the crimes the people whose place he had usurped had committed against the Jews, and he realized he was an outsider in his own home: "What had they to do with him, with this little Jew in the dressing-gown, holding up the candle and staring bewildered on all sides of him." Even time was foreign, as the clocks "slowly, musically, and with stately insistence, as if participating in a religious ritual", counted the hours. After dark, stricken with insomnia Max quit his pleasureless bed and padded about his gilded cage; as incongruous a sight on his throne as the Jewish tailor the mob called King of Poland:

> A small, shrunken figure, he cowered in the big armchair. The vast palace stretched on all sides of him. The clocks continued to chime out the hours with multiple melodies. The bronze Mephistopheles on a pedestal in a corner of the room grinned down at him.[19]

Just as Yakob's martyrdom was witnessed by an alien god, so Max's majesty was regarded with amusement by a Christian devil. In short, Max had sold his soul, and the abyss into which he had fallen was hell, although Max had yet to learn it.

Max was in Russia when the German army invaded Poland, and so he was not present to see his palace revert to a more appropriate occupier. Baron von Heidel-Heidellau, son-in-law of old Huntze, was appointed governor of Lodz, and naturally he requisitioned his father-in-law's former abode. The Baron turned out to be a sadistic, vain bully with pederastic inclinations and a taste for rosy-cheeked lieutenants. Nevertheless, the servants loved him, especially the butler: "After all these years in the service of a Jew who had no demands and who did not know how to treat a servant, it felt good to submit again to a real master." With the Baron in residence the house came alive again, its spirit was literally restored. Indeed, like the city of Lodz the palace had anthropomorphic characteristics which Baron von Heidel-Heidellau accurately reflected. As the Baron systematically stripped Lodz of all its valuables, Max was trying to regroup his machinery in Russia: "While the sick and the dying were being carried past him, while disease and hunger and chaos had descended on the world, he pursued with fantastic resolution his one obession — the gathering together of his organization, and its reconstruction in Petrograd." As a result of his will and energy he succeeded, and there developed "Lodz-in-Petrograd, with Max Ashkenazi as the uncrowned king". Here Max was at home, in a factory surrounded by machines, making huge profits out of Russia's war effort, "even turning out bandages and cotton-wool". Although he considered war ridiculous he regarded it as a "natural phenomenon which could be turned to advantage from the business point of view". But Max's refusal to consider the personal cost of his enterprises, either to his workers or his family, was about to backfire. He was about to learn that history was not a mechanistic but a vital process.

His first teachers were his workers. They went on strike. And this time it was not an isolated incident, but part of a revolution. When the Tsar was overthrown even Max began to worry, not because he respected the régime but because the Tsar was "the symbol of all ultimate force, stability, and authority, the sacred individual whose likeness was stamped on every gold coin in the Empire". Max was frightened because he saw that if the man whose head was stamped on gold could be overthrown like an ordinary mortal what hope was there for the uncrowned king of Lodz-in-Petrograd? He accepted that the working class was a force that could change history, just as his fellow manufacturers had changed the face of Lodz; but as Lodz now produced poisonous fumes, so that revolution created its own monsters. Ruthless power seekers who pushed aside dreamers such as Tevyeh and Nissan, and bent the "iron laws" to suit themselves. After the Bolshevik coup the plunderers were plundered, and Max was thrown out of his factory like an unwanted dog. He had nothing.

Foreseeing that paper would become worthless he had invested in property, but that too was confiscated. At last he learned that "there are no eternal things. Even houses and factories are not eternal things. He had thought to prepare himself against the worst by putting his money into solid, tangible possessions. Now they were all gone". He concluded that the tangibles — money, possessions, power — were in fact more insubstantial than an intangible such as love of family. In his imagination he rebuilt his life in Lodz, little knowing that that edifice had also collapsed, resolving to "be softer toward the world at large", and "not to sell himself again to this idol of gold". In addition to his reaffirmation of family life, Max Ashkenazi underwent a religious conversion. However, his prayers remained mingled with calculations; how to survive, who to bribe to let him go. Nevertheless, the prayers were answered: "The person for whom Max Ashkenazi prayed appeared suddenly; like a delivering angel he descended unannounced from the sky." In Bashevis's work desperate characters are frequently unable to distinguish between salvation and temptation, but in Joshua's more worldly novel Miron Markovitch Gorodetzky turned out to be an agent not of the devil but of the secret police. Therefore, despite reciting his prayers with extra devotion Max Ashkenazi was arrested whilst fleeing Russia. God also afforded him no protection. The only eternal thing is man's vulnerability to his fellow man.

Instead of reconciliation, Max's return to Lodz brought death to his brother and misery to his ex-wife and daughter. On the first day of mourning for Yakob, Max read from the book of Job: "Let the day perish wherein I was born." On the second day he could think only of the vanity of life. By the third, however, he was beginning to weigh up the responsibilities he owed Yakob's family. He became enthusiastic about Palestine, and dreamed of being textile king in the land of the Jews. But at length he decided to stay and regain Lodz. He recaptured the palace through the courts, not because he liked the place, but as a symbol "for his own prestige". Despite the discouragement of the Poles, Max was a success once more, and again penniless anti-Semitic aristocrats came begging for jobs. Max took revenge for his humiliation in the railway station:

> The power of Israel did not lie in physical strength, but in thought...often he had grown to such strength that the gentiles who despised him had been compelled to seek favours from him. This was the strength of the Jew, and this was his revenge.[20]

But even so the recrowned king of Lodz felt no happiness, and the "satisfaction which he had anticipated with the restoration of his position still eluded him". Moreover, he knew that this post-war prosperity was built on a "crazy paper bridge", and could foresee how the wild dance would end. Again Lodz was the evil genius that presided over the madness; just as its "hoggish gourmandizing" had once caused a slump through over-consumption, now "the fever of the inflation time turned hot in the veins of Lodz". But in this lunatic situation Max's foresight was no use, for the course of events was too illogical to allow for planning.

> Among lunatics the sane man is a fool. He had planned sensibly, far-sightedly. But these were times which mocked all plans. Neither shrewdness nor foresight nor reliability nor reputation nor all the other virtues of the solid industrialist and business-man counted now. Only chance ruled; or if it was something more than chance, it was a combination of all the qualities which made for failure in healthy and normal times: falsehood, unreliability, instability, and recklessness.[21]

Max Ashkenazi was now a helpless captive of historical events, "like the captain of a ship caught in a blind storm", kept going by the "worries which were killing him". Nor could he force his good intentions on his family; Ignatz, his son, had turned into a copy of the Huntze brothers, so that there was "nothing Jewish about him". He refused to have anything to do with the firm of Ashkenazi, and it was clear that Max's desire to perpetuate the name would be disappointed. Though Ignatz was only conforming to the tradition which Max began; as he dropped the Jewish names Simcha Meyer, Ignatz was shedding Judaism itself. During the long sleepless nights, as in his former reign, Max wandered "through the vast rooms of the palace, pausing always to return the sly grin of the bronze Mephistopheles". The Mephistopheles is bronze, for there is no need to make the devil flesh while men are prepared themselves to build hell-on-earth. The irony of this was at last apparent to Max; he had helped turn Lodz into a hell and he would reap his reward when the devil's minions took over the city that had been prepared for them. That was why the king of Lodz ate a beggar's breakfast.

At last the paper-chain broke and Lodz was paralysed. By now there was a complete identification between Max's health and the condition of the city, as if in recognition of the fact that just as Max was a self-made man so Lodz was a man-made mutant. Both Max and the builders of Lodz had been seduced by power and gold into doing the devil's work, which they thought was the inevitable progress of history. Like Max, Lodz was putrefying alive. Its new rulers were the swindlers and the fly-by-night speculators. And over its prostrate body crawled, "like blood-sucking vermin, the tax-collectors, who concentrated their activity on the Jews". Likewise, the peasants avenged themselves on the Jews who were "hoarding the gold of the country." This new anarchic society was the end product of so much work, which began with the arrival of the German weavers. Now all was reversed: "Once the roads had been thick with immigrants swarming into the growing city; now they were thick with emigrants swarming out of the dying city." And death, when it arrived, came simultaneously to Lodz and to the man who had acquired the title of King of Lodz:

> It was as though he had been unable to give up the ghost as long as the pulse of the city still beat, however faintly. But with the extinction of the last glimmer of vitality in Lodz, he, too, closed his eyes. He could not breathe the air from which the smoke of the factories had been wholly removed. He stifled in the tranquillity of the atmosphere.[22]

On his last night he sat beneath the picture of a satyr pursuing a naked girl, symbol of the pagan nature of the palace, reading from a tattered Hebrew Bible he had hidden among his gilt volumes of Gothic prose. The once-hated words of Ecclesiastes, "concerning the vanity of life and the insignificance of man", now seemed "strangely intimate and true". Like Calman, at the end of *The Manor*, Max found some solace in the Hebrew texts, but unlike Calman they gave him no protection. He remained trapped in his palace, watched over by no god but a priapic satyr. A pathetic victim of history and his own misplaced energy.

Max Ashkenazi is without doubt the most powerful character in *The Brothers Ashkenazi*, as his final impersonation of Lodz makes explicit. But it was Nissan who had to carry the burden of Joshua's personal disillusion. After all Max's fate, though cruel, was not unjust considering the harm he had done others. Nissan's final anguish was almost masochistic, however, because his struggle had not been for self-aggrandizement but for the advancement of the proletariat. And his defeat was more chilling, because it demonstrated the impossibility of introducing a more just society. It may be deduced from the number of "sayings" Joshua inserts on the circumstances of the weavers that his sympathies are with them, and with Nissan's campaign on their behalf. But even so Joshua was too sceptical or too honest to ignore the outcome of the Russian revolution, and so he was forced to make Nissan as much a dupe of Marx as Max was a fool for Mammon. All dialectics are open invitations to dictators and criminals, who are prepared to help history on its way. So Joshua found himself in something of a dilemma; giving emotional support to a movement he knew would lead to dictatorship. Hence his treatment of Nissan is akin to Bashevis's treatment of Ezriel Babad; in facing up to the full implications of Nissan's beliefs he is punishing himself.

In 1905 both Nissan and Max were hurrying to Lodz, both for their own purposes: "Like Max Ashkenazi, Nissan was being recalled to Lodz by those who needed his guidance and leadership in a crisis. Lodz was again one of the centres of the revolutionary movement." But Nissan's leadership and guidance were finally as illusory as Max's rule of Lodz. Equally illusory was the unity of the Jews; they also were divided by class, as Joshua learned in his grandfather's *beth din.* A major problem with the Jewish artisans, however, was their refusal to see themselves as workers. Ezra Mendelsohn in *Class Struggle in the Pale* recorded the feelings of a socialist leader:

> It was this tendency of the journeymen to become employers, their failure to recognize the class struggle, that made the early socialist leaders despair. Feliks Kon, the Polish socialist, disparagingly characterized the Jewish artisans as "journeymen who dream of becoming masters".[23]

"Since employer-staff relationships were more clearly defined in the larger establishments, workers naturally found it more difficult to alter their status," adds Mendelsohn. Which is precisely why Nissan decided that the hard-core of the revolution was not with the self-interested Jewish hand-loom weavers of Balut but in the steam factories where the workers "realized how impassable was the gulf between them and the owning class". Comparing this observation

with the quotation from Mendelsohn gives a glimpse of how accurate
was Joshua's presentation of the situation in Lodz. But even though
the Jewish artisans were hard to organize they were no less exploited
than their gentile co-workers. He is a strike proclamation quoted by
Mendelsohn:

> "Feival Janovsky", the [boycott] proclamation stated: "is a pious Jew;
> he goes to the synagogue regularly, and with all his heart prays to God.
> He is a Jewish nationalist, a patriot and perhaps even a Zionist. He no
> doubt is upset by the persecution of the Jews, and sheds crocodile tears
> over the Jews' desperate situation. But all this, as we see, does not
> prevent him from cruelly exploiting his Jewish workers."[24]

"The evidence suggests..." writes Mendelsohn, "that the struggle
between Jewish worker and Jewish employer, though often the
struggle of 'pauper against pauper', was extremely bitter. While
traditional historians, writing of Russian Jewry, have emphasized the
unity of the community as against its gentile oppressors, the
community was in fact rent by internal dissension of great
magnitude." Joshua was clearly aware of this fact, and demonstrated it
time after time; for example, the battle between the Jewish toughs
hired by the employers and the unionists. But no dissension was
greater than that between the Balut revolutionaries, led by Nissan,
and the capitalists led by Max. It was common practice for Jewish
factory owners not to employ Jews. Mendelsohn quotes the reason
given by a Jewish factory-owner in Smorgon: "The Jews are good
workers, but they are capable of organizing revolts...against the
employer, the régime, and the Tsar himself." Flederbaum also would
not employ Jewish workers because "Gentile workmen were more
obedient and respectful and less ambitious." Nor would Max
Ashkenazi in his steam factory. He could not understand why Nissan,
a Jew, should be leading a strike of his gentile workers, "putting all
sorts of ideas into their heads". "We know nothing about Jews and
gentiles," answered Nissan. "We know only of workers and
exploiters."

> "*You* don't know," said Max Ashkenazi scornfully. "But ask the
> gentiles *their* opinion. *They* know the difference between Jews and
> gentiles. Unity! Unity! Just try to get one Jewish worker into a steam
> factory, and he'll come out in a hurry, and not walking on his own legs,
> either."[25]

Nissan retorted that these were nationalistic orations, but secretly he
knew that Max was right. Anti-Semitism overrode class allegiance.
Later this scheme was repeated in radically different circumstances.
The location was Russia. Max was still a factory owner, but Nissan

was now a workers' delegate. With a gesture of helplessness Max conceded defeat: "It turns out you were right, and not I." Emphasizing their shared Jewishness he quoted from the Talmud: "Who is the wise man? He who foresees the unborn." But Max's congratulations were premature, the child was a mutant that consumed its progenitors. Nissan rejected Max's overtures, replying in Russian not Yiddish, but his looks belied his actions. By remarking that Nissan's Jewish beard and whiskers gave him the appearance of a pietist Joshua was confirming Max's earlier point. The Jews may indeed have their own class divisions, but these were non-existent in the eyes of the anti-Semites; they did not distinguish between Jewish capitalists and Jewish communists. Indeed, as Ezra Mendelsohn points out:

> The history of Jewish politics in the Russian Empire is largely the story of how members of this intelligentsia forged an alliance with the Jewish masses to create specifically Jewish political movements. Such an alliance was, at first, rather unlikely. For many Russian Jewish intellectuals were, by their very nature, estranged from the Jewish masses, having abandoned both the language of the masses, Yiddish, and religious orthodoxy. As they themselves had left traditional Jewish life behind, their most natural inclination was, often enough, to advocate the integration of Jews into Russian society and to participate in general political movements. This inclination, however, was sorely tested by the all-pervasive nature of Russian anti-Semitism.... The "General Jewish Workers' Union ('Bund') in Russia and Poland" ("Lithuania" was added later) was founded in Vilna in 1897. Its history illustrates the pattern discussed above.... This alliance eventually obliged the intellectuals to voice not only socialist slogans, but specifically Jewish demands.[26]

Despite all his political convictions to the contrary, the events Joshua described forced him to the same conclusion. Charles Madison, in his book *Yiddish Literature*, described a trip Joshua made to the Soviet Union in 1926. "What troubled him particularly," writes Madison, "were evidences of anti-Semitism and its effect on many Jews." The most ironic "effect" is reported thus: "...on visiting a secluded midnight celebration of 'Lubavishe' Hasidism he was surprised to find among them engineers, students and other enlightened men who had become pious *after* the revolution." But unlike Bashevis, Joshua refused to see a realistic alternative in hasidism. He was not impressed by gestures. Which is why he remained suspicious of the alliance formed between intellectuals and workers, described by Mendelsohn above.

One such intellectual made an appearance at the grand funeral of

Bashke, daughter of Tevyeh, who died a heroine of the movement. "He was a famous orator, this revolutionary leader — a splendid specimen of a man, tall, dark-eyed, his head crowned by black locks." With his noble gestures and his voice under perfect control he soon had the crowd in his hands. And the more his audience responded to him, "lifted to heights of enthusiasm...plunged into an abyss of sorrow", the more he became "enamoured of his role". But Tevyeh actually saw his daughter die, heard her cry, "I'm choking! Save me!" and was haunted by her "wide-open rolling eyes". The squalid reality of her death compared to the grandeur of her funeral made the orator's every word feel like "a separate knife-thrust" to Tevyeh. "It was on his Bashke's grave, on the fresh earth which covered the dead body of his daughter, that this performance was taking place." Finally, when the speaker raised Bashke's blood-stained blouse, Tevyeh could stand the theatricality no longer. He snatched the blouse and pressed it "convulsively to his heart". This spontaneous outburst of passion was a great disappointment to the assembled workers, who felt that "the fine mood created by the orator" had been ruined. Clearly Joshua wanted to demonstrate how easy it was to be blinded to the truth by rhetoric. More, he wanted to show how quickly a crowd can forget suffering in order to indulge in self-righteousness. Of course, his revolutionary leader was a phony, an actor playing a part, working to satisfy his own ego. Such a leader, Comrade Daniel, played a central and insincere role in Joshua's next novel, *East of Eden*, but even this brief scene is sufficient to display Joshua's scepticism. It is not the theory of Marxism he found so objectionable, but rather the people who exploited it for their own ends.

Even so Joshua's scepticism should not be confused with the expediency of Colonel Konitzky, who was given the task of pacifying Lodz after the assassination of Jurgoff and its concomitant riots. Konitzky's technique was based upon the need to alienate the masses from the intelligentsia, which may seem to be in accord with Joshua's own observations. "I was easily won over by the intellectuals, as so many others have been," he told a new prisoner. "But I was lucky enough to see through them in time and drop them." As he continued he could well have been describing the anonymous orator at Bashke's funeral: "They look down on the proletariat and have an inner contempt for it.... These intellectuals come from rich homes; they aren't acquainted with the working-man, they don't feel his emotions. Their so-called revolutionary passion is something born in the imagination, out of boredom and idleness and out of the fashionableness of being a radical." But Joshua could hardly be in sympathy with a man who is last seen, having transferred his allegiance from the Tsar to the new Polish republic, still working against the people: "the strong he repressed brutally, the weak he corrupted". Colonel Konitzky was based upon the figure of S.V. Zubatov, head of the Tsarist secret police, active around the turn of the century, who, according to Mendelsohn, was the originator of police socialism. His declared aim was to persuade the Jewish workers that they could not hope to profit from an alliance with the intelligentsia, who "all too often tried to engage workers in a senseless political struggle which could only defeat their demands for economic and cultural improvements".

> These demands, Zubatovism insisted, could only be won were workers to abandon illegal schemes and ally themselves with the government. In short workers should establish unions, based on democratic principles, and should not permit the interference of the intelligentsia; the government itself would willingly support their struggle for decent wages, shorter hours, and better cultural opportunities.[27]

Both Zubatov and Konitzky appealed to the "enlightened self-interest" of the Jewish workers, assuming them to be capitalists who merely lack capital. Their real purpose was not amelioration, but the painless preservation of the status quo and their own skins. In short, their deeds were disconnected from any emotion save self-interest, which is all they could recognize in others. Joshua, on the contrary, sensed that a more communal way of life was possible, but he was unable to ignore the empirical evidence supplied by human nature and history, which makes *The Brothers Ashkenazi* so pessimistic. And nothing occurred during Joshua's last years that gave him cause to reconsider.

4
Politics

ALTHOUGH THIS is a book about literary relationships, it is difficult not to remark upon the fact that Bashevis did not begin any substantial work in America until after Joshua's death. The few critics who have interested themselves in this matter have invoked biblical archetypes, comparing the brothers to Esau and Jacob; or psychology, concluding that Bashevis "was working in the shadow, not the light of his older brother". Certainly, it is impossible not to observe the difference between the brothers in contemporary photographs. A portrait of the two of them taken in Warsaw shows Bashevis physically overwhelmed by his brother's commanding bulk. Joshua's expansive hands are clasped around his knees, while Bashevis's retire to his lap; Joshua stares boldly at the camera, while Bashevis's glance is sidelong. Maurice Carr, who was instrumental in organizing the earliest English publications of his uncles (for example, the 1938 anthology *Jewish Stories of Today* in which Bashevis dropped his surname so as not to trade upon his brother's fame), gave some credence to those who sought undertones in the relationship.

It was not so much the relationship of an elder brother to a younger but [that of] a wise father to a lost child. And Isaac, I believe, smarted under that but accepted it, because he is, at bottom, a very practical man. He knew that I.J. Singer was terribly vain. He also knew that people were trying to spoil the relationship between himself and I.J. Singer.... And he was very, very careful to play second fiddle...to accept the role of the lost child who is listening to the wisdom of his father. He was even, I think, ready to flatter I.J. Singer, because his older brother had wonderful qualities, but he also had one quality that marked the entire Singer family with the exception of the father — my grandfather — and that was tremendous vanity. Isaac has his vanity, but he's able to mask it. I.J. Singer had this vanity, but he was not able to mask it. And Bashevis was very, very careful to keep on the right side of I.J.....very, very careful indeed. Not until I.J. Singer's death...did Isaac's talent really blossom forth. It was as if some kind of clamp had been taken off him spiritually and he was free and he was able to develop. I don't want to give the impression that Isaac did not love his elder brother...but

within this love there were all sorts of complex emotions and fears and
jealousies and attachments and enslavements.[1]

Families have their politics, just as nations; and in a family of writers
there will be as many views as there are members, as we have already
seen.

When Bashevis joined his brother at Seagate on Coney Island he
"felt terribly confused".

> I saw that here Yiddish was not becoming richer but poorer. I saw
> hundreds of objects for which Yiddish had no name. Because Yiddish
> was created in Poland, not here. I lived through a real crisis. I stopped
> writing for six or seven years, doing only articles for the *Forverts*. But
> then after a few years I said to myself, if I have something to say, or a
> story to tell, I should do it instead of going around in despair, worrying
> why we are not as rich in every way as others are. Poverty is nothing to
> be ashamed of, even if it is a spiritual poverty. But Yiddish is not
> spiritually poor. It has certain treasures which other languages don't
> have (just as the others have treasures which we don't have).[2]

Bashevis's position in New York was a replica of his situation in
Warsaw. Once again Joshua was his protector. Joshua arranged a deal
with *Forverts* whereby they would serialize Bashevis's next novel.
This caused his fellow immigrants, especially the writers, to remark
that he had "gotten off 'on the right foot in America'". The latter
adding, under their breaths, that he owed it all to his brother. This
stung Bashevis who knew "full well how true this was". Whatever the
reason he found it almost impossible to deliver a worthy successor to
Satan in Goray. Instead of working Bashevis spent nights wandering
around Seagate, exiled both from his heritage and his talent.

> What now? I asked myself. I felt like laughing at my own helplessness. I
> turned back and saw the house with the two white columns. It had
> materialized as if from the ground. I came up to the house and spotted
> my brother outlined within the illuminated window. He sat at a narrow
> table with a pen in one hand, a manuscript in the other. I had never
> thought about my brother's appearance, but that evening I considered
> him for the first time with curiosity, as if I weren't his brother but some
> stranger. Everyone I had encountered in Seagate this day had been
> sunburned, but his long face was pale. He read not only with his eyes
> but mouthed the words as he went along. From time to time, he arched
> his brows with an expression that seemed to ask, How could I have
> written this? and promptly commenced to make long strokes with the
> pen and cross out. The beginning of a smile formed upon his thin lips.
> He raised the lids of his big blue eyes and cast a questioning glance
> outside, as if suspecting that someone in the street was observing him. I
> felt as if I could read his mind: It's all vanity, this whole business of

writing, but since one does it, one must do it right. A renewed surge of
love for my brother coursed through me. He was not only my brother
but my father and master as well. I could never address him first. I
always had to wait for him to make the first overture.[3]

Being a father-figure made Joshua an impossible confidant. And
Bashevis continued to protect his privacy, fearful of his brother's
judgement. Such caution was unnecessary concerning his writing, for
Joshua praised *Satan in Goray,* even though he never saw the
manuscript. Joshua was not so shy; indeed, he used Bashevis as
something of a research assistant on *Yoshe Kalb* when it came to the
superstitions of Galicia. On the other hand, Bashevis was probably
wise to be discreet about his relations with women. There is a
character in *East of Eden*, the novel that followed *The Brothers
Ashkenazi,* called Soloveitchik who bears a passing resemblance to
Bashevis. "He is not what you would call handsome; he is red-headed,
his face is covered with freckles, but there's an irresistible charm about
him." Moreover, he is "a great teller of stories and the delight of the
children; for he can crow like a cock, cluck like a hen struggling to get
out a big egg, coo like a pigeon making love". Joseph Singer, Joshua's
son, remembered that his uncle "was always rather playful.... He
used to run through the house, barking like a dog and quacking like a
duck". And what is Soloveitchik's role in *East of Eden?* He is a
seducer. He takes the virginity of Sheindel, sister of the novel's main
character, then abandons her. There are no consequences for
Soloveitchik, who disappears from the novel, but poor Sheindel is left
with a bastard. By coincidence, when Bashevis came to America he left
behind a woman named Runya, the mother of his only child. They
were married, though "never...by a rabbi". The trouble with Runya
was that she was a fervent communist, and when the talk was of
leaving Poland her promised land was Russia. Indeed, after Bashevis
had sailed for America, she took their child to the Soviet Union, "that
new haven which turned out to be a butcher shop". Eventually she
was exiled for Zionist activities and made her home in Israel. Bashevis
felt that a relationship with such a woman was dangerous. If
Soloveitchik was an implied criticism of his brother's morals, at least
Joshua had no cause to worry about Bashevis's politics.

At the end of *Steel and Iron* Benjamin Lerner forfeited his
individuality, which had hitherto been sustained by his scepticism, as
he became a trooper of the new Soviet republic. Also, in those last
pages, Joshua freed him from the harness of autobiography; Lerner's
future is unwritten, anonymous. However, Joshua, though rid of
Lerner, found himself unable to close his mind to the broken promises
of the new age of man. *East of Eden* took its title from a quotation in

Genesis: "So he drove out the man; and he placed at the east of the garden of Eden Cherubims, and a flaming sword which turned every way, to keep the way of the tree of life." Throughout the novel the Soviet Union is referred to as "paradise", and the masses are told: "Look to the East!" And Daniel, the handsome orator of the revolution in Poland, sees the future as "fresh and sweet, like a meadow in spring, like a garden, like an immense orchard, filled with flowing waters and blossoming fruit". As with the revolutionaries in *The Brothers Ashkenazi*, so in *East of Eden*; communism became an exact replacement of Judaism, demanding the same single-minded devotion, and borrowing the same imagery; as orthodox Jews bowed eastwards in the direction of Jerusalem, so the workers turned their eyes to Moscow. But the title suggests the inevitable fall of these hopes, the impossibility of recreating a time when, "Peace would reign; human beings would live with the gentleness of sheep, wrapped round with love and goodness." Joshua had no quarrel with the idea of original sin. In fact, he was an outright determinist, for nothing determines the future quite like pessimism with its simple rule: if you hope, expect the opposite. Naturally, this would sound defeatist in the ears of a Daniel who was an optimistic determinist, a prophet of the dialectic of history.

Thus Joshua arrived at another artistic problem: how to retain the tension of unpredictability in a novel when all hopes were doomed to failure, or how to put a mirror to determinism and show more than a world through a looking-glass. A sceptical hero was unsatisfactory, because Joshua wanted to portray the seductive appeal of a messianic ideology, so he decided to experiment with a gullible central character. Benjamin Lerner's fate was his starting point. In effect, he decided to rework *Steel and Iron*, making use of everything he had learned subsequently. The original Yiddish title, *Chaver Nachman*, speaks of his intentions no less ironically than its English counterpart. *Chaver* means "comrade" and Nachman, the hero's name, derives from *nachem*, which is Hebrew for "to comfort". Unfortunately, by the novel's end Nachman is a comrade to no one and a comfort to nobody. So what Joshua produced was an out-and-out political novel, disguised as an epic of realism, but actually a bitter parable in the manner — but not the spirit — of Peretz's "Bontsha the Silent". Joshua's *kleyne menshele* received no reward in "paradise", on the contrary the guardians of "Eden" inflicted even greater punishment upon him. What we have in Nachman Ritter is a Yiddish Candide.

It is worth recalling that at much the same time, in a different neck of the woods, another writer was taking on a similar artistic problem; the chief difference being that instead of attacking the utopian nightmare his enemy was the American Dream. Nathanael West's conclusion was *A Cool Million*. His *kleyne menshele*, Lemuel Pitkin, was no more fortunate than Nachman Ritter, nor was Shagpoke Whipple, his manipulator, any more admirable than Daniel; both, like Pangloss, see in their beliefs the best of all possible worlds. Of course, Nachman and Daniel seem more realistic, but this is an illusion born of Joshua's *trompe-l'oeil* presentation; instead of taking metaphors and turning them into an absurd reality, he painstakingly contrasted the rhetoric of the revolutionaries with actuality. West more or less rewrote American history, providing an image of the nation extrapolated from propogandist's clichés, whereas Joshua carefully implanted the events of *East of Eden* into recent history. If *A Cool Million* was finally a greater artistic coup than *East of Eden*, it was perhaps at the expense of its political impact. In the thirties the American Dream was but a whisper in an awakened people, while the Soviet Union still retained its allure for many intellectuals disenchanted with capitalism. What Dan Jacobson said of Bashevis's characters is equally true of West's people; they have the transparency of celluloid, while Nachman and Daniel give off the solid whiff of greasepaint. Indeed, the same Daniel who breathes the fire of communism is actually given this motivation:

> This had been his life's longing: to be admired and applauded by masses. This was what had made him follow Polish actors through the streets when he was a little boy, and this had impelled him, in his student days, to hang on the outskirts of the Polish labour movement. If he could not be an actor he would at least be a leader, a great orator.[4]

Joshua was no less a prestidigitator than Nathanael West, but he learned his tricks upon the Yiddish stage of New York rather than at the movie sets of Hollywood. And it is this dramatic solidity which makes the fate of Nachman and his family so moving. Nachman failed to realize that he was participating in a drama that required acting ability not sincerity. Likewise, the reader must recognize that while the scenery of *East of Eden* is realistic, the *dramatis personae* who act out their inevitable fates are not.

Nachman's father was called Mattes. He was a pedlar, who wandered from village to village with a sack upon his back. Sentimentalists would have us believe that in spite of poverty and squalor men such as Mattes were Biblical scholars. Mattes was certainly poor, dwelling in the street of the beggars, and devout enough to refuse food offered by a peasant, but he was "no scholar, and unacquainted with the finer points of ritual". He was a regular worshipper in the synagogue, but once inside "stood near the door...among the beggars, the wanderers, and the homeless, and he strained himself to catch the words of the cantor". He was so insignificant that whenever he celebrated the birth of a child, one unconsidered daughter after another, the beadle always forgot his name. His Sabbath meal consisted of beans and dumplings. Joshua, never one to obscure the unsociable effects of poverty, noted how rapidly his daughters ate, "in part because they were hungry and in part because each one feared the other would eat up more". But for all the shame of his poverty Mattes never questioned the rules of society or the justice of God. Indeed, he adhered to the latter with masochistic intensity. The novel begins on a Friday. It was a morning of torrid heat, but Mattes had taken no breakfast, for he would not eat until he had said his prayers, and to find a suitable place in the unfriendly countryside was not easy. So Mattes staggered onward, bent "so low under his burden that the tip of his dust-covered beard almost brushes against the rope which girdles him". Eventually he had to pause, because it was almost noon. Once he had begun to pray he would not stop, even when stoned by Polish peasants. Thereafter he must hurry back to Pyask, so as to arrive in good time for the Sabbath. Such was the working life of Mattes the pedlar.

> Five days he was on the road every week, among the peasants, five days of homelessness and dry food, five nights passed in stables and barns, five days without a sight of his wife and children and without a friendly conversation in Yiddish.[5]

But even in Pyask he was given no respect, instead he was mocked by the more prosperous householders who "smiled at the sight of this man who combined two proverbial misfortunes: no money and nothing but daughters".

Therefore Nachman's birth was a moment of triumph for Mattes. "May he be the comfort of our life," he said to Sarah, his wife. And despite a multitude of subsequent calamities, including the death of Sarah (once again in childbirth), Mattes continued to construct a future upon dreams of Nachman's achievements.

> Trudging the Polish roads under the weight of his pack, chased by dogs and mocked by shepherd lads, Mattes the pedlar dreamed great dreams. He saw Nachman first a God-fearing, learned youth on whom rich fathers of marriageable daughters had fixed desirous eyes.... Shortly after the wedding Nachman is invited to become the rabbi of a large town.... He enters the synagogue and delivers his first sermon, which is so filled with wisdom and scholarship that the congregation is struck dumb.... Everyone now envies him, Mattes the pedlar.[6]

He even imagined himself in the hereafter, standing before the same tribunal that judged Bontsha the Silent. At first the demons beleaguer him with fiery whips, until the famous Rabbi Nachman says the prayer for his father's memory, whereupon the demons are shamed and silenced and the following miracle occurs:

> Mattes the pedlar is lifted out of the grave; they lead him by the hand into paradise, where the floors are of pure gold and the walls sparkle with precious stones. They show him his throne in the midst of the great and learned men of old; and when one of them asks: "Who is that base and common person who had insolently placed his throne in our midst?" the echo of the Divine Voice sounds sweetly through all the heavens: "Suffer him to sit with you, for this is Mattes, a pedlar and wanderer in villages; though he himself is a common person, he has raised a son who is a scholar and a saint."[7]

But in *East of Eden* no dreams are destined to be fulfilled, least of all those of Mattes, or of Nachman in his turn, who imagines a similar reception in the Soviet Union. Mattes was even denied a Jewish funeral, despite all his precautions. When he was conscripted to fight for Russia in the Great War he wrote the following words upon a piece of canvas which he sewed on his fringed ritual garment, worn next to his skin. "I am Mattathias, son of Arye Judah Mattes, of the congregation of Warsaw. He that finds my body let him bring it to a Jewish grave." But Mattes was killed in his first skirmish and dumped in a mass grave.

> He was thrown along with the rest into a shallow pit, quicklime was poured on all of them, and the common grave was covered hastily. An officer put up a rough cross, made of two branches; he peeled away the bark from one side of the upright, took out a pencil, and, wetting it several times between his lips, wrote out: "Glory to the heroes who have fallen for Czar and fatherland."[8]

But by then Mattes had already seen the end of his grand dream, destroyed as a direct consequence of Sheindel's own dreams, which were rudely pricked by Soloveitchik.

After Sarah's death, Sheindel became surrogate mother, until Mattes was bullied into a disastrous second marriage. His wedding to Eva was solemnized beneath a tablecloth held aloft by four broomsticks. And Eva certainly turned out to be a witch, for with her appearance "hell had come into their house". She immediately humiliated Nachman by exposing him to his classmates as a bedwetter. Later Nachman was horrified when Mattes would defend neither himself nor his son against Eva's onslaughts. "Mattes did not even defend the boy, and Nachman, shamed to the soul by his stepmother, grew ashamed of his father, who would not stand up for

himself and his own children". And when Eva finally walked out on
Mattes, after forcing him to become a beggar, Nachman burned "with
shame for his father's sake, and for his own sake. As long as he could
remember, his father had brought him only humiliation, in the
synagogue, in *cheder*, here at home. He knew obscurely that in a sense
he loved his father; but he knew also that he hated and despised him
for his weakness, for his readiness to put up with everything". These
were the harsh lessons Nachman was learning alongside his religious
studies. He saw that timidity was no virtue, nor "patient submission to
the burdens of life", that it was necessary to assert one's individuality
to achieve self-respect; conclusions he unknowingly repressed in his
subsequent blind loyalty to communism. Meanwhile, Sheindel had
made a similar discovery: that even she had a unique value in the eyes
of men. When she was molested by the driver who was taking her to
Warsaw in his wagon she was both grateful and revolted, for no one
had ever called her beautiful or kissed her before. Similarly, the crude
bakers who worked in the house where she found employment as a
servant, "frighten her, yet awaken something in her". Thus the way
was opened for Soloveitchik to play the seducer.

Before her downfall Sheindel returned to Pyask. The inhabitants
were astonished at her transformation into a sophisticated city girl,
and some of her glamour rubbed off on Mattes, who felt an
uncharacteristic boldness.

> Mattes no longer stands at the door of the synagogue during prayers.
> Because of his daughter Sheindel, but much more because of his son
> Nachman, the Talmudic student, he has taken courage and approached
> the pulpit. A new sense of dignity shows itself in his deportment. He
> blows his nose no longer into a corner of his capote, as he used to, but
> into the new kerchief which his daughter brought him from Warsaw.[9]

"God has been good to me. I have not merited such good children," he
said to his neighbours. But God unfortunately had a blind spot when it
came to the future of Mattes Ritter and his family, for the small
happinesses that came to them were invariably followed by disaster.
Sure enough, the next time Sheindel visited Pyask she was a scandal.
She succumbed to Soloveitchik because she allowed herself to dream,
even though she knew that "it is too good, too wonderful, and it can
never happen to her", she fought against his seductive promises of
marriage but "she feels her senses dying and her mind slipping from
her...and she knows that she is losing herself". Moreover, she was
aware "in her heart of hearts" that Soloveitchik was lying to her, that
the accounts of his past "varied from one Saturday to another". But
she could not help herself, "his words were too sweet". Like Malkah
before her she was in the grip "of a will deeper than her own, the will

which glazes the eyes of animals in rutting-time, and sends the fish headlong upstream against currents and cascades". She went under, where the words reached her "blood rather than her ears". It was a victory for passion over reason, the animal over the human. Sheindel had been tricked by a performance.

When her shame was revealed to the people of Pyask they passed judgment upon her, usurping the role of the divine arbiter, so that the consequence of her mistake was social; it forced Mattes to take his family to Warsaw. And here his dream was finally crushed by the economic realities of city life. "I'd like Nachman to go on with his studies of the Holy Word. He's gone a long way already, and he's got a good head," Mattes fearfully mumbled. But Sheindel, the new boss, was blunt: "This is Warsaw. Here everybody works." Mattes made no response, "but during the grace after the meal his voice quivers, and...heart-breaking sighs tear their way out between the words". The lesson was simple; be an actor not a dreamer. This was easy enough for the irresponsible Soloveitchik and the opulent revolutionary, but economic necessities strictly limited the roles available to Mattes and his children; Mattes was destined to be a pedlar even in Warsaw, and Sheindel had destroyed her chances and Nachman's opportunity to reach the one goal that could have raised him above his circumstances. Nachman's response to his new life as a baker was ambiguous; when he threw away his capote, cut his hair, and missed prayers he was scared, "But together with the fear something else stirred, a feeling of joy and abandonment, a foretaste of sweet liberation from the yoke of the commandments." But such sweet liberation was an illusion, only economic revolution could give a choice of roles to one such as Nachman. But that is yet another illusion.

At first it seemed as though Nachman would be content as a baker; he learnt his trade well, he was promoted, he purchased the first new clothes he had ever owned.

> He looked at himself in the greenish mirror of the emporium and was astounded. The salesmen, dancing around him, kissed their fingertips and sang their praises.... But he walked home as in a dream, carrying under his arm the bundle of rags which had been his only clothes till then.[10]

But the rules of the novel never vary; one dream destroys another. To celebrate his new appearance Nachman's fellow workers took him to the little house of Auntie Fradel. Here he lost his virginity to a grotesque whore amid the gasps and giggles of his comrades and their tarts, and all his "secret dreams and hopes, his boyish imaginings of love, were drowned in a sea of filth". Nevertheless, Nachman recovered from the self-loathing and self-contempt occasioned by this folly, and regarded himself with a sense of achievement and responsibility. "Plans and hopes danced in his head", but as may be anticipated, they did not endure long. This time the obstacle was more substantial; the German occupation of Warsaw. Nor had the Germans improved since *Steel and Iron,* they were still "a vast unreasoning and ruthless force". It was their unreasonableness that broke the population of Warsaw, just as it was Sheindel's lack of reason that destroyed her family's future. Indeed, Sheindel was one of the many victims of the Germans; in the claustrophobia of the occupation she unwisely married one of Nachman's colleagues, the only worker left in the bakery. Her plan was unambitious: to provide some sort of home, some sort of security, for his sisters, for Nachman, and for her little son. On the contrary, her marriage accelerated the disintegration of her family; for Manassah, her husband, was a gambler and a drunkard. In addition he was violently jealous of her affair with Soloveitchik. Finally, Manassah was driven out of work by the Germans, and he took his humiliation out upon Sheindel. Whereupon Nachman struck him. The blow had no less effect upon Reisel, his younger sister; she felt herself "free from the burden of obedience... and her heart expanded with hope and expectation." And what was her reward? After a series of misadventures Reisel was forced to carry the yellow ticket of a prostitute. At the same time, Nachman was suddenly faced with the "promise of unexpected, unmerited happiness". He had met Hannah, "the girl with the blue eyes and the red cheeks", who had initiated their courtship with a handful of revolutionary pamphlets.

Like Deborah, the heroine of Esther Kreitman's novel, Nachman was drawn into revolutionary politics by a romantic attachment. "He saw the workers' movement in her and through her, and he made himself part of it because it meant so much to her." When Hannah told him about Comrade Daniel, her idol and leader, he agreed with everything she said and meant it with all his heart. Like Sheindel with her soldier, Nachman could not believe his luck; "helplessly, timidly, he kept asking her whether it was true, whether he was not a wholly unwanted creature on earth". He need not have worried, no one could have been prouder than Hannah when Nachman was arrested by the Germans after a foolhardy May Day demonstration, she cheered deliriously when Daniel made the following declaration: "Comrades... if you're chopping down a forest you must expect splinters to fly!" But when Hannah became pregnant her delirium wore off, she was transformed from the revolutionary girl into a typical Jewish housewife — such was fate's joke upon Nachman. "She discovered in herself an instinctive devotion to housewifely duties, a peculiar, unsuspected pleasure in making the bed perfectly, smoothing out the sheets so that not the tiniest wrinkle showed." She no longer wanted turmoil but security. But by then it was too late — this was fate's joke upon her — for Nachman's loyalty to the cause had transcended its beginnings. His behaviour had become a secular variation upon his father's religious abnegation, seeking his reward not in paradise but in the Eden to the east. Ironically, his transformation was accomplished by an experience that Mattes had already undergone, down to the last detail but one. As Mattes was conscripted by the Russians to fight the Austrians, so Nachman (after his release from Germany) was conscripted by the new Polish Republic to attack the Bolsheviks. His company was also ambushed, his officers also fled, his comrades also followed, and the local Jews were hung once again as spies; finally Nachman was also shot. But unlike Mattes, Nachman returned from the war, his souvenirs being "a rushing noise in the ears, a medal in reward for his wound, and an implacable hatred of the unjust, existing order". So as Hannah's enthusiasm for Daniel waned, Nachman's waxed.

Actually, Daniel had a brief previous existence in *The Brothers Ashkenazi,* as the famous orator who spoke the eloquent elegy over Bashke's grave. But now Joshua made explicit what was only implicit in *The Brothers Ashkenazi;* Daniel was a born actor. What prevented him from entering his chosen profession was the fact of his Jewishness; likewise, his religion "raised a wall between him and the Polish masses". So he turned to the Jewish workers for his audience. Nor had his old ambition left him, regard the care with which he chose his outfit for the performance that captivated Nachman:

> Comrade Daniel had no lack of white shirts, even silk ones, which Sophia kept in apple-pie order for him; but this evening he put on a simple black one. Nor was he short of excellent and expensive ties, most of them presents from his wife, but he did not wear one that evening. He even carried his simplicity so far as to leave the top button of his black shirt open, showing the length of his full, round neck and a little of his white, smooth chest. He knew that the workers liked him best in this black shirt, especially when it was slightly open at the top so that the agitation of his heart, when he soared aloft in an oratorical flight, became, as it were, visible to all of them. Nor did he fail to rumple his black locks with both hands as he stood in front of the mirror, admiring meanwhile the intemperate blackness of his hair, which almost shaded off into a blue.[11]

Such egotism — acceptable in an actor — contrasts strangely with the matter of his oratory. Yet without such histrionics the audience would have remained unmoved, if this historical testimony from Ezra Mendelsohn's *Class Struggle in the Pale* is any guide:

> Yashka was a passionate agitator.... With his ardent nature he won over all those to whom he spoke. I, too, was captivated by his inspired words (literally "hot breath") despite the fact that I understood nothing of what he said to me. I was agitated and stunned by the very fact that Yashka had taken me under his wing and had spoken to me.[12]

Joshua was naturally suspicious of such exhibitionism, the more so when the effects were completely premeditated. Charles Madison thought Daniel too far-fetched: "Although charlatans like Daniel are no rarity in real life, his unrelieved villainy and the absence of honest counterparts detract from his fictional credibility. Even harder to believe is Nachman's excessive naïveté." But he failed to spot the essential theatricality of the relationship; Daniel was the prompter and Nachman was his dummy. Exactly like the worker quoted by Mendelsohn, Nachman was enthralled by Daniel; although he too understood nothing of the discussion. No less than Soloveitchik, Daniel's fiery words appealed to the blood, and Nachman was "carried away by the lovely words of Comrade Daniel, by the vision of the happy future which was knocking at the door of the poverty-stricken workers in their garrets and cellar apartments". With such rhetorical flourishes Nachman was transported, both metaphorically and literally; for Daniel's popularity gave him the power to outflank the more cautious party theoreticians, who counselled against the rash May Day demonstration that led to Nachman's imprisonment in Germany. One such intellectual was Zalkind, who intended to make Daniel his mouthpiece, to use him as Daniel was to use Nachman; "the oratory would be Daniel's, but the ideas would come from Zalkind". But Zalkind miscalculated, underestimating Daniel's ambition and his support. Instead, it was Daniel who found a mouthpiece:

> Though he was perfectly capable of drawing up a ringing proclamation which should draw away the masses of the workers from Zalkind's party into his own, he conferred upon Nachman the distinction of writing an appeal to his comrades. More exactly, he permitted Nachman to append his signature, for the substance of the appeal was written by Comrade Daniel. He affected in it the simple, convincing phraseology of a plain working man; he even put mistakes of grammar and spelling into it so that there should be no mistake as to who had written it. The appeal was cast in the form of a confession from a worker in the ranks who had been blind for a time, had let himself be misled by false teachers, and had had his eyes opened so that he was able to perceive the light of the truth in good time. Nachman was breathless

> with excitement as Comrade Daniel began to read forth the
> proclamation which he was to sign; every word seemed to find its way
> into his blood and to spread like a balm through his body.[13]

Yet again the words strike the emotions rather than the mind, making
Nachman breathless and his blood race. Even so, he still felt some
qualms when Daniel, speaking through him, attacked Zalkind as a
paid servant of the bourgeoisie. Nachman's hesitation caused Daniel
to question his loyalty to the cause, whereupon Nachman denied his
doubts in the firm voice of a pietist. Thereafter, whenever he came
across any of Zalkind's followers (with whom he sympathized in his
heart) he shouted at them in Comrade Daniel's words. Thus Nachman
lost control of his individuality, so much so that he confused his own
importance with that of Daniel:

> For the first time in his life Nachman knew the thrill of achievement
> and exaltation.... Now he was among those who were masters of their
> own lives, directors of their own destinies. On those walls which had
> always been covered with the proclamations of the mighty,
> proclamations which demanded obedience, loyalty, service, and slavery
> from the masses, now appeared the proclamations of Comrade
> Nachman, the call of the oppressed to the oppressed. The government
> on one side, Comrade Nachman Ritter on the other!... Comrade
> Daniel wrote, Comrade Nachman signed and distributed and pasted
> up. An intense pride filled Nachman.[14]

But Conrad Lempowsky, Director of Internal Defence for the city
of Warsaw, knew better; he knew that no hair of Daniel's head might
be touched, while Nachman's skull could be split without a second
thought. For Lempowsky, like Colonel Konitzky, the pacifier of
Lodz, was aware that today's revolutionary leader could be
tomorrow's president. Consequently on the next futile May Day
demonstration engineered by Daniel, Nachman was clubbed, while
the instigator was spirited away by the secret police. To underline the
hypocrisy Joshua sent Lempowsky that same evening to a glittering
reception at the Soviet Embassy in the honour of the People's Day.
Nor was Hannah slow to point out to Nachman that while she lived in
poverty thanks to his revolutionary activities, Daniel's wife dressed in
silks and satins. Nachman's response was extraordinary: "Nachman
put his hand hastily on her mouth, with the gesture of a pious Jew who
hears his companion uttering incredible blasphemy against the
heavenly powers." He had reverted to the unquestioning obedience he
so despised in his father.

Thus even when Nachman knew very well that the decision to call
for a strike among Jewish bakers was folly, he allowed himself to be
silenced by Daniel's thunder. He tried "humbly to explain to his

leader and guide", pointing out the number of men who would be put out of work. Daniel's response echoed that of Aaron Lvovich to Lerner (when the former was about to leave his charges to join the Russian revolution): "We are not concerned with men.... We are concerned with the revolution. It's the revolution that matters! The party has decided there is to be a strike, and it's for you to carry out the party decision." Sir Isaiah Berlin's stern report upon Bakunin applies equally to Daniel and Lvovich: "Morally careless, intellectually irresponsible, a man who, in his love for humanity in the abstract, was prepared, like Robespierre, to wade through seas of blood; and thereby constitute a link in the tradition of cynical terrorism and unconcern for individual human beings, the practice of which is the main contribution of our own century, thus far, to political thought."[15] Nachman believed Daniel: "He was a soldier in the ranks. A soldier does not debate and question; a soldier carries out the instructions of his commanding officer." Without realizing it, Nachman had willingly turned himself back into the duped soldier whose injury he swore to avenge. Sure enough, the strike was defeated, and Nachman became a victim of his own prophecy. Once again Daniel provided comfort with his favourite axiom: "No matter.... When you chop wood, splinters are bound to fly." But Nachman was soon called upon to make even greater sacrifices.

A plot was discovered by Lempowsky to overthrow the government. Financed by an unnamed country to the east, it was, in fact, an invention, backed by agents provocateurs, to trap Daniel "the Jewish spider at the centre of the Red net", so that he may be exchanged for an important Polish cleric held by the Bolsheviks. Among the names upon the list of other conspirators arrested with Daniel occurred also that of Nachman Ritter, a baker. Although Daniel was sentenced to death while Nachman was given eight years, the latter's punishment was the heavier. During their respective interrogations Daniel was accorded every courtesy by Lempowsky, while Nachman was tortured in a dungeon at the dead of night. Daniel flung Lempowsky's lies back at him "confident of being rescued by the exchange which he declared to be impossible", while Nachman was crippled for the same act of defiance. He refused to sign a false confession, which he had not hesitated to do for Daniel, an irony lost on Nachman. Daniel's trial was immediate, a charade, "three whole days of manoeuvring and lying, of pretence and counter-pretence", while Nachman had to wait a year for his. By then Daniel was well established in the Soviet Union, living the life of a hero. Even his wife, who dyed her hair to conceal her Jewish origin, was impressed by the workers' state. Not so Hannah. After Nachman had been dragged off to prison shouting revolutionary slogans, she was left to look after herself and their son. He was named Mattes, as if to demonstrate the hopelessness of his destiny. When Nachman was introduced to his son for the first time, at the end of his sentence, Hannah used these ambiguous words: "This is your father, Mattes." And indeed Nachman saw before him a ragged yeshiva student. The fate of Manassah, Sheindel's husband, illuminated the folly of Nachman's obstinate courage. He went blind. Only then did he recognize his reprehensible former behaviour. He reformed. This is the opposite of the image Nachman used in his false confession, penned by Daniel. In fact Nachman still had much to suffer before his eyes were finally opened to Daniel's true nature, still had many confused hours of trying to reconcile what he could see with what the party told him was true. It is a symptom of his frail individuality that he will not accept the evidence of his own eyes, just as his son's reversion to orthodoxy is a comment upon the sterility of his ideals.

Like his father before him, Nachman was sustained through the dark years of captivity by a dream of a better life on the other side. After his release he could not wait to "set foot in the land to which he belonged". Unfortunately, no one else shared his enthusiasm; not his wife, nor his comrades (who called his a deserter), nor the Soviet embassy (which refused to grant him a visa), nor Daniel (who did not reply to his letters). So Nachman decided to smuggle himself into paradise, feeling that "he was leaving behind him that old, wicked, foolish, superstitious world into which he had been born", that "this was the last stage before that new, free, proletarian world which was the hope of mankind". But when he first saw the peasants of that happy land, Nachman was inclined to believe that his guide had tricked him and that he was still in Poland. However, his doubts disappeared when he approached the guardhouse; here was no icon but a portrait of Lenin, here were no anachronistic peasants but a soldier of the Red Army. Nachman ran towards him, to be greeted by these words: "Halt, you bastard, or I'll fire." Thereafter he was locked up as a spy, in conditions that closely resembled those of his captivity in Poland. Although it was a rude awakening, Nachman would not abandon his dream. His fellow prisoners were men who had offended the system. Nachman told them how lucky they were to be living in Russia, but all they were interested in was the price of bread in Poland. One, arrested for stealing cabbages, stopped Nachman's lecture thus: "I don't give a damn about the system.... Can you buy bread? Can you buy potatoes? That's all I want to know."

Nachman was interrogated in the middle of the night, as he had been in Poland, and likewise presented with false confessions for his signature. But Nachman maintained his innocence. His ingenuous faith in the power of reason seemed vindicated, however, when he was sent to Moscow under Daniel's patronage. Nevertheless, Nachman was left to linger in the Lubianka, until Daniel was able to find time in his busy schedule to arrange his release. When they met Daniel was "terrified lest the other should take it into his head to embrace him", while Nachman remained totally impervious to the irony that surrounded him. They had both changed; like Lemuel Pitkin, Nachman had been a little worn away by his troubles; not so Daniel, now growing a paunch. Nachman sustained his convictions because he refused to see the truth, Daniel was able to maintain his self-respect by neither listening to nor believing the complaints of the masses. Both were reassured by the spectacular May Day celebrations; formerly, on such days, Nachman was in danger of losing his liberty, now something even deeper was at risk. For he marched among the workers, "his body cleansed of its dirt, his face shaved, his clothes patched and washed", and along with those his memory was also wiped clean, so that "he had forgotten completely the wretched frontier crossing, cellar number one in the Cheka of Minsk, the hunger and dirt of his imprisonment". His mind was in thrall. "His blood sang in him." He had fulfilled the desire of Bakunin who wrote: "I do not want to be I, I want to be We." So Nachman happily concluded that "it had been worthwhile". But Nachman was lost. He had been robbed of his reason. Now the full importance of the theatrical metaphor becomes apparent, for all the moments that open the doors of unreason are the result of dramatic manipulation. From Soloveitchik to the Soviet Union, all are stage managers. They represent the triumph of artifice over reality, they manipulate reason by appealing to the emotions. They promise temporary glory, and demand the self in payment. Mattes, Sheindel, Nachman — all are fooled; worse, they are turned into enemies of their own selves. Such are the goals of seducers and totalitarian régimes alike.

Finally, after all his tribulations, Nachman was awarded a job as a baker in Moscow's Red Star Bakery.

The factory worked through the twenty-four hours of the day, in several shifts. It could not afford to pause. The capital of the Soviet Union was constantly expanding. Every month saw the addition of new factories, the arrival of new masses of workers. Bread was needed in ever increasing quantities. On the walls of the factory, placards announced: "With our aggressive tempo we will complete the Five-Year Plan in four years." Underneath the announcement appeared a set of figures which contradicted the arithmetical rules which the workers were given in their evening courses: "$2 \times 2 = 5$".[16]

This simple unequal equation plays a central role in the literature that ventures into the underworld of irrationality. Just as $2 \times 2 = 4$ seems to be the solid foundation upon which the status quo rests, so $2 \times 2 = 5$ is the rallying cry of iconoclasts. On the one hand, such a "reality instructor" (to use Saul Bellow's classification) as Senator McCarthy can declare that the threat of communism is obvious to "anyone who...can add two and two" (his definition of the "average American"),[17] while on the other, Dostoyevsky's man from the underworld can avow that "the formula 'Twice two make five' is not without its attractions". For him the correct equation is "an abomination, since it is a formula which wears an impertinent air as, meeting you on the road, it sets its arms akimbo, and spits straight in your face".[18] In the Russia portrayed in *East of Eden* such a reactionary figure would be called a saboteur. Thus it is possible to echo George Steiner, and see Dostoyevsky and Stalin linked by the very nature of Russian society which generates both "absolutist visions" and "apocalyptic determinism".[19] Consequently, in resisting the dangerous politics of illogicality, Joshua also had to close his mind to the imaginative freedom of irrationality. He was not able to "reassert the scandal and wonder of human freedom as against the dictates of mathematical postulates and the prohibitions of logic" (which is how George Steiner described Dostoyevsky's achievement in *Letters from the Underworld*).[20] But then Joshua must have been aware of pro-communist artists, such as Louis Aragon, whose aim was "scandal for the sake of scandal". After a visit to the Soviet Union in 1930 Aragon wrote a poem entitled "Red Front" which contained the following:

> Death to those who endanger the October conquest
> Death to the saboteurs of the Five-Year Plan.

Joshua's answer to Aragon was the case of Affanasiev, Nachman's most sympathetic fellow worker at the Red Star Bakery. But also a drunkard, and a saboteur. As Joshua succinctly noted, "Twice two did not turn out to be five."

> The rulers were profoundly perturbed. Something had to be given to the excited masses in order to still their fury. And they were given *blood*. They were given the blood of the scapegoat, which carries into the wilderness the sins of others.[21]

And so a new slogan spread throughout the country: "Proletarian comrades! Death to the saboteurs!" The same words as used by Aragon, the erstwhile surrealist. Joshua recognized the connection between art that used the unconscious as its inspiration, and politics that appealed directly to the blood of the masses. Therefore he kept a strict control over his imagination, denying himself the liberties Bashevis had taken in *Satan in Goray*. He would never evade the restraints imposed by logic with the ingenious dexterity of his younger brother, who gave an interviewer this example of how an artist can free himself with one bound: "When you say two and two is four, actually you don't know what this means. What does it mean this two and two is four? Two horses and two tables are not four; they have to be alike."[22] There is no doubt that *East of Eden* lacks the exhilarating dizziness found in works where the artist is taking risks with his powers, but it fulfils another important function — it bears witness. It is moving, rather than exciting.

Bashevis was able to dismiss the dogmas of his generation with a cunning image:

> Certainly I was very close to these people, and maybe that was the trouble: you know, sometimes when you see the cook, the food doesn't seem very appetizing. While the ideologies sounded very attractive, I was close enough to see who was preaching them and how these people fought for power among themselves. The truth is, if you ask me, that the aches and troubles of this world cannot be cured by any system.[23]

Later, in a short story, he wrote: "If there is such a thing as truth it is as intricate and hidden as a crown of feathers." At his best Bashevis is an inspired writer, he relies upon his imagination to provide the images that will translate his ideas into language; as a result he does not work as hard as Joshua in acquainting himself with the details of the political dogmas he has rejected, he is put off by the smell. However, in rejecting the "inspired condition" (Saul Bellow's phrase again) Joshua sacrificed spontaneity, wonder. One of the few novels that has attempted to reconcile the conflicting potentialities of the "inspired condition" is, in fact, Saul Bellow's *Herzog*. Even as Herzog "took seriously Heinrich Heine's belief that the words of Rousseau had turned into the bloody machinery of Robespierre, that Kant and Fichte were deadlier than armies", he also acknowledged that "Romanticism guarded the 'inspired condition', preserved the poetic, philosophical, and religious teachings, the teachings and records of transcendence and the most generous ideas of mankind, during the greatest and most rapid of transformations, the most accelerated phase of the modern scientific and technical transformation".[24] Although Herzog recognized the link between Rousseau and Robespierre, he could not dismiss the claim: "Je sens mon coeur et je connais les hommes." *Herzog*'s peripatetic narrative reflects this confusion, and its conclusion is quietude: "At this time he had no messages for anyone. Nothing. Not a single word." But Joshua would not allow himself the luxury of enjoying the "inspired condition", he knew his target, and the narrative of *East of Eden* proceeds directly, unambiguously, to its inevitable conclusion. As far as he was concerned, the "inspired condition" was a cheap dramatic trick, too dangerous for humanity. Even Bertrand Russell, having proved that two plus two must always equal four in *Principia Mathematica,* fell into the underworld. "Suddenly the ground seemed to give way beneath me, and I found myself in quite another region," he wrote in his autobiography. "At the end of those five minutes," he continued, "I had become a completely different person. For a time, a sort of mystic illumination possessed me."[25] Consider the construction, "a completely different person", and the word "possessed", both of which suggest a loss of self. This was the danger which obsessed Joshua.

It is no coincidence that an equally passionate novel, which won for its author the title "Maggot-of-the-Month" from the communist magazine *Masses and Mainstream,* had this sentence at its core: *"Freedom is the freedom to say that two plus two make four. If that is granted, all else follows."* Actually, George Orwell's *1984* took a sceptic, Winston Smith, who could not reject the evidence of his eyes and ears just because the Party told him to, and turned him into a believer; a career which was the reverse of Nachman's. Winston's conversion took place in a torture chamber, where O'Brien (the novel's equivalent of Daniel) attempted to persuade him that two plus two did not always make four. This was how O'Brien succeeded, by sleight of hand, since four fingers held aloft do not really represent the equation in question:

O'Brien held up his left hand, its back towards Winston, with the thumb hidden and the four fingers extended.

"How many fingers am I holding up, Winston?"

"Four."

"And if the Party says that it is not four but five — then how many?"

"Four."

The word ended in a gasp of pain....

"How can I help it?" he blubbered. "How can I help seeing what is in front of my eyes? Two and two are four."

"Sometimes, Winston. Sometimes they are five. Sometimes they are three. Sometimes they are all of them at once. You must try harder. It is not easy to become sane."

...

"How many fingers, Winston?"

"Four. I suppose there are four. I would see five if I could. I am trying to see five."

"Which do you wish: to persuade me that you see five, or really to see them?"

"Really to see them."[26]

O'Brien's triumph was based upon his unlimited ability to inflict pain. But however crude the methods the results were genuine; Winston's capitulation was tragic, as he wrote of his own volition, "TWO AND TWO MAKE FIVE." On the contrary, Nachman had no trouble accepting Stalin's new formulation. Indeed, what energy he had left after a day's work was spent trying to find a connection between "slogans and pictures and the people among whom he lived". For these people were "wicked, frightfully wicked", as ungrateful as were the refugees cared for by Lerner and Lvovich in *Steel and Iron*. Horrified, Nachman "wanted to lose himself in the sea of words, in the smooth, cheerful lines; he did not want to hear and see what was going on about him, all the ugliness and meanness". And when Hannah joined him in Moscow, bribing her way into an apartment, furnishing it with items purchased on the black market, Nachman was outraged by her cynical behaviour.

> He did not care that she spoke disparagingly of him, but he could not bear to hear her speak with disrespect of his country, the country of the workers who had thrown off the yoke of the oppressor and had become the masters. The party newspaper told him that the building industry had entered on immense developments, having far surpassed the figures laid down in the Five-Year Plan. There it was, black on white, with many figures and diagrams. Nachman believed every word, every figure, and every drawing, and he showed Hannah the newspaper, so that she might see for herself.[27]

But Nachman was no Daniel, try as he might he could not prevent the truth from speaking to his heart:

> Nachman does his best not to listen and not to see; he does not want to be a witness of the hatred and of the injustices. He goes to the meetings and listens to the cheerful reports of the speakers and the optimistic addresses of the leaders. He swallows the articles in the party newspaper, with their great plans, their magnificent achievements, and their encouraging promises. Thus, in the mass of the bigger things, he forgets the little ones. But when he leaves the meetings, when he is not reading the paper, when he takes his place in front of the oven, when he meets his fellow-workers in the kitchen or goes through the streets or returns to his home, then those alien worlds melt away in his mind. There is no correspondence between what he sees about him and what he hears at the meetings and reads in the paper. And his heart sinks lower and lower.[28]

Finally, the truth found a voice when his friend Affanasiev was arrested as a saboteur.

Affanasiev's expulsion from the Red Star Bakery is worth quoting in full, for the scene contains the novel in microcosm. Kulik the hatchet man speaks:

> "Comrades, our genius of a Leader, to whom we have sworn to carry out the Five-Year Plan in four years, is watching us. He tells us not to tolerate in our midst the counter-revolution and sabotage, which has crept like a snake into our factory. He warns us: 'Comrades, clean out your ranks! Drive out the mangy sheep from the healthy flock!' Which of us, comrades, will fail to heed the words of our glorious Leader?"
>
> Now Kulik did not have to wait for his applause.
>
> "Long live the great Leader! Down with the saboteurs!" came from Kulik's comrades.
>
> "Long live our great Leader!" echoed from the hall....
>
> Comrade Podolsky waited until the applause had subsided, and prepared to close the meeting in a businesslike way....
>
> "Comrades," he said, "we have just heard an expression of the resentment which all of us rightly feel against the saboteur Affanasiev, who ought to be thrown out of our ranks. Does anyone wish to add anything before we put the resolution to the vote?"
>
> Comrade Podolsky uttered these words rapidly and formally. He was quite sure that no one would wish to take the floor, and thus he would be able, as always in such cases, to finish early, get into his machine, and arrive home in time for dinner....
>
> "*Tovarich* Podolsky," said the voice, and the r in the *tovarich* had a soft Yiddish sound, "Comrade Podolsky, I want the floor." Podolsky, Kulik, the foremen, the secretaries and assistant secretaries, the librarians and collectors and professional organizers, and all the workers in the hall turned their amazed eyes in the direction of the voice, just as if it had resounded from heaven.
>
> "Who is that 'I'?" asked Podolsky, a note of anger in his voice.
>
> "It's I, Ritter," the voice replied, "Nachman Ritter."[29]

At last, in that dramatic moment, Nachman stepped forward to affirm his individuality, to claim his true identity; and this action, paradoxically, destroyed the carefully managed drama, demonstrated that a man's life was at stake — a real man with a name, not just another saboteur. Naturally, this act of individuality, this act of humanity, cost Nachman his party membership and then his freedom. Worse, in denying the Soviet Union, Nachman was left with neither paradise nor this world; he had reclaimed his individuality, but he had lost everything else. He had even seen through Daniel. Nachman visited him, seeking help. Daniel offered comforting words, but they no longer penetrated, "he shakes them off". He told Daniel what his fellow workers had always said to him: "You can't eat those figures." As ever, Daniel spoke of the "big point of view", until Nachman informed him that he had been expelled from the party, at which

Daniel panicked and instinctively reverted to Yiddish. The coward within was revealed; when he heard how Nachman defended Affanasiev he yelled: "Why the devil do you have to put your foot into it?... What damned business is it of yours? Why don't you think of your wife and child instead?" These were momentous words, they made a mockery of all Nachman's sacrifices. He had been fooled. Utterly disillusioned, Nachman drifted into his fate. When he was eventually picked up as a saboteur, Hannah went to Daniel and realized that "this man who had once been her idol" was terrified. She yelled a single word: "Skunk!" For the last time Nachman was handed a false confession to sign; tempted by his interrogator, moved by Hannah, no longer having any ideals, Nachman decided to sign.

This was the final irony; it made no difference. He was expelled and abandoned in no man's land, between Russia and Poland, banned from both places, his only companion being a dying horse. "A strange passionate sense of nearness to the dying animal filled Nachman, and he stroked its raw, wounded hide. In that abandoned, exhausted, used-up animal, gasping in its death agony, he saw himself, his whole life." *Steel and Iron* began with a carthorse licking Lerner's sweaty shoulder. The image had not changed. Revolution had done nothing for the working man.

There is a Jewish curse, "May his name be blotted out." The reverse is Yad Vashem, literally "A Place and a Name", a memorial to the lost Jews of Europe, where the Israelis have attempted to gather in the names of all those murdered by the Nazis. By this tragic route a majority of the Jews of Joshua's generation found their promised land at last. Joshua himself was dead by then, but these words from *The Family Carnovsky* demonstrate that he knew what those Jews who remained in Europe could expect, "The youths in boots had meant it when they sang in the streets about spilling Jewish blood. To them, these were not mere lyrics, as the inhabitants of West Berlin had assumed. With each passing day more blood dripped from their daggers — drop after drop after drop." Indeed, it is possible to see each of Joshua's novels as a systematic destruction of Jewish hopes; in every one a bit more of the ground collapses beneath their feet, or promises evaporate into thin air. These promised lands are no mirages, but a variety of hells. Finally, even enlightenment itself proves false. For Berlin, the headquarters of enlightenment, becomes the capital of the New Order. In *East of Eden* Joshua rarely used Stalin's name, preferring references such as Great Leader, and in *The Family Carnovsky* he managed to write a novel about the rise of Nazism in Germany without mentioning Hitler's name at all. When he is described for the only time, it is as a "scowling little man with the slack mouth and the mad, baggy eyes". This description, with its suggestion of spiritual weakness, physical deformity, and psychological infirmity, is representative of Joshua's treatment of all Nazis in the novel; they are failures (Hugo Holbeck), impotents (Dr Kirchenmeir), or homosexuals (Dr Zerbe), the remainder being typically thugs or whores. Even Jegor Carnovsky's attraction to Nazism is explained as a perverse result of neurosis; he is not misguided, like Nachman, but confused. Daniel has no equivalent in *The Family Carnovsky*, there is no eloquent champion of National Socialism. And although Joshua again hints at the irresistible charm of the mass movement, he is not anxious to give a rational account of its appeal to decent Germans. Thus one of the few sympathetic Germans, Frau Holbeck, soon regrets her support for the Nazis, which she attributes to mesmerism. "In the excitement that had attended the elections, when the city had been full of music and proclamations and oratory, she had been hypnotized into following the trend in favor of the men in boots who had promised prosperity and the re-establishment of a strong and vigorous Germany.... Yes, she had been tricked into voting for the New Order and she was ashamed." In general Joshua is unforgiving, and there is no doubt that the sentiments of Von Spahnsattel (an anti-Nazi) are his own: "You Jews still don't know us Germans. You keep on seeing us through your Semitic eyes. But I know my own people only too well because I am one of them. *Zum Wiedersehen*, Klein. God have mercy on you." As he speaks Von Spahnsattel's "steely eyes" fill with "anger and contempt". Joshua, likewise, did not spare his fellow Jews; the aforementioned Klein, who ignored Von Spahnsattel's advice to leave Germany before it was too late, ended up as a jar of ashes on display in his widow's apartment in New York.

But *The Family Carnovsky* is not a catalogue of the evils of Nazism, rather it is an attack upon the folly of enlightenment. Although the adherents of Nazism might be perverts, the phenomenon is not shown as an aberration, but as a logical consequence of history. Nazism merely confirmed all Joshua's fears of mass movements, which sanctified the brutal and bestial aspects of humanity, and habitually picked the Jews as scapegoats. His anger was directed at those enlightened Jews who refused to recognize the inevitability of the process; and it consequently involved a reconsideration of his own position. This reflected the times; *De Mishpokhe Karnovski* was published in Yiddish in 1943 (the first English edition did not appear until 1969). Aaron Zeitlin — one of the few men Bashevis admires without reservation — gave this summary of Joshua's mood: "The outward conditions of his life were good. To the world he appeared as a man satisfied with his achievement. Yet the illusion of the 'broad world' had long since vanished from the mind of the wise Singer, and only an inner bitterness replaced it."[30]

The conflict between father and son, between tradition and enlightenment, conditioned the careers of Joshua and Bashevis, and continued to influence their writing. Indeed, Joshua often used the family as a metaphor for Jewish history, until his interest in its internal relationships came to dominate his passion for external events. The two continued to be interrelated, of course, but the balance was different; Joshua had taken Nachman's lesson to heart. In *The Brothers Ashkenazi* the decline of the Ashkenazi family, from the stern patriarch through his assimilated sons to his semi-apostate grandson, was one of the many movements related to the development of Lodz; however, it became the dialectic of *The Family Carnovsky*, which was accordingly divided into three books, "David", "Georg", and "Jegor". The examples of communism and fascism convinced Joshua that it was impossible to change the world, all that remained was to protect the family. And as the Jews had to take the hostility of the world for granted, they could only turn to each other for security. When David Carnovsky is reconciled to his son he says, "Be of courage, my son, as I am and as are all the men of our generation. We have borne persecution since the beginning of time and we shall continue to bear it, as Jews always have." Without a family a Jew is destined to be an outcast, doomed to loneliness. This is the discovery of Elsa Landau, a revolutionary firebrand, and an independent woman.

> Her father had warned her of what happened to a woman who shunned the natural course of marriage and motherhood. She had scoffed at him then, but it seemed that he knew life better than she. The wives of the workers whose homes she visited seemed to lead lives of fulfillment. Their days were taken up with their children and their household tasks.... How did all her triumphs and fame measure up against the thrill of motherhood?[31]

Obviously the word "seemed" should not be overlooked, but there is no doubting the reality of Elsa's despair as she "buried her face in the pillow and cried the desperate tears of a woman alone". This is the same Joshua who wittily charted Hannah's transformation from an idealistic girl into a dull housewife, driving poor Nachman to distraction with her wifely demands. Nor is it any coincidence that the middle Carnovsky, Georg, is an obstetrician; having taken the advice of Elsa's father.

However, these are the sentiments of experience. For the novel commences with David Carnovsky, newly married, disrupting the household of his in-laws. His father-in-law was the biggest lumber merchant in Melnitz. Like most Polish Jews of his status Leib Milner was a hasid; although of similar background, David Carnovsky was a rationalist. On his first visit to the synagogue he antagonized the congregation by "reciting the chapter of Isaiah in the Book of Prophets in a Lithuanian accent and with such grammatic precision that the Hasidic Jews in the house of prayer became irked". The rabbi attempted to chide David, pointing out that the prophet Isaiah was neither a Litvak nor an anti-hasid. But David thought otherwise: "If Isaiah the Prophet had been a Polish Jew and a Hasid, he would have been unfamiliar with the rules of grammar and his writings would have reflected the erroneous Hebrew used by all ignorant Jews and Hasidic rabbis." Such a riposte did not make David very popular. Eventually he was discovered reading from the Pentateuch of Moses Mendelssohn. In the eyes of the world Moses Mendelssohn was a great philosopher, but to the Melnitz rabbi he was "that Berlin apostate". Leib Milner attempted to make peace, but David "was ready to take on the world for his convictions". He defended his guide so skilfully that he enraged the hasidim and was thrown out of the synagogue with the words, "Go to that Berlin convert, cursed be his memory!" And this is just what David did, much to the despair of his wife's family. As far as David was concerned the Jews of Melnitz were "savages and ignoramuses ... benighted denizens of the Dark Ages, idolators, asses".

> Not only did he want to abandon the town that had so disgraced him, but all of Poland, which was steeped in darkness and ignorance. For a long time he had been drawn to Berlin — the city in which the sainted Moses Mendelssohn had once lived and from which he had spread his light across the world. From early childhood, when David Carnovsky had studied German from Mendelssohn's Pentateuch, he had been drawn to that land across the border that was the source of all goodness, knowledge, and light. Later, when he was older and helped his father in the lumber business, he often had to read German letters from Danzig, Bremen, Hamburg, and Berlin. Each time he did this, a strange feeling of sorcery came over him. The *Hochwollgeborn* that preceded each name breathed of great nobility and grace. Even the colorful postage stamps bearing the portrait of the strange Kaiser evoked within him a longing for this alien yet familiar land.[32]

There is no escaping the irony of these sentences; for example, Germany as "the source of all goodness, knowledge, and light". Nor was David Carnovsky spared the consequences of Germany's "sorcery", which caused him to eat his own words. Years later, now an exile in New York, David Carnovsky "vented his rage at the rabbi of

Sha Mora just as he had once vented it at the rabbi of the synagogue in Melnitz". It so happened that the rabbi of Sha Mora was the same Dr Speier who had so impressed David when he had first come to Berlin. David Carnovsky spat out the "sweetened poison" of enlightenment, but the ironic turn of history cannot negate its initial attraction; perhaps that is why Joshua sent the Carnovskys to America, rather than back to Melnitz (as Bashevis might have done), although they do enter a kind of little Melnitz in New York. Joshua could never endorse a return to hasidic narrowness, but the failure of enlightenment to combat Nazism made him appreciate orthodoxy's spiritual strength. It was one thing to be let down by communism, which was iconoclastic, but more frightening to be abandoned by enlightenment, which had seemed to be the foundation of the world. It meant that no philosophies were proof against the demonic energy of an ideologue. Of course such conclusions were no more apparent to the young Joshua than they were to the young David Carnovsky.

David was besotted with Germany. He adopted the dress of an affluent Berlin Jew, "a derby and a jacket cut to the knees", with a top hat for Sabbaths and holidays, he trimmed his beard to a point and he abandoned Yiddish. "German to him signified light, culture, Moses Mendelssohn, and the highest form of Jewishness, while Leah's jargon reminded him of the rabbi of Melnitz, the cult of Hasidism, of stupidity and ignorance." Even in "the emotion of love" David whispered endearments to his wife in German, which offended Leah since, in her opinion, "they did not contain the true flavor of love". Only in moments of anger did he forget his grammatical German and revert to "homely Melnitz Yiddish". Such a moment occurred when he learned that his son, Georg, was consorting with a *shiksa*. It did not occur to him that such an attachment was the logical outcome of Georg's upbringing. At birth Georg was given two names, "Moses, after Moses Mendelssohn, a name by which the boy would be called up to the Torah when he grew older; and a German name, Georg, a corruption of his father's name, Gershon, a name with which he could go among people and use in business." The word "corruption" suggests the fate of David's intentions which he phrased thus ("in both Hebrew and German"): "Be a Jew in the house and a man in the street." Dr Speier and the other distinguished Jews who attended Georg's circumcision "nodded their heads in approval", for this was their notion of the "golden mean": "A Jew among Jews and a German among Germans." Later, in New York these same Jews (now exiles) invoked the same "golden mean" in opposition to the election of David Carnovsky as the beadle of Sha Mora, for in his argument with Dr Speier David had forsaken moderation. But it was left to Ephraim

Walder, last of the German-Jewish sages, to give voice to the fallacy of
the "golden mean": "Life is a terrible prankster, Reb Carnovsky. It
loves to play tricks on people. German Jews wanted to be Jews in the
house and gentiles in the street but life turned this ambition
completely topsy-turvy. The fact is that we have become gentiles in
the house and Jews in the street."

Certainly, Georg had no desire to maintain a dual identity; from
childhood he rejected his Jewish persona. Whenever Leah called him
by his Hebrew name he cried, "I'm not Moshele, I'm Georg," while
Hebrew itself caused him to be overcome with laughter. Nevertheless,
in the eyes of his peers Georg was a Jew, nor was there a shortage of
those willing to teach him about anti-Semitism. Even Emma, the
Carnovskys' Catholic maid, took Georg secretly to a Sunday service
where she showed him images of "bad men with the wicked eyes and
the crooked noses". She explained that they were "the Christ-killers,
the Jews". Naturally, Georg immediately questioned his father,
"Why did the Jews crucify the Lord Jesus?" Horrified, David
attempted to give a rational response "about good people and bad,
about educated, intelligent people who loved peace and friendship and
about the wicked and stupid ones who sought only hate and conflict".
Finally, he counselled Georg to be "a good person and a good
German". German? Georg pointed out that his companions told him
that he was a Jew. So David repeated the "golden mean": "You are
that in the house, child...but in the street you are a German."
Ironically, when Georg and David argued over Georg's affair with
Teresa Holbeck, his gentile nurse, it occurred in the street.

Georg's best friend during his schooldays was Kurt, son of the
janitress, who epitomized freedom to the boy burdened with the need
to study; like Leo in Roth's *Call It Sleep,* Kurt represented lack of
responsibility — to parents, to teachers, to the world. So Georg would
not concentrate upon his studies, and brought home poor grades
which enraged his father. In particular, Georg antagonized his history
master, Professor Kneitel, to whom David made a humble apology.
Nor would Georg take his *barmitzvah* seriously; when questioned
about the Book of Proverbs by Dr Speier he replied that "he did not
remember such nonsense". Moreover, he continued to refuse to
recognize his Jewish name. "My name is Georg, Herr Doktor." To
which the rabbi responded with the "golden mean": "Georg you are
to the world, my son.... In the synagogue you are Moses." But Georg
was adamant: "I am always Georg." When David heard of this
exchange, "he flew into such a temper that he even forgot his beloved
German and began to scold his only son in the same Yiddish words
that his father had used to castigate him". David was not quite

enlightened enough to realize that he was participating in the ancient conflict between father and son, one that he had precipitated by giving Georg a name that was a corruption of his own father's. So the row in the street between David and Georg over Teresa was also a conflict over Georg's Jewish identity. For all Georg had done was to take his father's advice literally; he was in the street, he was a German.

> Georg saw that it was up to him to remain calm and reasonable. But he and his father were too much alike. The moment he started talking, he too lost control and soon they were locked face to face like images in a mirror, despising in each other what they despised in themselves.[33]

The argument overflowed into Georg's apartment; here the final break occurred when David saw a photograph of Teresa. The golden mean was unbalanced, as was inevitable; the street had invaded the home. But the picture of father and son "locked face to face like images in a mirror" actually outweighed all the angry words, for National Socialism did not recognize the slow progress of the generations. David's "golden mean" and Georg's freedom of choice were equally illusory; they were Jews, whether they liked it or not. Thus the Nazis effected a reconciliation between father and son.

After years apart Georg visited his father. " 'No more reason to be angry, Father,' he said with an ironic smile. 'Now we are all Jews alike.' " However, Reb Ephraim was incorrect when he advised David: "Fathers have never been satisfied with their children. It's a long time since I was a boy and I recall how my father, may he rest in peace, used to tell me how disrespectful I was and how in *his* day things had been different. Even the Prophet Isaiah complained about it: 'I have raised them and they have sinned against me....' " For Georg comforted himself with similar sentiments when, in his turn, he was called to his son's American school to answer complaints. "He smiled, recalling the time his father had been summoned to school by Professor Kneitel. He was glad that he was able to treat the matter more lightly than had his father. Like most middle-aged people, he was also struck by the swift passage of time. How long was it since he himself had been bickering with his father? With a philosophical smile he mused about the evanescence of life." But his "philosophical" smile soon disappeared when Jegor's headmaster told Georg of his son's Nazi sympathies. Returning home he thrashed Jegor, as David had thrashed him. But Jegor was not like Georg, he was no mirror image, instead part-Jew, part-gentile, "a mixture of his two strains. His eyes were blue and his complexion fair like the Holbecks, but his brows and hair were raven black and the nose prominent and stubborn like a true Carnovsky". Georg's two names have been personified, and they are at war. In effect, Jegor was a living example of the "golden mean", and he was completely unbalanced by Nazism.

Shaken by Georg's marriage and the victories of the Nazis in the streets, David himself began to question the "golden mean". Not only was he disappointed in his son, but also in the gentiles and even the enlightened Jews of Berlin. His son had married a *shiksa*, the gentiles had elected the Nazis, and the enlightened Jews had failed him when he was marked as an alien by the authorities during the Great War, even though his son was an officer in the army, and he was the complete Germanophile. There was a certain justice in this, for like his erstwhile compatriots David had despised all reminders of the East, whence he came, estranging himself from his wife by refusing to mix with her cronies from Melnitz. One of these, Solomon Burak, was designed to make the Berlin Jews shrink with embarrassment; above all, he refused to conceal his Jewishness. David was full of sayings such as, "The future is no mystery to a scholar," yet it was only Solomon Burak who was able to see through the polite façade of the German political system. He told his detractors that "even though they were long-settled and Germans for many generations back, they were despised by the gentiles every bit as much as he, the stranger, and as were all Jews". This was a truth the Jews of Berlin did not like to hear, least of all "from the lips of a former peddler". In their uneasiness they blamed the Solomon Buraks rather than the anti-Semites themselves for any ill-feeling; these undisguised Jews "who with their names, conduct, and business tactics caused the gentiles to lump them, the long-settled and German-assimilated Jews, in the same category. They were afraid because of these recent arrivals who resurrected the very Jewishness that they, the old settlers, had for so long masked and concealed". When Georg answered Dr Speier back, the urbane rabbi had no hesitation in putting it down to "his Eastern origin from whence emanated all of Jewry's bad traits". Accordingly, Dr Speier had no problem in brushing off David, when the latter was declared of questionable loyalty.

Now, in his confusion, David was not so positive about "the vileness of Melnitz and the spirituality of Berlin". Indeed, the following passage reads a little like an apology to Pinchos Mendel, Joshua's own father:

> David Carnovsky felt deceived by the city of his idol, Moses Mendelssohn. The Melnitz rabbi had been right after all. The ways of the philosopher led only to evil. It began with enlightenment and involvement in the gentiles' world; it ended with apostasy. As it had happened with Moses Mendelssohn's descendants, it was happening with his. If Georg would not himself convert, his children surely

would. Perhaps they would even become anti-Semites, as converts
often did.[34]

Like Bashevis after him, Joshua seems to be endorsing the absolute
logic of his father; that enlightenment is a social process with no
brakes, that the ultimate destination of a journey begun in the intellect
is an emotional crash. For the simple truth is that human nature is not
controlled by reason, and even a child can be completely out of the
reach of his father; no philosophical book could "provide clues as to
what went on in the mind of a five-year-old boy who was afraid of the
dark". This was most movingly demonstrated when Georg stood over
his sleeping child, unable to protect him from the terrible nightmares
that tormented him:

> He looked at the sleeping boy. His lids were closed, his wasted arms
> awkwardly sprawled over the blanket, his forehead beneath the lank,
> dark hair was pale and lined with bluish veins. A wave of pity came over
> Georg. What was his son thinking? What went on in that childish
> brain? What visions appeared there when he was asleep? What fears
> haunted him? As a surgeon, Georg knew every tissue and cell of the
> human brain. But what was it actually, that small pile of matter, blood
> and veins? Why did it differ so radically from person to person,
> encompassing every degree of brilliance and stupidity, coarseness and
> spirituality? Why did it bring joy and fulfillment to one, fear and
> torment to another? There lay his son, his own flesh and blood.
> Although he was a mere baby he was already burdened with dark
> thoughts and morbid fears.... Man's semen was full of hidden forces —
> good and evil, wisdom and stupidity, cruelty and mercy, health and
> sickness, joy and sorrow, genius and insanity, ugliness and beauty — all
> borne along in a tiny drop of liquid propelled by some mysterious force.
> This was nature, his colleagues explained, but what did it actually
> mean, this word?[35]

Such unanswered questions are common in the writings of Bashevis,
but they make very infrequent appearances in the work of his sceptical
older brother; Joshua was not one to over-use such phrases as "hidden
forces", or "mysterious forces". More surprisingly they come from a
rationalist, a doctor; but a rationalist who rationalized his son's
circumcision thus: "The little ceremony that, incidentally, was
medically beneficial, might serve to win over his father and lead to a
reconciliation. He would show him that a younger man could be more
sensible and tractable, and that an egg could indeed be wiser than the
hen." (Coincidentally, Joshua's own son has said that he "wouldn't
even have been circumcised if it hadn't been that my mother insisted
on it".)[36]

Feeling that he was the last of a generation, David Carnovsky took

his doubts to Reb Ephraim, who was more philosophical, as if Joshua
were trying to sooth his own uncertainties (though don't forget what
happened to Georg's "philosophical" smile). Reb Ephraim would not
blame the ideas of Moses Mendelssohn, but rather "the rabble" who
"always corrupted the ideas of a saint". However, as Joshua had
concluded, it was impractical to separate an idea from those who
espouse it. Reb Ephraim believed in the immortality of ideas, "What
has remained has not been the mobs but the teachings", but the fate of
his own life's work contradicted him. He was writing two
manuscripts:

> One was in Hebrew, with its elaborately carved characters and an
> embellished title page that was inscribed *The Book of Knowledge*. This
> was a work that reorganized nearly the entire Torah, beginning with the
> Scriptures and including the Babylonian and Jerusalem Talmuds.
> With extraordinary logic and remarkable ingenuity, Reb Ephraim
> cleared up all the errors and inaccuracies that had been perpetrated in
> transcribing the Torah throughout the centuries.... Reb Ephraim's
> second manuscript was written in German, with pointed Gothic
> characters and ornate capital letters at the beginning of each chapter.
> This work was aimed at the gentiles, for Reb Ephraim was convinced
> that all the Christian hatred for the Jew was based on a lack of
> understanding of the Jewish Torah and scholarship. Once initiated into
> the treasures of the Torah, the eyes of the gentiles would open to its true
> light that would illumine their minds and hearts.[37]

Unfortunately, even as he wrote, mice were devouring the pages;
moreover, since he was trapped in Germany, it was obvious that the
mice remained the only beneficiaries of his wisdom. Reb Ephraim,
cloistered in his room, "heard nothing, saw nothing, and remained
completely aloof", and was thus unaware that life had more than a
prank in store for the Jews; to him the Nazi atrocities were part of an
old, familiar story. David had no argument with the old man's logic,
but he also knew that the Nazis were beyond logic; besides, they were
more than a mob, including students and educated people as well. As
National Socialism made a mockery of David's "golden mean" so it
made Reb Ephraim's logic irrelevant. Pinchos Mendel called
suffering "the greatest secret of all", and Reb Ephraim said, "Our
minds are too limited to cope with it, but there must be a reason for it
as there is a reason for everything else." When Joshua wrote *The
Family Carnovsky* it seemed that there was no reason for anything, that
suffering was the final inheritance of the Jews.

Georg's unpromising adolescence came to an abrupt end when he
was initiated into sex with the cooperation of the Carnovskys' maid,
Emma. This occurred while his parents were otherwise occupied,

working guests at Dr Halevy's Maternity Clinic. When they returned
with the new baby, Rebecca, their son was a changed person. Just as
Joshua's physical appearance improved when he began work on *Yoshe
Kalb,* so did Georg's when he found a somewhat dissimilar outlet for
his creative impulses. Sex provided an all-purpose cure for acne,
frenzy, and Oedipal problems; Georg's face became "smooth and
clear", his eyes "were calm and serene", his behaviour was "calm and
relaxed" and he kissed his mother "willingly". Moreover, he "even
began to apply himself to his schoolwork and brought home excellent
grades". Much later, when Georg's career as an obstetrician had been
terminated by the Nazis, and his own son's face "was sprinkled with
acne", he began to consult "many volumes on psychology and
psychoanalysis, sciences that had never particularly interested him, a
practising surgeon more concerned with anatomy than with the
psyche". But now that the enlightened world had gone mad, and
divided his son against himself so that "Jegor Holbeck despised
everything about Jegor Carnovsky", these concepts "seemed
reasonable and appropriate". Joshua must have read the same books,
for Jegor exhibits the textbook symptoms of an Oedipus complex.
Jegor entered puberty unconsciously, while prostrate with a nervous
illness, and recovered to discover that he looked like one of "the
typical *Itziks* caricatured in the newspapers". This was his review of
his altered state: "God, how awful I look! So ugly and Jewish!" Thus
he associated his Jewishness with his growing sexuality, of which he
felt ashamed. For this, however, he had sufficient reason. Unlike his
father Jegor was a sickly child, but otherwise his development was
similar; instead of Kurt he idolized Karl, the Carnovskys' gentile
gardener, and Hugo, his weak-willed uncle, both of whom gave the
boy nightmares with their war stories. Jegor was also secretly taken to
church by his grandmother Holbeck, while he made fun of his other
grandmother's mixture of Yiddish and German. This tortured
upbringing was rather like Rechele's in *Satan in Goray*; Jegor was also
visited by terrible nocturnal creatures invented by the gardener, his
grandmother, his uncle, and the maid; they included "horned
devils...long-haired witches with pointed chins who rode on brooms,
sorceresses in red cowls who slid down chimneys". Like Rechele he
"closed his eyes to avoid seeing the terrible creatures but the tighter he
squeezed his lids, the thicker they came charging at him". Of course,
after puberty these repressed devils became sexually motivated, when
they caused acne and much worse. Like Bashevis, Joshua linked
repressed sexuality with hysteria and political madness. Jegor became
infatuated with National Socialism because of his failure to develop
fully as a man.

In fact, he was only set free by an act of violence, as he aped the behaviour of Georg toward a homosexual playmate of his youth. Just before his tumultuous encounter with Emma, Georg was kissed by "doglike" Helmut, who got a bloody nose as a result. When, at the end of the book, Jegor was kissed by that "loathsome reptile" Dr Zerbe "full on the mouth" he crushed his skull with the ebony statue of an African goddess blessed "with exaggerated breasts". But in Joshua's eagerness to fill the Nazi party with every kind of sexual pervert he included the sexually promiscuous, who can hardly be called repressed; for example, Lotte with the "firm, pointed breasts" that "jiggled with her every gesture", who finally initiated Jegor. What is the difference between the African goddess's liberating bosom and Lotte's free agents? For when Jegor ran with Lotte's Nazi friends in Yorkville his life was described as "completely free and unrestricted". Hitherto, Joshua had hinted that homosexuality was somehow bound up with anti-Semitism, but in *The Family Carnovsky* it came to symbolize the pathological deficiencies that the Nazis, in their envy, required a scapegoat to disguise. In short, as with Jegor, anti-Semitism was a symptom of self-loathing. But Joshua also wanted to demonstrate that National Socialism was a consequence of the irrational let loose, of logic abandoned, of taboos ignored, of unrestrained social licence. The two explanations are contradictory; it is hard to imagine National Socialism as both Oedipal and rampant. If the self becomes absorbed into a larger mass, then individual motivations also slacken. This contradiction may be excused by Joshua's understandable determination to make National Socialism as unattractive as possible, but it weakens the landscape of the novel. On the other hand, the psychological approach offers an interesting reversal of Bashevis's distinction between rabbi and man. For the manhood represented by the victors is something less than that demonstrated by the Jews.

Like his father before him, Jegor frequently denied his Jewishness. But this did not impress Dr Kirchenmeir, the newly appointed principal of the Goethe Gymnasium, whose first action was to replace the portrait of the eponymous writer with that of his fuehrer. His next was to order that Jegor "be isolated from the rest of the pupils and informed in no uncertain terms of his status under the New Order". Kirchenmeir was a typical specimen of Joshua's Nazis; a failed teacher of biology (the opposite of Georg, a successful obstetrician), he was easily tempted by the powerful promises of National Socialism. As a biologist he knew that their theories of racial purity were poppycock but he closed his eyes to them and the other "pseudoscientific nonsense". He was able to accept their financial explanations by abandoning his usual logic. But once he was installed as headmaster, and could revel in his authority, he soon "began to believe in many of the things he had previously considered pure drivel". As a result he decided to prove "the race theory before the entire school with a live model". What followed was Jegor's humiliation. It was the culmination of a series of mock rapes that began with the genital examination that concluded Gitta's appearance in *Steel and Iron*. Before an auditorium filled with his fellow pupils and scattered with invited dignitaries Jegor was used by Dr Kirchenmeir to demonstrate all the racial deficiencies of the Jews.

> "The audience will see from the figures on the blackboard the difference between the structure of the Nordic dolichocephalic skull — the long and handsome head that projects racial beauty and superiority — and that of the Negroid-Semitic, brachycephalic skull — the stubby and blunted head that resembles that of an ape and typifies racial deformity and inferiority. But in the case of our subject, it is particularly interesting to note the influence of the Negroid-Semitic strain on the Nordic. As you can clearly observe, the mixture has created a kind of freak. It may occur at first glance that the subject resembles the Nordic type, but this impression is strictly illusory. From the anthropological viewpoint one soon realizes that the Negroid-Semitic strain, which is always predominant in cases of mongrelization, has very subtly allowed the Nordic strain to dominate the external appearance in order to mask its own insidious influences."[38]

In other words, the fact that Jegor did not look especially Jewish was the greatest possible proof of the inherent knavery of the Jewish gene. But the poppycock was garnished with scientific quotation and Latin expressions, so that the distinguished visitors and the students were deeply impressed. Poor Jegor, ready to faint, was then told to disrobe. Since he refused he was dragged into a backroom by Kirchenmeir's assistant, Storm Trooper Herman, who willingly stripped "the garments from the girlish body". Jegor's struggles only served to arouse "his cruelty and sadism, along with vague sexual feelings". Jegor was dragged back to the stage where other parts of his anatomy were shown to be of inferior manufacture, including "the genitalia, whose premature development emphasized the degenerate sexuality of the Semitic race". By now the subject of the demonstration was an object, not a person but an "it". Nonetheless, Jegor responded like a human being, so much so that the traumatic experience touched his sanity and "madness...emanated from his...eyes". Dr Kirchenmeir, too, responded like a man to the success of his lecture; that night he even tried to make love to his wife, "but the long years of abstinence had left him impotent".

Georg tried to cure his son by applying the methods advocated in the psychological text books, but Jegor refused to believe a word his father said: "It didn't make sense that a whole country should suddenly conspire to lie simultaneously. It was his father who was the liar." Gimpel the Fool gave a similar reason for believing the people of Frampol: "A whole town can't go altogether crazy." When Gimpel discovered that a whole town could deceive him, he was tempted by the devil, and only saved by the intervention of his wicked wife's ghost. In *The Family Carnovsky*, Jegor acted as if his father were the devil, and he used the memory of his torment — "every exquisite moment" — to exorcize his words. "Rather than hate his tormentors, he loathed himself." When Gimpel was called a fool he had the strength of character to maintain: "I don't think myself a fool. On the contrary." But Jegor was infected by the lunacy of Germany, which provided the grotesque images that his Oedipus complex required. In her clinging nightgown his mother seemed "a divine yet voluptuous idealization of the perfect Aryan woman", and she provided the prototype for the women in "his sexual dreams". Consequently, Jegor "couldn't stand the lustful and rapacious way his father looked at her", and he used every "excuse to disturb his parents in their bedroom". Jegor shunned his father, but he would kiss Teresa "passionately and brutally, leaving bruises on her delicate skin". He copied drawings out of Nazi newspapers, one of which showed "a blonde angel being raped by a fat curly-haired *Itzik*". When Georg discovered this caricature he struck his son. And it was Jegor's response — "Jew!" — that prompted his decision to take his family to America. But Jegor showed no improvement in America. He told the immigration officer that he was "a Holbeck and a Protestant", and he called America a "Goddamn filthy hellhole!" aping Uncle Hugo's "description of foreign countries he had seen during the war". Georg tried to reason with him: "The city won't adjust to you — you'll have to adjust to the city. That's simple logic." "You and your logic!" was all Jegor could manage by way of a response.

He hated his father and his grandfather who had become "the complete Jew" in America, and he begged his mother to take him back to Germany.

> He had abandoned all reality and had begun to live in a dream world, to wish for things that his logic knew were impossible. The more he took refuge in the world of make-believe, the more credible his reveries seemed. In his dreams he saw himself on the other side, marching with the rest of the aroused nation. Women and blonde young maidens threw flower petals that he crushed beneath his hob-nailed boots.[39]

The only obstacle to the fulfilment of these sexual fantasies, and his

elopement with his mother, was his father. Consequently, "he began
to long for the only thing that he thought would make her his alone —
his father's death". But his father would not oblige, he was far too
strong; he could slap Jegor with impunity, as he did when he returned
from the interview with his headmaster. The only revenge of which
Jegor was capable was to cry out "Jew!" and run off to Yorkville to
join the Nazis. Joshua had been there already.

> My father looked like a one hundred percent Kraut. He used to go to
> those Nazi rallies in Yorkville — to gather material for a piece he was
> doing on the American Nazi movement in the thirties — and he could
> go out with these guys and talk to them. I mean, he knew German and
> drank beer with them, and they never caught on. If Isaac had tried that
> they would have spotted him right away and lynched him.[40]

Joshua led Jegor into the Young German Clubs, where he felt slightly
uncomfortable when they used Uncle Moe caricatures for target
practice, introduced him to Lotte, transported him to a camp in the
country, where Lotte whispered into his ear, "Sweet, precious *Bube*."
Words which astounded Jegor, who considered himself "the ugliest
and most repulsive creature alive". This was Jegor's first glimmer of
self-respect, though Lotte did not remain faithful for long. But it was a
beginning, the end of which came when he was clubbing Dr Zerbe to
death. He had a vision:

> Jegor's eyes opened wider and wider and suddenly saw double — two
> faces at once. One moment it was Dr Zerbe's; the next, Dr
> Kirchenmeir's. The wrinkles, the murky eyes and naked skulls, even
> the rasping voices seemed one and the same. He felt the tremendous
> surge of revulsion, hate, and strength that possesses one when facing a
> particularly loathsome reptile.[41]

At last Jegor recognized the real enemy. They had much in common,
Dr Zerbe and Dr Kirchenmeir. The latter divided Jegor against
himself, taught his to hate his cunning Jewish self, while the former
employed Jegor to spy upon the Jews (especially Elsa Landau). Both
profited from widening the split in his personality, which could only
be reunited by this final act of violence. Even then Jegor was not free
from the urge to self-destruction. Her shot himself outside his
parents' house. But when he spoke to his father, his words were full of
love. It was a bizarre reconciliation; Jegor upon a makeshift operating
table "so close to death, yet, in a way, completely cured", Georg and
Teresa (erstwhile doctor and nurse) working into the dawn to save his
life. Nachman ends up in darkness in no man's land, while Jegor
(though barely alive) greets a new dawn in America.

The Family Carnovsky is filled with the intimations of other possible

novels. Perhaps this is best illustrated by the story of Dr Landau and
Elsa, his daughter. Dr Landau was a doctor who worked exclusively
for the poor, a member of the workers' party until revolted by its
bellicosity at the outbreak of the Great War. The mood of the party
was paralleled by Elsa's behaviour; on the day of Georg's departure
for the front she forsook her independence and squirmed beneath him
like a bitch on heat (as Georg vengefully recalled the event). Love for
Elsa led Georg into medicine, his experiences in the war directed him
(with Dr Landau's aid) towards obstetrics. Unlike her father Elsa
remained within the party, abandoning both her medical career and
Georg for the sake of politics. Like Nachman she put the happiness of
millions before her own; and her lesson was the same as Nachman's.
When the Nazis began to win over the working classes she warned her
leaders, but they called her too pessimistic and attributed her attitude
to an "inherent Semitic cowardice". And when she tried to convince
her constituents "no logic could prevail". Her photograph was
constantly in the newspapers, and after Georg too became famous she
sent him a note in a "strong masculine script", which attested to the
perils of spinsterhood. Nevertheless, Georg was stirred. Would the
affair begin anew? Although Elsa also escaped to America, after a
harrowing sojourn in a concentration camp, she and Georg never met
again. Dr Landau (like Georg) was not allowed to practise medicine in
the States, but was eventually given a chicken farm to run. Here
occurred the final encounter between a Landau and a Carnovsky,
families whose destinies had once seemed linked. Wandering around
the country like a vagrant Jegor passed "a chicken farm where a white-
haired and white-bearded old man who hopped among his birds like
Santa Claus among his helpers waved to him good-naturedly".
Neither knew who the other was, it was as if they now belonged to
different novels.

   On the rebound from Elsa's independence, Georg married his over-
docile nurse. At the cultivated salon of the convert Rudolf Moser
(where Dr Zerbe and Dr Klein exchanged the insults of intellectuals)
Georg admitted to himself that he was bored to death with Teresa.
Consequently, he fell easy prey to the rapacious Frau Moser who
knew "how to exploit every nuance of love. She was submissive,
violent, brazen, and inventive to such a point that even he, a woman's
doctor, was astounded". But it was marital fidelity thereafter. It was as
though the consequences of National Socialism not only robbed the
Jews of their options to misbehave but also persuaded Joshua to limit
the possibilities of his novel. Certainly, after the immigration to
America all the varieties of story are reduced to a single one: Jegor's
flirtation with National Socialism. It was left to Bashevis to follow up

the affair between Georg and Herta Moser, and explore its complications in *The Estate*; for surely Georg Carnovsky was an earlier incarnation of Ezriel Babad, just as Rudolf Moser and his environment were an equivalent of Wallenberg and his high society. Joshua was dead, but Bashevis remained to breathe life into the literary examples of his brother. The course of *The Family Carnovsky* seems to mimic the fate of Berlin's Jews; it begins leisurely, as if it has all the time in the world, expanding into the numerous sub-plots an epic format allows, fooling itself, like the Jews of Berlin, that the end is nowhere in sight. But then, abruptly, all the stories evaporate, as though only one really mattered: the Nazi persecution of the Jews. Joshua seemed to be turning his back on fiction, just as David Carnovsky abandoned enlightenment. When David set upon Dr Speier in Sha Mora Synagogue he all but accused him of hiding the truth about Germany's treatment of the Jews with the words: "This is the time to speak, even to shout, Rabbi Speier." But Dr Speier was horrified at the thought, it was a "private affair...not one to be dragged through the streets...before strangers and outsiders". For Dr Speier did not want to put ideas into the heads of Americans, or want them to think he was connected with Asiatic Jews. Of course David was wiser, "We are all Jews...regardless of whether we come from Frankfurt or Tarnopol!" David had no time for the foolish intrigues of his one-time mentors, just as Joshua eschewed the frivolities of fiction; both were left with one object: to rage against the Nazis. David became more and more the Melnitz Jew he once despised, and Joshua took his talent back to Leoncin. His last book was *Of a World That Is No More*.

Israel Joshua Singer died in New York City on 10 February 1944. Bashevis called this "the greatest misfortune of my entire life. He was my father, my teacher. I never really recovered from this blow. There was only one consolation — whatever would happen later would never be as bad as this". About a year after Joshua's death Bashevis at last began to work on a second publishable novel. When he finally completed *The Family Moskat* Joshua was the obvious dedicatee. There are numerous instances of Joshua's influence in *The Family Moskat*. The very beginning, with the old patriarch Meshulam Moskat marrying for the third time, is reminiscent of *Yoshe Kalb*. Meshulam Moskat, though no Rabbi Melech, was a millionaire and king among Jews. Instead of by a *gabbai* his affairs were managed by a bailiff, Koppel, also the enemy of Moskat's envious offspring. In fact, the destruction of the rabbinic court at Nyesheve provided a model for Bashevis's more ambitious project: the end of Jewish life in Warsaw. In a similar fashion, *The Brothers Ashkenazi* set a precedent for linking the fate of the Jews with that of a city. Thus the funeral of Meshulam Moskat, like the funeral of Max Ashkenazi, was more than that of a single man; it was that of a community. "Old Meshulam Moskat had been a king among Jews; and, with all their faults, his sons had managed to stay Jews. But the grandchildren had completely alientated themselves from the old ways.... More than twenty years had gone by since old Moskat had died, and the Jewish kingdom over which he had ruled on Gzhybov Place had long been in ruins."

Towards the end of the novel, the remnants of the family gathered for the last time. It was Passover. They prayed for an end to the exile, and hoped against hope for the coming of the Messiah. Instead the Nazis invaded Poland. As the bombs dropped upon Warsaw two confused intellectuals had the following conversation: "Hertz Yanover burst into tears.... He hesitated for a moment and then said, in Polish: 'The Messiah will come soon.' Asa Heshel looked at him in astonishment. 'What do you mean?' 'Death is the Messiah. That's the real truth.'" Asa Heshel Bannet was a sceptic, the very thing Bashevis complained of in Benjamin Lerner, hero of *Steel and Iron*; although, unlike Lerner, Asa Heshel's scepticism came very close to being selfishness.

As with many of Bashevis's central characters Asa Heshel was a self-portrait, which is by no means the same thing as saying that *The Family Moskat* was autobiographical. Asa Heshel, a spiritual refugee from the religious life of Tereshpol Minor, arrived in Warsaw with a copy of Spinoza's *Ethics* in his hand and this thought on his lips: "Is it here I will learn the divine truths?" Two failed marriages later Asa Heshel told his new mistress: "I'm sick. Physically and spiritually." Barbara, the mistress, advised a psychiatrist. To which Asa Heshel responded: "Then every Jew in the world would have to go to one. I mean every modern Jew." Finally Adele, his first wife, realized what was really the matter with Asa Heshel: "He was one of those who must serve God or die. He had forsaken God, and because of this he was dead — a living body with a dead soul." Not only was Asa Heshel a failure in marriage; he also failed to become a Professor or even finish his dissertation, "The Laboratory of Happiness". Asa Heshel's theory was very simple, even if his chapters sounded complicated: since there was no higher philosophy the only valid intellectual activity was the pursuit of happiness. Life was Asa Heshel's laboratory, just as this world is God's (or the novel Bashevis's). This was too much even for Asa Heshel's mistress. When Asa Heshel told her, "I doubt whether I could be happy with anyone," she snapped back: "It's good you know it. It's true — you could never love anyone. You're a victim of your own philosophy. If pleasure is all that counts, there is no reason for ever giving. Only for taking." According to Asa Heshel this was "the quintessence of all civilization". Barbara, a communist, didn't agree. Asa Heshel's character was the opposite of Gimpel's. Gimpel said, "Shoulders are from God, and burdens too," while Asa Heshel's ambition was "to rest, to forget for a while all worries and burdens". Among the burdens Asa Heshel wanted to shed was that of family, time after time he complained of the responsibilities of family life, shouting at Hadassah (his second wife): "I'm sick of all this family stuff."

After her eventual departure, Asa Heshel's life "took on the pattern he had long wanted". He was rid of his two wives, his children, his mother (for whom he had "even neglected to put up a stone on her grave"). Incidentally, Bashevis got rid of Asa Heshel's father by using the expedient his own father never quite dared: taking shelter with his doting mother and sending a bill of divorcement to his wife. According to Maurice Carr, if Bashevis had his way he "wouldn't be anybody's uncle, brother, son, husband, father, or grandfather". Certainly, family life in *The Family Moskat*, unlike *The Family Carnovsky*, demonstrates nothing that is positive about the institution; the Moskats squabble about the estate after the old man's death, and Asa Heshel's family in Tereshpol Minor (based upon Bashevis's uncles and aunts in Bilgoray) "small as it was, was compact with hatred, intrigue, and jealousy". Nevertheless, as the Germans approached Warsaw Asa Heshel returned to be with his family; at the last, the "eternal deserter" was prepared to shoulder his responsibilities. Indeed, in a final chapter published only in the Yiddish edition of the novel, Asa Heshel also returned to orthodox Judaism.[42]

Everything about *The Family Moskat* is suggestive of Joshua, as if Bashevis had anticipated Dan Jacobson's remark and was determined to create something as substantial as his brother. Even some of Asa Heshel's adventures in the Great War and its revolutionary aftermath are related to Joshua's own experiences, for Bashevis was too young to have been conscripted during the war or to have travelled to the Soviet Union after it. Similarly, there is a whiff of personal guilt in Asa Heshel's decision to remain in Warsaw and return to the ways of his fathers, as if Bashevis had more than one debt to repay. Even so, the strength of *The Family Moskat* is Bashevis's determination to remain consistent to his own vision; Asa Heshel is a self-portrait, and his concerns are essentially those of a writer. As in *Satan in Goray* Bashevis is examining the importance of the written word. Doubtless he admires the strength of Asa Heshel's saintly grandfather, Reb Dan Katzenellenbogen, rabbi of Tereshpol Minor, who burns his manuscripts when exiled from his village by the Russians with the words: "The world will survive without them." But he is too much like Asa Heshel, who hides his manuscript of "The Laboratory of Happiness" in a stove (without igniting it) when he thinks the police are after him. Thus, while *The Family Carnovsky* and *The Family Moskat* cover the same period, they have a fundamental difference; Bashevis was unable to abandon the illicit joys of literature. "Certainly, if my brother would have lived another twenty or thirty years, which he should have, he would have developed more and more, and he would have published stunning books — I'm absolutely convinced of that."[43] It was left to Bashevis himself to fulfil this prophecy.

Notes

INTRODUCTION (pages 7-9)

1. *World at One*, BBC Radio 4, 5 October 1978,
2. Letter to the author from the Friends of Yiddish, 2 January 1978, written on behalf of A.N. Stencl by D.L. Berman.
3. I.B. Singer, *Nobel Lecture*, London, 1979.
4. Letter to the author from I.B. Singer, 12 November 1977.
5. C. Sinclair, "My Brother & I, A Conversation with Isaac Bashevis Singer", in *Encounter*, February 1979, p. 21ff.

CHAPTER ONE: FATHERS AND SONS (pages 11-48)

1. I.J. Singer, *Of A World That Is No More*, translated by J. Singer, New York, 1979.
2. E. Kreitman, *Deborah*, translated by M. Kreitman, London, 1946 (republished 1983).
3. I.B. Singer, *In My Father's Court*, translated by C. Kleinernan-Goldstein, E. Gottlieb and J. Singer, New York, 1966.
4. In conversation with the author, Tel Aviv, Israel, 5 January 1980.
5. I.J. Singer, *Of A World That Is No More*, pp. 29-30.
6. E. Kreitman, *Deborah*, p. 31.
7. I.J. Singer, *Of A World That Is No More*, p. 30.
8. J. Blocker and R. Elman, "An Interview with Isaac Bashevis Singer", *Commentary*, November 1963.
9. I.B. Singer, *Der Bal-Tshuve*, Tel Aviv, 1974.
10. E. Kreitman, *Deborah*, p. 43.
11. ibid.
12. I.B. Singer, *In My Father's Court*, p. 15.
13. I.B. Singer, *Gimpel the Fool*, New York, 1969, pp. 22-3.
14. I.B. Singer, *A Young Man in Search of Love*, New York, 1978, p. 149.
15. I.B. Singer, *In My Father's Court*, p. 160.
16. ibid., p. 160.
17. C. Sinclair, in *Encounter*, op. cit.
18. I.B. Singer, *In My Father's Court*, p. 57.

19. ibid., p. 219.
20. ibid., p. 151.
21. E. Kreitman, *Deborah*.
22. ibid., p. 96.
23. I.J. Singer, *Of A World That Is No More*, pp. 140-1.
24. E. Kreitman, *Deborah*.
25. Letter to the author from Maurice Carr, 12 February 1982.
26. I.B. Singer, *In My Father's Court*.
27. C. Sinclair, in *Encounter*, op. cit.
28. I.J. Singer, *Of A World That Is No More*, p. 81.
29. E. Kreitman, *Deborah*.
30. I.B. Singer, *In My Father's Court*, p. 269.
31. I.J. Singer, *Of A World That Is No More*, p. 72.
32. ibid., pp. 118-20.
33. ibid., p. 130.
34. ibid., p. 131.
35. I.B. Singer, *In My Father's Court*, p. 273.
36. I.B. Singer, *A Little Boy in Search of God*, New York, 1976, pp. 103-4.
37. I.L. Peretz, *My Memoirs*, translated by F. Goldberg, New York, 1964, p. 183.
38. I.B. Singer, *In My Father's Court*.
39. I.J. Singer, *Of A World That Is No More*.
40. ibid., p. 218.
41. ibid., p. 220.
42. ibid., p. 233.
43. ibid., p. 237.
44. C. Sinclair, in *Encounter*, op. cit.
45. ibid.
46. ibid.
47. I.B. Singer, "The Gentleman from Cracow", collected in *Gimpel the Fool*, p. 29.
48. ibid., p. 31.
49. ibid., p. 35.
50. ibid., p. 39.
51. I.B. Singer, *In My Father's Court*, p. 56.
52. E. Kreitman, *Deborah*, p. 66.
53. ibid., p. 87.
54. ibid., p. 71.
55. ibid., p. 113.
56. ibid., p. 101.
57. ibid., pp. 66-7.
58. ibid., p. 198.

59. ibid., pp. 213, 215-16.
60. Letter to the author from Maurice Carr.
61. I.B. Singer, *In My Father's Court,* p. 155.
62. ibid., pp. vii-viii.
63. ibid., p. 256.
64. C. Sinclair, in *Encounter,* op. cit.
65. Israel Joshua Singer's entry in S.J. Kunitz and H. Haycraft (eds), *Twentieth-Century Authors,* New York, 1956.
66. I.B. Singer, *In My Father's Court,* p. 232.
67. ibid., p. 240.
68. C. Sinclair, in *Encounter,* op. cit.
69. J. Blocker and R. Elman, in *Commentary,* op. cit.
70. I.B. Singer, *A Little Boy in Search of God,* p. 47.
71. Both stories collected in *Old Love,* New York, 1979.
72. I.B. Singer and I. Moskowitz, *The Hasidim,* New York, 1973, p. 17.
73. I.B. Singer and I. Howe, "Yiddish Tradition vs. Jewish Tradition, A Dialogue" in *Midstream,* June/July 1973.
74. I.B. Singer, *Gimpel the Fool,* p. 23.
75. I.B. Singer and I. Howe, in *Midstream,* op. cit.
76. I. Howe and E. Greenberg (eds), *A Treasury of Yiddish Stories,* New York, 1973, p. 224.
77. I.B. Singer and I. Howe, in *Midstream,* op. cit.
78. J. Blocker and R. Elman, in *Commentary,* op. cit.
79. In conversation with the author, New York, 25 May 1978.
80 I.B. Singer, *A Young Man in Search of Love,* p. 34.

CHAPTER TWO: REPUTATIONS (pages 49-85)

1. Charles Madison, *Yiddish Literature, Its Scope and Major Writers,* New York, 1971, p. 456.
2. In conversation with the author, Tel Aviv, 5 January 1980.
3. I.J. Singer, *Yoshe Kalb,* translated by M. Samuel, New York, 1965, introduction p. vii.
4. E. Kreitman, *Deborah.*
5. I.J. Singer, *Yoshe Kalb,* Introduction, pp. vi-vii.
6. I.B. Singer, *In My Father's Court.*
7. I.J. Singer, *Blood Harvest,* translated by M. Kreitman, London, 1935. Introduction, p. vii.
8. I.J. Singer, *Steel and Iron,* translated by J. Singer, New York, 1969.
9. ibid., p. 49.
10. ibid., p. 215.
11. ibid., p. 254.

12. ibid., p. 45.
13. ibid., p. 55.
14. ibid., p. 71.
15. ibid., p. 80.
16. ibid., p. 110.
17. ibid., p. 112.
18. I.B. Singer and I. Howe, in *Midstream,* op. cit.
19. I.J. Singer, *Steel and Iron,* p. 125.
20. ibid., pp. 161-2.
21. ibid., p. 225.
22. ibid., pp. 237-8.
23. C. Sinclair, in *Encounter,* op. cit.
24. I.J. Singer, *Yoshe Kalb,* Introduction, p. vii.
25. Paul Bailey, presenter, "Isaac Bashevis Singer: A Story No One Else Can Tell", BBC Radio 3, 1975 (repeated 1978).
26. Collected in I.B. Singer, *A Crown of Feathers,* New York, 1973.
27. C. Sinclair, in *Encounter,* op. cit.
28. C.L. Grossman, "The Story of Isaac", *Tropic (The Miami Herald),* 25 May 1980.
29. C. Sinclair, in *Encounter,* op. cit.
30. I.J. Singer, *Of a World That Is No More,* pp. 193-4.
31. C. Sinclair, in *Encounter,* op. cit.
32. Quoted in the souvenir programme to "Maurice Schwartz's Production of I.J. Singer's Play 'Yoshe Kalb' ", presented to the British Library by its editor, Maximilian Hurwitz, 4 February 1933.
33. I.J. Singer, *Yoshe Kalb,* p. 59.
34. ibid., p. 70.
35. ibid., p. 75.
36. ibid., p. 103.
37. ibid., p. 104.
38. ibid., p. 103.
39. ibid., p. 115.
40. ibid., p. 147.
41. ibid., p. 221.
42. ibid., p. 224.
43. ibid., p. 225.
44. S.J. Kunitz and H. Haycraft (eds), op. cit.
45. C. Sinclair, in *Encounter,* op. cit.
46. Quoted in Hurwitz's *Yoshe Kalb* programme.
47. C. Sinclair, in *Encounter,* op. cit.
48. ibid.
49. Quoted in P. Kresh, *Isaac Bashevis Singer, The Magician of West 86th Street,* New York, 1979, p. 116.

50. I.B. Singer, *Satan in Goray,* translated by J. Sloan, New York, 1955, pp. 55-6.
51. ibid., p. 59.
52. ibid., pp. 66-7.
53. ibid., pp. 206-7.
54. I.J. Singer, *Yoshe Kalb,* p. 114.
55. I.B. Singer, *Satan in Goray,* pp. 234-5.
56. ibid., p. 4.
57. G.G. Scholem (ed), *Zohar, The Book of Splendor,* New York, 1963, pp. 89-90.
58. I.B. Singer, *Satan in Goray,* p. 239.
59. ibid., p. 91.
60. ibid., p. 107.
61. ibid., p. 138.
62. ibid., p. 139.
63. ibid., p. 147.
64. ibid., p. 162.
65. ibid., p. 176.
66. ibid., p. 183.
67. ibid., p. 194.
68. ibid., p. 200.
69. ibid., p. 238.
70. C. Sinclair, in *Encounter,* op. cit.

CHAPTER THREE: POLAND (pages 86-119)

1. C. Sinclair, in *Encounter,* op. cit.
2. In conversation with the author, London, 9 November 1979.
3. I.B. Singer, *The Estate,* translated by J. Singer, E. Gottlieb and E. Shub, London, 1970, p. 349.
4. I.B. Singer and I. Moskowitz, *The Hasidim,* p. 17.
5. ibid., p. 20.
6. Collected in I.B. Singer, *A Crown of Feathers.*
7. I.B. Singer and I. Moskowitz, *The Hasidim,* pp. 11-12.
8. I.B. Singer, *The Manor,* translated by J. Singer and E. Gottlieb, New York, 1967, p. 250.
9. C. Sinclair, in *Encounter,* op. cit.
10. I.B. Singer, *The Manor,* p. 113.
11. ibid., pp. 126-7.
12. I.B. Singer, *The Estate,* p. 188.
13. I.B. Singer, *The Manor,* p. 25.
14. ibid., p. 63.
15. I.B. Singer, *The Estate,* p. 349.
16. ibid., p. 249.

17. I.J. Singer, *The Brothers Ashkenazi,* translated by M. Samuel, New York, 1936, pp. 642-3.
18. I.B. Singer, *Nobel Lecture,* London, 1979, p. 13.
19. I.J. Singer, *The Brothers Ashkenazi,* p. 467.
20. ibid., p. 610.
21. ibid., pp. 625-6.
22. ibid., p. 639.
23. E. Mendelsohn, *Class Struggle in the Pale, The Formative Years of the Jewish Workers' Movement in Tsarist Russia,* Cambridge, 1970, p. 9.
24. ibid., p. 91.
25. I.J. Singer, *The Brothers Ashkenazi,* pp. 383-4.
26. E. Mendelsohn, op. cit., Introduction, p. viii.
27. ibid., p. 140.

CHAPTER FOUR: POLITICS (pages 120-160)

1. Quoted in P. Kresh, op. cit., p. 128.
2. C. Sinclair, in *Encounter,* op. cit.
3. I.B. Singer, *Lost in America,* translated by J. Singer, New York, 1981, p. 118.
4. I.J. Singer, *East of Eden,* translated by M. Samuel, London, 1939, p. 195.
5. ibid., p. 9.
6. ibid., p. 91-2.
7. ibid., pp. 92-3.
8. ibid., p. 158.
9. ibid., p. 114.
10. ibid., pp. 166-7.
11. ibid., p. 192.
12. E. Mendelsohn, op. cit., p. 69.
13. I.J. Singer, *East of Eden,* p. 224.
14. ibid., p. 226.
15. I. Berlin, *Russian Thinkers,* London, 1978.
16. I.J. Singer, *East of Eden,* p. 367.
17. Senator J. McCarthy, from speech to the army's McCarthy Hearings, 1954.
18. F. Dostoyevsky, *Letters from the Underworld,* translated by C.J. Hogarth, London, 1964, p. 40.
19. G. Steiner, "Russia: the search for Utopia", in *Sunday Times,* 8 January 1978.
20. G. Steiner, *Has Truth a Future?,* London, 1978, p. 8.
21. I.J. Singer, *East of Eden,* p. 443.
22. Marshall Breger and Bob Barnhart, "A Conversation with Isaac

Bashevis Singer", printed in I. Malin (ed), *Crictical Views of Isaac Bashevis Singer,* New York, 1969, p. 38.
23. J. Blocker and R. Elman, *Commentary.*
24. S. Bellow, *Herzog,* Conn., 1969, pp. 204-5.
25. *The Autobiography of Bertrand Russell,* London, 1967, p. 146.
26. G. Orwell, *1984,* London, 1964, pp. 200-2.
27. I.J. Singer, *East of Eden,* p. 399.
28. ibid., p. 417.
29. ibid., pp. 425-6.
30. Quoted in *Yiddish Literature* by C. Madison, op. cit., p. 474.
31. I.J. Singer, *The Family Carnovsky,* translated by J. Singer, New York, 1969, p. 210.
32. ibid., pp. 7-8.
33. ibid., p. 149.
34. ibid., p. 158.
35. ibid., p. 186.
36. Quoted in P. Kresh, op. cit., p. 147.
37. I.J. Singer, *The Family Carnovsky,* p. 56.
38. ibid., p. 238.
39. ibid., p. 318.
40. Quoted in P. Kresh, op. cit., p. 146.
41. I.J. Singer, *The Family Carnovsky,* p. 401.
42. I.B. Singer, *The Family Moskat,* translated by A.H. Gross, M. Samuel, L. Mearson and N. Gross, New York, 1950.
43. C. Sinclair, in *Encounter,* op. cit.

Bibliography

AGNON, S.Y., *Twenty-One Stories* (ed. Nahum Glatzer), London, Gollancz, 1970.

ALEICHEM, Sholom, *Tevye's Daughters* (trans. Frances Butwin), London, Vallentine, Mitchell, 1973.

——, *Stories and Satires*, New York, 1960.

ASCH, Sholom, *Mary*, New York, Putnam, 1949.

BABEL, Isaac, *The Collected Stories* (trans. Walter Morison), New York, Meridian, 1974.

BANAS, Josef, *The Scapegoats, The Exodus of the Remnants of Polish Jewry*, (trans. Tadeusz Szafar, ed. Lionel Kochin), London, Weidenfeld & Nicolson, 1979.

BAUMGARTEN, Murray, *City Scriptures, Modern Jewish Writing*, Massachusetts, Harvard University Press, 1982.

——, "Dual Allegiances: Yiddish as theme and value in modern Jewish writing", paper delivered at the First International Conference on Research in Yiddish Language and Literature, Oxford, 6-9 August 1979

BELLOW, Saul, *Herzog*, Connecticut, Fawcett Crest, 1969.

BERLIN, Isaiah, *Russian Thinkers*, London, The Hogarth Press, 1978.

BILIK, Dorothy Seidman, *Immigrant-Survivors, Post-Holocaust Consciousness in Recent Jewish-American Fiction*, Connecticut, Wesleyan University Press, 1981.

——, "Isaac Bashevis Singer's 'Positive Capability'", paper delivered at the First International Conference on Research in Yiddish Language and Literature, Oxford, 6-9 August 1979.

BLISHEN, Edward, "A Watchful Small Boy", *The Times Educational Supplement*, 24 September 1982.

BLOCKER, Joel, and ELMAN, Richard, "An Interview with Isaac Bashevis Singer", *Commentary*, November 1963.

BUBER, Martin, *Tales of the Hasidim*, New York, Schocken, 1975.

BUCHEN, Irving, *Isaac Bashevis Singer and the Eternal Past*, New York University Press, 1968.

CAHAN, Abraham, *The Rise of David Levinsky*, Massachusetts, Peter Smith, 1969.

——, *The Education of Abraham Cahan,* New York, 1969.

CHAPMAN, Abraham (ed.), *Jewish-American Literature,* New York, Mentor, 1974.

COHEN, A. (ed.), *The Soncino Chumash,* London, 1956.

COHEN, Sarah Blacher, "Isaac Bashevis Singer's Realistic Women", paper delivered at the First International Conference on Research in Yiddish Language and Literate, Oxford, 6-9 August 1979.

DOBROSZYCKI, Lucjan, and KIRSHENBLATT-GIMBLETT, Barbara, *Image Before My Eyes, A Photographic History of Jewish Life in Poland, 1864-1939,* New York, Schocken, 1977.

DUBNOW, S.M., *History of the Jews in Russia and Poland, From the earliest times until the present day* (trans. I. Friedlaender), Philadelphia, The Jewish Publication Society of America, 1920.

FRANKEL, Jonathan, *Prophecy and Politics, Socialism, Nationalism, and the Russian Jews, 1862-1917,* Cambridge University Press, 1982.

GILBERT, Martin, *The Jews of Russia,* London, 1976.

GOLD, Michael, *Jews Without Money,* London, Searl, 1948.

GROSSMAN, Cathy Lynn, "The Story of Isaac", *Tropic* (colour magazine of *The Miami Herald*), 25 May 1980.

HANDLIN, Oscar, *The Uprooted,* New York, Grosset & Dunlap, 1951.

HOWE, Irving, *The Immigrant Jews of New York, 1881 to the Present,* London, Routledge & Kegan Paul, 1976.

—— (ed.), *Jewish-American Stories,* New York, Mentor, 1977.

——, "A Yiddish 'Modernist' ", *Commentary,* October 1960.

——, "The Other Singer", *Commentary,* March 1966.

HOWE, Irving and GREENBERG, Eliezer (eds.), *A Treasury of Yiddish Stories,* New York, Schocken, 1974.

——, *A Treasury of Yiddish Poetry,* New York, Schocken, 1976.

——, *Voices From the Yiddish,* New York, Schocken, 1975.

HUBMAN, Franz, *The Jewish Family Album,* London, Routledge & Kegan Paul, 1975.

HUGHES, Ted, "The Genius of Isaac Bashevis Singer", *The New York Review of Books,* 22 April 1965.

HURWITZ, Maxmilian (ed.), "Maurice Schwartz's Production 'Yoshe Kalb' by I.J. Singer", New York, 1933.

JACOBSON, Dan, "The Problem of Isaac Bashevis Singer", *Commentary,* February 1965.

KAFKA, Franz, *The Complete Stories* (ed. Nahum Glatzer), New York, Schocken, 1971.

KARP, Abraham (ed.), *Golden Door to America,* New York, Penguin, 1977.

KAZIN, Alfred, *New York Jew,* London, Secker & Warburg, 1978.

KREITMAN, Esther, *Deborah* (trans. Morris Kreitman), London, Foyles, 1946; republished, Virago, 1983. (First published in Yiddish as *Der Szejdym Tanc*, Warsaw, 1936.)

——, *Yichus*, London, Narod Press, 1949.

——, *Brilliantin*, London, Foyles, 1944.

KREITMAN, Morris, *Jewish Short Stories*, London, Faber & Faber, 1938.

——, "My Uncle Isaac", *Jerusalem Post*, 4 July 1965.

KRESH, Paul, *Isaac Bashevis Singer, The Magician of West 86th Street*, New York, Dial, 1979.

KUNITZ, Stanley J., & HAYCRAFT, Howard (eds.), *Twentieth-Century Authors*, New York, H.W. Wilson, 1956.

LEA, Martin, *The House of Napolitano*, London, Rich & Cowan, 1938.

LEFTWICH, Joseph (ed.), *Yisroel: The First Jewish Omnibus*, London, Heritage, 1933.

——, *The Peacock Anthology*, London, Anscombe, 1939.

——, *An Anthology of Modern Yiddish Literature*, The Hague, Mouton, 1974.

LIND, Jakov, *Numbers*, London, Jonathan Cape, 1972.

MADISON, Charles, *Yiddish Literature, Its Scope and Major Writers*, New York, Schocken, 1971.

MALIN, Irving, *Isaac Bashevis Singer*, New York, Frederick Ungar, 1972.

—— (ed.), *Critical Views of Isaac Bashevis Singer*, New York University Press, 1969.

MENDELSOHN, Ezra, *Class Struggle in the Pale, The Formative Years of the Jewish Workers' Movement in Tsarist Russia*, Cambridge University Press, 1970.

METZKER, Isaac (ed.), *A Bintel Brief*, New York, Ballantine, 1977.

NISBET, BAIN R. (ed.), *Cossack Fairy Tales*, London, Harrap, 1916.

NEUGROSCHEL, Joachim (ed.), *Great Works of Jewish Fantasy*, London, Picador, 1978.

ORWELL, George, *1984*, London, Penguin, 1964.

OZICK, Cynthia, *The Pagan Rabbi*, London, Secker & Warburg, 1972.

——, "Fistfuls of Masterpieces", *The New York Times Book Review*, 1982.

PERETZ, Isaac Leib, *My Memoirs* (trans. Fred Goldberg), New York, The Citadel Press, 1964.

——, *Stories*, (trans. Sol Liptzin), New York, Hebrew Publishing Co., 1947.

PINSKER, Sanford, *The Schlemiel as Metaphor*, Carbondale, Southern Illinois University Press, 1971.

PRAGER, Leonard, "Ironic Couplings: The sacred and sexual in Isaac

Bashevis", paper delivered at the First International Conference on Research in Yiddish Language and Literature, Oxford, 6-9 August 1979.

REZNIKOFF, Charles, *Family Chronicle*, London, 1969.

RISCHIN, Moses, *The Promised City*, New York, Harper, 1970.

ROTH, Henry, *Call it Sleep*, New York, Avon, 1973.

ROTH, Philip, *The Ghost Writer*, London, Jonathan Cape, 1979.

ROSKIES, Diane K., & David G., *The Shtetl Book*, New York, Ktav, 1975.

RUBIN, Ruth, *Voices of a People*, New York, Yoseloff, 1963.

SCHOLEM, Gershom, *The Messianic Idea in Judaism*, New York, Schocken, 1974.

——, (ed.), *Zohar, The Book of Splendor*, New York, Schocken, 1963.

SCHULZ, Bruno, *The Street of Crocodiles*, New York, Penguin, 1977.

——, *Sanatorium Under the Sign of the Hourglass*, London, Hamish Hamilton, 1979.

SCHWARZ, Leo (ed.), *The Jewish Caravan*, New York, Schocken, 1976.

SCHWARZ-BART, André, *The Last of the Just*, London, Secker & Warburg, 1961.

SEFORIM, Mendele Mocher, *The Travels & Adventures of Benjamin the Third*, New York, Schocken, 1968.

SHMERUK, Chone, "Bashevis Singer — In search of his autobiography", *The Jewish Quarterly*, Winter 1981/2.

SHULMAN, Abraham, *The Old Country, The Lost World of Eastern European Jews*, New York, Scribners, 1974.

SINCLAIR, Clive, "My Brother and I. A Conversation with Isaac Bashevis Singer", *Encounter*, February 1979.

——, "Half a Devil", *London Magazine*, April/May 1980.

——, "Paperback Writer, Isaac Bashevis Singer", *Sunday Times Colour Magazine*, 26 May 1980.

——, "At the Mercy of Demons", *The Times Literary Supplement*, 16 July 1982.

——, "The Sceptic and the Visionary: The influence of Hasidism upon the fiction of Israel Joshua and Isaac Bashevis Singer", paper delivered at the First International Conference on Research in Yiddish Language and Literature, Oxford, 6-9 August 1979.

——, Introduction to E. Kreitman, *Deborah*, London, Virago, 1983.

SINGER, Isaac Bashevis, *In My Father's Court* (trans. Channah Klienerman-Goldstein, Elaine Gottlieb and Joseph Singer), New York, Farrar, Straus & Giroux, 1966 (*Main Tatn's Beth-Din Shtub*, New York, 1956).

——, *A Day of Pleasure*, New York, Farrar, Straus & Giroux, 1969.

——, *A Little Boy in Search of God* (illus. Ira Moskowitz), New York, Doubleday, 1976.

——, *A Young Man in Search of Love* (trans. Joseph Singer), New York, Doubleday, 1978.

——, *Lost in America* (trans. Joseph Singer), New York, Doubleday, 1981.

——, *Nobel Lecture,* London, Jonathan Cape, 1979.

——, *Satan in Goray* (trans. Jacob Sloan), New York, Farrar, Straus & Giroux, 1955.

——, *The Family Moskat* (trans. A.H. Gross, Maurice Samuel, Lyon Mearson and Nancy Gross), New York, Alfred Knopf, 1950.

——, *The Slave* (trans. the author and Cecil Hemley), London, Jonathan Cape, 1973.

——, *The Magician of Lublin* (trans. Elaine Gottlieb and Joseph Singer), New York, Bantam, 1965.

——, *The Manor* (trans. Elaine Gottlieb and Joseph Singer), New York, Farrar, Straus and Giroux, 1967.

——, *The Estate* (trans. Elaine Gottlieb, Joseph Singer and Elizabeth Shub), London, Jonathan Cape, 1970.

——, *Enemies, A Love Story* (trans. Aliza Shevrin and Elizabeth Shub), London, Jonathan Cape, 1972.

——, *Shosha* (trans. Joseph Singer), New York, Farrar, Straus & Giroux, 1978.

——, *Der Bal-Tshuve,* Tel Aviv, Peretz, 1974.

——, *Collected Stories,* London, Jonathan Cape, 1982.

——, *Gimpel the Fool,* New York, Avon, 1969.

——, *The Spinoza of Market Street,* London, Jonathan Cape, 1973.

——, *Short Friday,* London, Secker & Warburg, 1967.

——, *The Seance,* London, Jonathan Cape, 1970.

——, *A Friend of Kafka,* London, Jonathan Cape, 1972.

——, *Passions,* London, Jonathan Cape, 1976.

——, *A Crown of Feathers,* New York, Farrar, Straus & Giroux, 1973.

——, *Old Love,* New York, Farrar, Straus & Giroux, 1979.

——, *Zlateh the Goat,* London, Kestrel, 1975.

——, *Mazel and Shlimazel or The Milk of a Lioness,* London, Jonathan Cape, 1979.

——, *The Fools of Chelm and Their History,* London, Abelard, 1975.

——, *Naftali the Storyteller and his Horse, Sus,* Oxford University Press, 1977.

——, *When Schlemiel Went to Warsaw,* London, Longman, 1974.

——, *The Power of Light,* New York, Farrar, Straus & Giroux, 1980.

——, *The Hasidim* (illus. Ira Moskowitz), New York, Crown, 1973.

——, *Reaches of Heaven,* New York, Farrar, Straus & Giroux, 1980.

——, *Elijah the Slave*, New York, Farrar, Straus & Giroux, 1970.

SINGER, Isaac Bashevis, and HOWE, Irving, "Yiddish Tradition vs. Jewish Tradition, A Dialogue", *Midstream*, June/July 1973.

SINGER, Israel Joshua, *Steel and Iron* (trans. Joseph Singer), New York, Funk and Wagnalls, 1969. A new translation of

——, *Blood Harvest* (trans. Morris Kreitman), London, Sampson Low, Marston, 1935. (Originally published in Yiddish as *Sztol un Ajzn*, Vilna, 1927.)

——, *Yoshe Kalb* (trans. Maurice Samuel), New York, Harper & Row, 1965. (Originally published in English as *The Sinner*, New York, 1933.)

——, *The Brothers Ashkenazi* (trans. Maurice Samuel), New York, Alfred Knopf, 1936. New translation by Joseph Singer, New York, Atheneum, 1980. London, Allison & Busby, 1983.

——, *East of Eden* (trans. Maurice Samuel), London, Putnam, 1939.

——, *The Family Carnovsky* (trans. Joseph Singer), New York, Vanguard, 1969.

——, *Of A World That Is No More* (trans. Joseph Singer), New York, Vanguard, 1979. (Originally *Fun a Welt Wos Is Nishto Mer*, New York, 1946.)

——, *The River Breaks Up* (trans. Maurice Samuel), New York, Vanguard, 1966.

SINGER, Brett, *The Petting Zoo*, New York, Simon and Schuster, 1979.

SOLTES, Mordecai (ed.), *The Yiddish Press: An Americanizing Agency*, New York, 1930.

SONNTAG, Jacob, "Problems of Translation from Yiddish into English", paper delivered at the First International Conference on Research in Yiddish Language and Literature, Oxford, 6-9 August 1979.

STEINER, George, *Has Truth a Future?*, London, BBC Publications, 1978.

——, "Russia: The Search for Utopia", *Sunday Times*, 8 January 1978.

TOBIAS, Henry J., *The Jewish Bund in Russia, from its origins to 1905*, Stanford University Press, 1972.

VISHNIAC, Roman, *Polish Jews, A Pictorial Record*, New York, Schocken, 1965.

WEST, Nathaniel, *Miss Lonleyhearts and A Cool Million*, London, Penguin, 1966.

WIRTH, Louis, *The Ghetto*, University of Chicago Press, 1928.

WISSE, Ruth, *The Schlemiel as Modern Hero*, University of Chicago Press, 1971.

ZAMOYSKI, Adam, "The Jews of Poland", *History Today,* Summer 1976.

ZAMYATIN, Yevgeny, *We,* London, Penguin, 1972.

ZBOROWSKI, Mark, and HERZOG, Elizabeth, *Life is with People,* New York, Schocken, 1974.

ZWEIG, Stefan, *The World of Yesterday,* London, Cassell, 1943.

Index

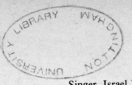